D1711825

CONTEMPORARY
*B*lack
*B*iography

ISSN-1058-1316

CONTEMPORARY
*B*lack
*B*iography

Profiles from the International Black Community

Volume 49

THOMSON

GALE

ST. PHILIP'S COLLEGE LIBRARY

Detroit • New York • San Francisco • San Diego • New Haven, Conn. • Waterville, Maine • London • Munich

Contemporary Black Biography, Volume 49
Sara and Tom Pendergast

Project Editor
Pamela M. Kalte

Image Research and Acquisitions
Robyn V. Young

Editorial Support Services
Nataliya Mikheyeva

Rights and Permissions
Margaret Abendroth, Margaret Chamberlain,
Edna Hedblad

Manufacturing
Dorothy Maki, Rhonda Williams

Composition and Prepress
Mary Beth Trimper, Gary Leach

Imaging
Lezlie Light, Mike Logusz

ISBN 0-7876-7921-6
ISSN 1058-1316

Printed in the United States of America
10 9 8 7 6 5 4 3 2 1

Advisory Board

Contents

Introduction

Contemporary Black Biography provides informative biographical profiles of the important and influential persons of African heritage who form the international black community: men and women who have changed today's world and are shaping tomorrow's. *Contemporary Black Biography* covers persons of various nationalities in a wide variety of fields, including architecture, art, business, dance, education, fashion, film, industry, journalism, law, literature, medicine, music, politics and government, publishing, religion, science and technology, social issues, sports, television, theater, and others. In addition to in-depth coverage of names found in today's headlines, *Contemporary Black Biography* provides coverage of selected individuals from earlier in this century whose influence continues to impact on contemporary life. *Contemporary Black Biography* also provides coverage of important and influential persons who are not yet household names and are therefore likely to be ignored by other biographical reference series. Each volume also includes listee updates on names previously appearing in *CBB*.

Designed for Quick Research and Interesting Reading

- **Attractive page design** incorporates textual subheads, making it easy to find the information you're looking for.

- **Easy-to-locate data sections** provide quick access to vital personal statistics, career information, major awards, and mailing addresses, when available.

- **Informative biographical essays** trace the subject's personal and professional life with the kind of in-depth analysis you need.

- **To further enhance your appreciation** of the subject, most entries include photographic portraits.

- **Sources for additional information** direct the user to selected books, magazines, and newspapers where more information on the individuals can be obtained.

Helpful Indexes Make It Easy to Find the Information You Need

Contemporary Black Biography includes cumulative Nationality, Occupation, Subject, and Name indexes that make it easy to locate entries in a variety of useful ways.

Available in Electronic Formats

Diskette/Magnetic Tape. Contemporary Black Biography is available for licensing on magnetic tape or diskette in a fielded format. Either the complete database or a custom selection of entries may be ordered. The database is available for internal data processing and nonpublishing purposes only. For more information, call (800) 877-GALE.

On-line. Contemporary Black Biography is available on-line through Mead Data Central's NEXIS Service in the NEXIS, PEOPLE and SPORTS Libraries in the GALBIO file and Gale's Biography Resource Center.

Disclaimer

Contemporary Black Biography uses and lists websites as sources and these websites may become obsolete.

We Welcome Your Suggestions

The editors welcome your comments and suggestions for enhancing and improving *Contemporary Black Biography*. If you would like to suggest persons for inclusion in the series, please submit these names to the editors. Mail comments or suggestions to:

The Editor

Contemporary Black Biography

Thomson Gale

27500 Drake Rd.

Farmington Hills, MI 48331-3535

Phone: (800) 347-4253

Stephanie Allain

1959—

Independent film producer

In the 1990s Stephanie Allain became one of the most respected and powerful producers in Hollywood, holding positions at Warner Brothers, Columbia, and Jim Henson Productions. She became known for her ability to create independent-style films within the studio system, making a huge impact at Columbia as producer of *Boyz N the Hood*, the 1995 debut of writer and director John Singleton. Before Singleton arrived at Columbia, Allain was one of twelve readers at the studio, and one of only two black readers. She was influential in encouraging and developing a black filmmaking community in Hollywood that began to flourish at the start of the late 1990s. Between 1996 and 1999 Allain presided over Jim Henson Productions, where she was responsible for overseeing such quirky children's movies as *The Adventures of Elmo in Grouchland* (1999) and *Muppets from Space* (1999). Allain's talent has always been best applied to hard-hitting movies with "street" influences. In 2002 she was named as one of the top fifty power brokers in entertainment by *Black Enterprise* magazine. Since 2002 she has directed her energies to her own production company, Homegrown Films.

Stephanie Allain was born in New Orleans, Louisiana, on October 30, 1959, to Dr Charles Allain, a biochemist, and Gwen Allain Miller, an educator. She has a sister, Pamela, and a brother, Greg. During her early childhood the family moved from New Orleans to Pittsburgh, Pennsylvania, eventually settling near Los Angeles, California, in 1965. Allain was educated at Catholic schools in and around Inglewood, first at the Cathedral Chapel School and later at St. Mary's Academy for Girls. After graduation she attended the University of California, Santa Cruz, graduating with a bachelor's degree in English and creative writing. She considered signing up to the master's program in critical analysis, but was attracted by the opportunity to write and study dance in San Francisco. By 1985 Allain's ambition and drive was beginning to surface; she was disillusioned with the poor rewards available to dancers and moved back to Los Angeles. She married Mitch Marcus in 1988 and they have two children, Wade and Jesse. They divorced in 1999.

When Allain arrived in Los Angeles in 1985 she was pregnant and desperate to find work she could do while looking after a baby. Almost immediately she picked up some work as a freelance script reader for various agencies including Creative Artists Agency (CAA); within three months she had landed a staff position reading scripts three days each week at CAA. She joined the Story Analyst Union in 1987. Allain had a talent for reading and assessing scripts and quickly earned a reputation for accurate judgments. She worked at CAA for a year before being hired by Amy Pascal at 20th Century Fox as a reader. When Pascal moved on, Allain applied to Warner Brothers and was hired as a reader and analyst on a salary of 75 thousand dollars in 1988. But the twenty-two week strike by Hollywood writers that year meant that studios cut back and Allain was one of the first to lose her job. She was again hired by Amy Pascal, by then working at Columbia, and as she explained to *Contemporary Black*

Biography (*CBB*) she became Pascal's "mouthpiece and record keeper."

Brought Street Culture to Columbia

In 1989, within a year of being hired, Allain was promoted to creative executive at Columbia, with responsibility for shepherding movies through the production process. She told *CBB* that she became a "golden retriever" for Columbia executive Dawn Steel, seeking out promising projects and bringing them to the table. One of the projects Allain rounded up was John Singleton's groundbreaking *Boyz N the Hood*. She explained that at the time Columbia was in the process of being bought by Sony and about to move to new premises at Culver City. There was very little activity at the studio, which was "in disarray." When Singleton's script arrived she described being overwhelmed by its power. Set on the streets of South Central Los Angeles, the movie portrayed an environment familiar to Allain. She was determined to champion Singleton and his project, which arrived at exactly the right time: "After nothing happening, suddenly there was this *big* thing."

Boyz N the Hood was a groundbreaking movie for its hard-hitting realism and its "street" outlook. It also brought black ghetto culture into mainstream movie theaters, so the process of persuading Columbia to make such a new type of movie was far from easy.

Allain described to *CBB* how she pitched the project to each of the Columbia executives in turn, persuading them to read the script. Most of the feedback was positive, but when it came to the final meeting none of the executives who had expressed support were willing to go through with it. It finally came down to the deciding vote of Frank Price, an industry veteran with a reputation for conservatism. Despite the movie's violence, its attitude, and its non-mainstream ghetto edginess, Price actually liked it. Once approved, the movie went into production within two months, showing at Cannes within a year. *Boyz N the Hood* was a huge hit, winning its writer/director John Singleton two Oscar nominations and several other awards. Costing between five and six million dollars to make, it brought in around 60 million dollars and established Allain with a reputation for being able to make what she described as "independent movies in the studio system."

Made Muppet Movies

Allain stayed with Columbia until 1996, supervising over a dozen films in her time there and rising to Senior Vice President of Production, the highest position ever held by an African American in the organization. Her choice of projects at Columbia reflected her interest in small-scale productions with a big impact. For example *El Mariachi* (1992) was originally budgeted at just seven thousand dollars but managed to gross over 2 million dollars and in the process make a name for its writer/director Robert Rodriguez. Allain teamed up with Singleton again to produce 1995's *Higher Learning*, a campus movie with a charateristically hard edge. Then in 1996, after the birth of her second son, Allain moved to Jim Henson Productions, where she produced *Muppets From Space* (1998), and *The Adventures of Elmo in Grouchland* (1998). The difference between the decidedly adult movies she worked on at Columbia and *Muppets from Space*, which carried the tagline "Space: it's not as deep as you think," is significant. But when asked about it Allain told *CBB* that she brought a more adult tone to the Muppet brand. Despite its perceived lack of success, *Muppets from Space* grossed over 127 million dollars at the box office.

Allain admitted that her time at Jim Henson Productions was a career mistake. She thrives on networking and contact with people, and the small-scale, isolated world of what she described as "basically a repertory company" left her cut off from contacts in the rest of Hollywood. In 1999 she quit Jim Henson Productions and spent almost a year away from the industry, writing scripts and a novel; she also took hip-hop dance classes with her son. In 2000 she took charge of 3 Arts Entertainment, developing projects with Chris Rock and Matthew Broderick, among others. Over the course of two years she rebuilt contacts and, as she put it, was "reintroduced to the crowd." In 2002 she started her own production company, Homegrown Films.

Began Homegrown Films

Allain's commitment to making movies, and her excitement at being involved in what she sees as an "explosion" in black Hollywood in the first few years of the twenty-first century, drove her to sell her home to bankroll her production company. Her first movie as an independent producer was *40*, a short film by writer/director Michael Caleo that made its theater debut at the Los Angeles Film Festival in 2002. In the meantime she also produced *Biker Boyz* (2003) for Dreamworks, citing her time on set on this movie as what made her an independent producer "by accident." In 2004 Allain was focusing on *Hustle and Flow*, the work of first-time writer/director Craig Brewer, a white, Southern filmmaker for whom she had high hopes. After several years of trying to find backers for *Hustle and Flow*, Allain finally teamed up again with John Singleton to make the movie.

Allain's career has taken her from high-level executive positions in major studios to battling for money in the independent filmmaking scene. She also teaches producing in the Entertainment Studies division of the University of California Los Angeles. With *Hustle and Flow* she told *CBB* she is "poised to be a real producer," making the movies she wants to make. Despite the problems of being outside the major studios she said she is "pleased to be out...if I'm sleepless at night thinking about the movie I'm happy."

Selected works

Films as producer

Boyz N the Hood, 1991.
Poetic Justice, 1993.
El Mariachi, 1994.
Higher Learning, 1994.
Desperado, 1994.
I Like it Like That, 1995.
The Craft, 1995.
Buddy, 1996.
Muppets from Space, 1998.
The Adventures of Elmo in Grouchland, 1998.
Rat, 2000.
40, 2002.
Biker Boyz, 2003.
Good Boy!, 2003.
Hustle and Flow, 2004.

Sources

Periodicals

Black Enterprise, December 2002.

On-line

Biker Boyz, www.bikerboyz.com (October 28, 2004).

Other

Additional information for this profile was obtained through an interview with Stephanie Allain on October 28, 2004, and from material supplied by her.

—Chris Routledge

Ayi Kwei Armah

1939—

Writer

Ghanaian novelist Ayi Kwei Armah attained international renown for his fiction in the late 1960s and early 1970s. Despite his fame Armah maintained an intensely private life and rarely gave interviews and distanced himself from discussions of his craft. Though critics disagreed about the literary merit of his English-language works, his six novels and numerous short stories provide a glimpse of life in Ghana in the tumultuous years following its independence from Britain.

Armah was born in 1938 in Takoradi, a seaport on Ghana's coast. His heritage was Fante, one of the major ethnic groups in the country, and he came from an elite family. At the time of his birth, the West African nation was a colony of Britain, but the first twenty years of his life coincided with Ghana's long battle for independence. On March 6, 1957, Armah's land became the first colonial African country to win the sovereignty struggle. Around this time, Armah was a student at the Achimota College, a secondary school in Accra, Ghana's capital, and in 1959 won a scholarship to the Groton School in Massachusetts, a prestigious boarding school for boys whose alumni include President Franklin D. Roosevelt as well as numerous Wall Street titans. From there, Armah went on to Harvard University, where he earned a degree in sociology. His first published short story appeared in a 1964 *Harvard Advocate* issue.

During this period of his absence, Ghana descended into political chaos. Its socialist, one-party rule was overthrown by an army coup, and years of internal wrangling and instability followed. Keeping his distance from the turmoil for a time, Armah lived in Algeria and worked as a translator for *Révolution Africaine* magazine in 1963 before coming back to take a job as a scriptwriter for Ghana Television. He also taught English at the Navrongo School in Ghana's city of the same name in 1966 before leaving for Paris to edit *Jeune Afrique* ("Young Africa"), a French-language weekly news magazine, for a year.

Armah's first novel, *The Beautyful Ones Are Not Yet Born,* was published in 1968. It begins with a bus ride taken by its anonymous main character through Accra, where he sees this inscription that serves as the title. "By implication it refers back to the Teacher's story of Plato's cave," according to an essay on Armah's work in *Contemporary Novelists,* "where the one man who escapes from the cave and returns to tell his fellow sufferers of the beautiful world outside is thought to be mad by those in the 'reassuring chains.'" The man in question is a railway clerk, but refuses to take bribes, which keeps his family in poverty and incites their scorn. His old friend Koomson, meanwhile, has become wealthy as a government minister thanks to the endemic corruption. In the end, the man helps Koomson escape certain death when he becomes one of the hunted in crackdown on corrupt officials.

In his next novel, *Fragments,* Armah once again cast a critical eye on modern Ghanaian society. The protagonist in this 1970 work is Baako, who had been living in America but has returned in order to become a screenwriter in his homeland. His family and friends clamor to see genuine proof that he has gone abroad and prospered, but Baako is disillusioned by their rampant new

At a Glance . . .

Born on October 28, 1939, in Takoradi, Ghana. *Education:* Harvard University, AB, Sociology; Columbia University, New York, MFA, Creative Writing, 1970.

Career: *Révolution Africaine* magazine, Algiers, Algeria, translator; Ghana Television, scriptwriter; Navrongo School, Ghana, English teacher, 1966; *Jeune Afrique* magazine, Paris, editor, 1967-68; Teacher's College, Dar es Salaam, and universities of Massachusetts, Amherst, Lesotho, and Wisconsin, teacher.

Addresses: *Office*—Heinemann Educational, Ighodaro Road, Jericho PMB 5205, Ibadan, Oyo State, Nigeria. *Home*—Dakar, Senegal.

materialism. His grandmother, Naana, represents traditional village ways, and he worries that the wisdom of the elders will soon vanish in the rush to attain consumer goods. "Traditional ceremonies, such as Baako's baby nephew's outdooring, have lost their spiritual significance and become an opportunity for ostentation and avarice," noted the *Contemporary Novelists* essay about *Fragments,* and "the plot suggests that Naana's fears for the baby as the victim of this irreligious display are justified, for he dies in the course of it."

With Ghana still mired in political chaos, Armah kept moving: he taught at the University of Massachusetts and then settled in Tanzania in 1970. For several years he taught African literature and creative writing at the College of National Education in Dar es Salaam, the capital city. After 1976 he taught at the National University of Lesotho, a country located within South Africa. He continued to produce essays for various journals, including *Black World* and *West Africa,* on literary and political topics, while working on his third novel, *Why Are We So Blest?* The work was issued by Doubleday in 1972, and centers on Modin, who has been educated abroad and comes back to Africa eager to take part in its new revolutionary struggle. His involvement with a white woman, however, contributes to his horrific mutilation in the midst of a guerrilla war. Aimée and the other white women in the novel are not sympathetically presented, and instead seem to be depicted as sexual predators.

Critics often group Armah's first three novels together, for their literary style and themes seem to reflect the writer and exile's struggle to understand his homeland. They also contain a dark humor that betrays Armah's less-than-favorable appraisal of what happened in Ghana after independence. "Bereft of any sense of community or direction, the educated élites and the masses are shown as actively engaged in their own betrayal, collaborating in the neo-colonial plunder and impoverishment of their national heritages," summarized S. Nyamfukudza of Armah's early works in a critical essay that appeared in the *New Statesman* in 1980.

Armah's fourth book, *Two Thousand Seasons,* published in 1973, featured a new style of prose that borrowed more heavily from folk tales than of Western literary constructs. Its time is hard to place, but its setting is Africa, and the plot centers around a group of people who are fleeing some Arab invaders. The Africans head south, only to meet European slave traders making raids. Some of the group are taken, but later escape from the slave ship. The story seems to grapple with the idea of Africa and its destiny as shaped by outside people's forces. Armah's next work, *The Healers,* also deals with the past: in this case, the fall of the once-mighty Ashanti empire in Ghana, as does *Osiris Rising: A Novel of Africa Past, Present, and Future.* Though written in English, it was not published in the West after its 1995 issue by a Senegalese house. Armah lives in the capital of Senegal, Dakar.

Selected writings

The Beautyful Ones Are Not Yet Born, Houghton Mifflin, 1968.
Fragments, Houghton Mifflin, 1970.
Why Are We So Blest?, Doubleday, 1972.
Two Thousand Seasons, East African Publishing House, 1973.
The Healers, East African Publishing House, 1978.
Osiris Rising: A Novel of Africa Past, Present, and Future, Per Ankh, 1995.

Sources

Books

African Writers, vol. 1, Scribner's, 1997.
Contemporary Novelists, 7th ed., St. James Press, 2001.
Dictionary of Literary Biography, Vol. 117: Twentieth-Century Caribbean and Black African Writers, Bernth Lindfors and Reinhard Sander, eds., Gale, 1992.
Fraser, Robert, *The Novels of Ayi Kwei Armah,* 1980.
Ogede, Ode, *Ayi Kwei Armah, Radical Iconoclast,* Ohio University Press, 2004.

Periodicals

New Statesman, March 7, 1980, pp. 362-363.

—Carol Brennan

Roosevelt Barlow

1917-2003

Fire captain, civil rights activist

Roosevelt Barlow was among a small group of African-American firefighters to integrate the Philadelphia Fire Department, enduring extremely harsh treatment and fighting against entrenched institutional racism. He risked his life to help his brothers in the department and to help his community become a better place for all minorities. Barlow was among the first African Americans in the department to be promoted to lieutenant and captain, and his work is known by many throughout the city, even being mentioned in the Fireman's Hall Museum in Philadelphia. He is a key figure in the story of integration in the city and came to be loved by many for his dedication and caring.

Barlow was born on October 13, 1917, in Sandersville, Georgia, the eldest child of Eldridge and Lucy Barlow. "My mother-in-law was the sweetest woman and my father-in-law was lovable," Barlow's widow, Virginia, said in an interview with *Contemporary Black Biography* (*CBB*). "My husband got a lot of his traits from his father." The family moved to Philadelphia when Barlow was very young. Central Philadelphia was a rough place to grow up in at that time, and although the schools were integrated, often a black child would find himself alone in an all-white classroom. There Barlow met Virginia, who would become his high school sweetheart, at Simon Gratz High. He graduated in 1937 and married Virginia in 1938. The couple was blessed with a son, Raymond, and would spend 65 years together before Barlow passed away in 2003.

During high school Barlow took a job as a busboy and short order cook. But he really wanted to become a firefighter. Upon graduation he decided to test for both the fire and the police departments. When the fire department called, Barlow began work at Engine 11 (E-11), an all black station known among firefighters as the Jim Crow Station. In the early 1940s, black firemen could only work there or on the fireboat. Barlow and his co-workers suffered degrading insults and appalling treatment from whites in the department. There was some solace in the fact that their boss was an African American. "Jim Davis, the first black fire captain in Philadelphia, was tough but he taught his men well and that's when black firefighters started progressing," Virginia Barlow told *CBB*. The men believed in him.

"The department was integrating in 1952 and as black firefighters moved into white fire houses many whites did not like sharing living quarters with them," said Lt. Claude Smith, Barlow's good friend and president of Club Valiants, an international organization of black firefighters the two men helped to found. The nature of the work required that the men live together. Some white firemen had no trouble making blacks feel unwelcome. Black firemen were not allowed to use the same restrooms as whites, and whites would break dishes that the black men used. Once, Barlow was given a horse blanket to sleep on instead of a bed at one of the white stations. But Barlow fought discrimination where he found it and stood his ground. In later years he would find some of the memories too difficult to talk about. Even though the black firefighters' job was to help save homes and lives, sometimes the very people they tried to help were the one's who shunned them. In

1952 Barlow became a lieutenant, a well-earned promotion for a man known among his peers for speaking out against bias. In 1961 Barlow became one of the first black captains in the department.

Facing bias through the years Barlow knew personally the obstacles black firefighters would face as more joined the department, and he knew they needed to work together to fight racism. Barlow and a group of fellow firemen from E-11 and Fire Boat #1 began plans to create Club Valiants to fight the battle together. The organization would be vital to their survival as they were split from their comrades to move out across the city in the name of integration. The men had found themselves being mistreated and sometimes ignored at other stations. Club Valiants would create a fellowship and source of information for black firefighters and eventually began to counsel its members, donate to charities, and set out to educate the community about fire prevention. As promotions and hiring practices were scrutinized by the city it was determined that bias did exist and a class action suit was brought against the department. The Civil Rights Act of 1964 helped but did not allow discrimination cases to be brought against a city department, and many blacks felt that the department practiced discrimination openly. Despite these obstacles, the Valiants' work eventually paid off and many more minority members were hired and promoted as a result. Club Valiants would later become the founding chapter of a larger national group. In 1970 firefighters from stations across the country met in Hartford, Connecticut, to form the International Association of Black Professional Firefighters to help other blacks get hired, to fight discrimination, to foster promotions, and to support the dissemination of information about their work.

Conditions did change as Virginia Barlow recalled, "The people that he worked with soon found out that my husband was nothing to play with. But they also learned that people could get along regardless of who they were. He was a very kind man and believed in doing right. People found he was earnest in everything he did. They came to love him. Even today I meet people and they tell me he was well liked."

Barlow extended his kindness and concern for a life without discrimination beyond his vocation. He was active with Fellowship Farms, a non-profit, human relations group which helps educate the community about diversity. The group set up the Roosevelt Barlow Scholarship Fund to honor his work and to help disadvantaged kids.

Barlow was also a member of the National Organization of Concerned Black Men, a group dedicated to helping the disadvantaged with problems such as teen pregnancy, HIV, and substance abuse. The group offers many services, including tutoring and mentoring to young people. In addition Barlow was a board member, for more than 20 years, of Big Brothers Big Sisters of America, a youth mentoring program.

Barlow retired from the fire department in 1968. He worked for more years, however, as a human resources specialist at a local hospital. In his spare time he listened to jazz and classical music, a testament to the nature of this gentle and intelligent man who is remembered and loved by many in Philadelphia. Being an avid reader, he loved history, and indeed now he is a part of history.

Sources

On-line

"The Roosevelt Barlow Scholarship Fund," *Fellowship Farm,* www.fellowshipfarm.org/memorial.htm (November 18, 2004).

"History," *Club Valiants, Inc.,* www.clubvaliants.org (November 18, 2004).

Other

Additional information for this profile was obtained through an interview with Mrs. Virginia Barlow on October 30, 2004, and an interview with Lt. Claude Smith on November 4, 2004.

—Sharon Melson Fletcher

Don Berrysmith

1936—

Psychotherapist, social worker

During the first 20 years of his life, Don Berrysmith encountered a broad range of the African-American experience. From segregated Louisiana to liberal, but largely white, Seattle, and from Texas boot camp to the bistros of Paris and Copenhagen, Berrysmith learned about racism from the overt to the subtle. In Europe, he also got a glimpse of another world, where the color of his skin did not automatically define him as inferior to the white people around him. Always sharply observant, he developed an understanding of the impact that poverty and racism had on mental and emotional health. He not only forged a graduate degree and a lifelong career out of his experiences, but he also worked to give those most overlooked by the mental health system a voice in their own care.

Don Reginald Berrysmith was born in the tiny town of Jeanerette, Louisiana, in early March 1936. His mother, Neotha Rochon, worked as an elementary school teacher in Jeanerette. His father, Chester Berrysmith, was the school principal in nearby New Iberia. Educational prospects for African Americans were bleak in 1930s Louisiana, but Chester had been able to rise to the office of principal even though he had only attended college for a year.

Berrysmith spent the first seven years of his life with his family in New Iberia. Then, as the United States was swept up in World War II, Chester Berrysmith heard of good job opportunities working in the shipyards in Seattle, Washington. Leaving his family behind, he headed for the Pacific Northwest, where he got a job making three times what he had made as the principal

of a Southern black school. A year later, in 1943, he sent for his family, and the Berrysmiths made Seattle their home.

Grew up in the Pacific Northwest

In the 1940s, Washington had been a state for less than sixty years. Before the arrival of European settlers, Indian tribes like the Duwamish and the Suquamish had fished the shores of Puget Sound where Seattle is located. Many Scandinavian immigrants settled in the area, drawn to similarities in terrain and weather as well as jobs cutting timber or outfitting prospectors for the Alaska gold rush in the late 1890s. The population in the 1940s was diverse; there were still Native people living in and around the city, and many Asian immigrants lived and worked in Seattle. However, the city had a very small black population. In the 1940s, the war industry drew a steady stream of black workers from the South, but Seattle still remained predominately white. This white world came as a shock to a seven-year-old child from a black community in segregated Louisiana. Berrysmith found himself the only black student in his entire school.

Like many people from the French-influenced state of Louisiana, Neotha Berrysmith was a devout Catholic, so her children attended Catholic schools. Throughout his schooling, Berrysmith was among no more than a few other African American students, and often found himself harassed by white boys. Since he and his brother had few allies, they learned to defend themselves. Don was thin and small, but soon became angry

At a Glance . . .

Born Don Reginald Berrysmith on March 6, 1936, in Jeanerette, Louisiana; married LaVonne Mc-Gee, 1966 (divorced); married Ann Shigeta, 1981; children: three children. *Education:* University of Washington, MA, social work, 1974.

Career: Harborview Hospital Psychiatric Ward, orderly, 1952; Harborview Hospital, orderly, 1960-61; Luther Burbank, cottage supervisor, 1963-66; Echo Glen, cottage supervisor, 1967-68; Seattle Mental Health Institute, director of citizen participation, associate director, 1968-79; private practice psychotherapist, 1980-2001.

Memberships: National Association for the Advancement of Colored People; Seattle Metropolitan Urban League; National Association of Social Workers, Children's Hospital Guild.

Awards: Central Seattle Community Council, Man of the Year, 1969.

Addresses: *Home*—Seattle, WA.

and tough enough that the bullies learned to leave him alone. His self-image of strength and independence was reinforced when his parents divorced when he was eleven years old. As the oldest son, Berrysmith considered himself the man of the house.

Throughout his years at Catholic school, Berrysmith continually fought for respect from both students and teachers. When one of the Catholic Brothers who taught him at O'Dea High School refused to allow him to participate in an oratory contest, he only became more determined to succeed. The following year, he not only competed in the contest, but also won the trophy, defeating the students sponsored by the Brother who had kept him out of the competition.

Throughout his education, Berrysmith received conflicting messages from his parents. His father believed strongly that education was important, especially for black Americans trying to improve their lives. Berrysmith remembered in an interview with *Contemporary Black Biography* (CBB) that his father would tell his children repeatedly: "Knowledge is power." Neotha Berrysmith, on the other hand, often described a black man with a higher education as, "another janitor with a degree," as Berrysmith recalled to *CBB*. She considered education a waste of time, since she felt that blacks would never be allowed to rise to top jobs. She encouraged her son to learn a trade, get a good job, and work hard.

Traveled to Europe in the Air Force

In 1951, when Berrysmith was 15, his world changed in several fundamental ways. His mother remarried, and her oldest son found it hard to accept a new man in the house. Around the same time, an even larger change took place in Berrysmith's thinking. Raised in Catholic schools by a devout mother, Berrysmith had always been a religious young man. He had been an altar boy, helping the priest serve mass, and, during his first two years of high school, had been on the honor roll. A trip back to Louisiana to visit his mother's family caused him to question the church in which he had placed his faith.

Attending mass back in New Iberia, Berrysmith noticed something strange. He leaned over and whispered to his mother, "There aren't many white Catholics in Louisiana, are there?" When his mother explained that there were indeed many white Catholics, who were attending mass at the white cathedral across town, Berrysmith was stunned. He felt he could no longer trust a church that could teach brotherly love and yet practice segregation. When he returned home to Seattle, he withdrew from the church.

He also withdrew his energy from his studies. He became rebellious, challenging his teachers, his new stepfather, and the other adults in his life, who he had begun to feel were all hypocrites and liars. He was expelled, first from O'Dea High School, then from Garfield, his neighborhood public high school. The altar boy who had attended mass every day began hanging out on the streets, looking for trouble.

At the age of 17, Berrysmith joined the Air Force. His mother opposed the idea, but his father persuaded her that the discipline of the service would help their rebellious son. After a grueling 13-week boot camp training in San Antonio, Texas, Berrysmith was assigned to serve as a medic in the base dental clinic. However, he had no desire to stay in the South, and as soon as possible, he took a tour of duty in Europe.

When he went to France in 1954, Berrysmith found a very different world from that in which he had been raised. Though some discrimination existed, the entrenched anti-black racism he had experienced did not. Though still in the Air Force, he maintained a full social life. He traveled, met interesting people, went to clubs, gambled, listened to music, and enjoyed life in general. He even planned to continue living in France after he got out of the Air Force. However, some trouble with military authorities resulted in his being sent back to the United States, where he was discharged in 1958.

Began Social Service Work

When he returned to the United States, he made a brief stop in New Iberia, where he enjoyed his new status as "man of the world." However, he soon realized that he did not have the temperament to endure the blatant racial discrimination practiced in Louisiana during the 1950s. With his pride and quick temper, he knew that life in the segregated South would be dangerous for him. By 1959 he had returned to Seattle, where racial bias was present, but in a much less obvious way.

Before he entered the Air Force, Berrysmith had worked as an orderly in the psychiatric ward of Seattle's public hospital, Harborview. There, he had seen the pain and degradation of mental patients who had few treatment options besides being tied in restraints and given electric shocks. On his return, he again took a job at Harborview. Though treatments were somewhat less violent by the early 1960s, new psychiatric drugs like Thorazine left patients sluggish and unresponsive. Berrysmith watched them with sympathy and thought there must be a better way to treat those who suffered from mental and emotional pain.

Around this time, he began to visit a friend who worked at Luther Burbank School, a juvenile detention facility. He liked helping out with the boys who had been sentenced to stay at the school, and soon he left Harborview and went to work at Luther Burbank full time as a cottage supervisor. It made him angry that society seemed so easily to discard the young men of color who made up much of the school's population. He saw much of himself in the troubled youths, and he offered them discipline, respect, and friendship. They responded by respecting Berrysmith in turn, by winning most of the school's sports competitions, and by gaining their releases from the facility. Though proud of his students' successes, Berrysmith was disturbed by how many returned to detention after facing poverty, discrimination, and violence in the world outside.

Berrysmith continued to work with delinquent youth for the next six years, first at Luther Burbank, then at a new facility called Echo Glen. In 1968 he left Echo Glen, anxious to become part of a growing nationwide social reform movement that was seeking change in everything from the status of African Americans to the mental health system. He was hired in July 1968 to be a "community outreach worker" at Seattle Mental Health Institute (SMHI), a community mental health center.

The psychiatrists in charge of SMHI took advantage of the federal Model Cities program to gain funds for their center. Model Cities, initiated during the late 1960s by President Lyndon Johnson, was an ambitious plan to fight crime, unemployment, poverty, and other urban problems by funding community-based social programs. In 1967 Johnson had also provided government funds for the Community Mental Health Centers Act, which was part of the same broad government program to improve conditions for people living in poor communities. Though SMHI received money from the National Mental Health Institute (NMHI) through the Community Mental Heath Centers Act, and though they hired a black outreach worker, they had little idea how to create a really community-based center.

Did Groundbreaking Work in Community Health Care

However, Don Berrysmith did have ideas. He had grown up in the Central District of Seattle, the same area served by SMHI, and he was bursting with exciting plans for improving the mental health of his community. His first step was to re-define his job. Instead of a low-level outreach position, which might involve passing out flyers and attending meetings in the community, Berrysmith demanded a whole department devoted to getting the community involved in its own mental health care. He called it the Department of Citizen Participation. He would be the head of the department, and he would report directly to the head of the agency. The SMHI board of directors agreed, and the Department of Citizen Participation began its work.

Berrysmith then began to do outreach, not only to the community, but also to federal agencies, like the National Institute of Mental Health. He contacted various local committees of the Model Cities Program, such as the law and justice task force, the poverty task force, and the housing task force. Berrysmith proposed that a citizen participation task force be added to these groups. Not only did the Model Cities Program agree, but they made Berrysmith co-chair of the task force on health.

Having taken citizen participation into the organizations, Berrysmith then began to do outreach into the community, "I wanted to take the message to the community that the mental health center belonged to them," he said. He encouraged members of the community to let the center know what services were needed. His work on the various Model City task forces became even more important, because issues like poverty, housing, and law and justice are at the very center of mental health issues of poor people of color. As Berrysmith himself had experienced, both in his own life and in his work with delinquent children, poverty and discrimination led to anger and depression. That anger and depression, Berrysmith noted, too often led the poor and oppressed to prison or mental hospitals.

Berrysmith and Julia Bassett, his assistant at SMHI, worked hard to accomplish the changes they thought were necessary to create a truly community-based mental health center. However, it seemed that small reforms would not be enough. Most of the doctors and members of the board of directors in charge of SMHI were wealthy white people who did not live in the neighborhood the center served. Berrysmith began to feel that they could not understand the community's needs and would never make the necessary changes in the center. He called on the many powerful people he had worked with in the Model Cities Program to put pressure on SMHI to use the federal money grants it had received for more innovative and community-based programs.

This federal pressure combined with Berrysmith's base of support in the community began to make the SMHI management uncomfortable. The head of the agency resigned, followed by much of the rest of his administration. These department heads were soon replaced with more community-oriented workers. The board of directors was reorganized to include members of the local community. Berrysmith himself headed a committee of three to seek a new director for the agency. They hired Myron Kowals, who had written the original grant that gained government funds for SMHI. Berrysmith became his associate director.

Under the new administration, SMHI flourished. Exciting new programs were instituted, such as a working gas station, where mental health patients could learn job skills and responsibilities. In addition, Berrysmith set up an extensive volunteer program, where community members could work in all areas of the center and participate in meetings on an equal basis with paid staff. He also continued to work for racial balance on the center's staff and to do anti-racism work within the community.

Earned Master's Degree

While working at SMHI, Berrysmith continued to develop his own career. He had never finished high school, but passed a General Educational Development test while in the Air Force that gave him the equivalent of a high school diploma. Later, he attended high school classes in Seattle so that he could earn an actual diploma. Though he had taken courses at Edison Technical School (now called Seattle Central Community College), the University of Washington, and Olym-

pic College in the nearby town of Bremerton, he had never earned a college degree. However, citing his studies and his varied work experience, he petitioned the University of Washington to accept him as a graduate student. The university agreed, and in 1974 Berrysmith received his master's degree in social work.

In 1979 he left SIMH to go into private practice as a counselor. In 1980 he put to use the skills he had learned while restructuring the mental health center. He won a contract from the National Mental Institute of Mental Health to travel to 15 mental health centers in California and Arizona to train their boards of directors in the issues of community mental health. He also joined the faculty of the University of Washington for a time as a visiting lecturer, teaching medical school students about a topic which was very important to him, "Politics of the Powerless."

At the same time, he developed a thriving counseling practice, focusing on couples and families. During the mid 1980s, he was contracted by the Seahawks football team for counseling and drug treatment. In 1990 together with two other therapists, he began another innovative program, domestic violence treatment aimed at batterers. For eight years, Berrysmith and his associates took on the difficult and often unappreciated task of teaching those who had been violent towards family members more constructive ways of expressing anger. Courts often referred those convicted of domestic violence to Berrysmith's group for counseling.

In 2001 Don Berrysmith retired. He has continued to live in Seattle and to participate in community events. His retirement has provided him with more time to devote to his family, his travels, and his Harley-Davidson motorcycle.

Sources

Other

Information for this profile was obtained through an interview with Don Berrysmith on November 10, 2004.

—Tina Gianoulis

Eric Bibb

1951—

Blues guitarist

Bibb, Eric, photograph. Jo Hale/Getty Images.

One of the most imaginative modern musicians working within the blues tradition, Eric Bibb is also one of the least recognized in proportion to his talent, at least in his home country of the United States. Bibb is a singer, songwriter, and guitarist with deep roots in American music, roots that come from his family background and also from his own journey as a musician. But in the early 1970s, Bibb made the decision, as had many African-American musicians before him, to leave the United States and settle abroad.

Bibb was born in New York City on August 16, 1951. Music ran deep in his family; jazz pianist John Lewis of the Modern Jazz Quartet was his uncle, and his father Leon Bibb was an actor and singer who got involved in the rising folk scene in New York's Greenwich Village in the 1950s and early 1960s. Bibb grew up surrounded by folk music royalty. Singer and activist Paul Robeson was his godfather, and such nationally famous singers as Pete Seeger and Odetta were family friends. Another guest, when Bibb was 11, was Bob Dylan. "When I found out that he had arrived I snuck downstairs in my pajamas and had a talk with him about guitar playing. He told me to keep it simple—forget all

the fancy s–t," Bibb told the *Irish Times.*

Steered Toward Blues by Jazz Musician

While a student at New York's High School of Music and Art, Bibb was enthusiastic about music but indifferent in his other classes. He delved into all kinds of music, including classical guitar. Bibb's father taught him about various kinds of black music, but was his uncle John Lewis who did the most to expose him to the blues—which was somewhat ironic in view of the fact that Lewis was known for a very sophisticated type of jazz with strong classical influences. "I was fascinated to learn how enamored he was of the blues, and I mean gut-bucket blues…. I'd go to his house and he'd talk about Muddy Waters and stuff like that," Bibb told the London *Independent.*

Every time he got the chance, Bibb headed for Greenwich Village to spend time in the area's vibrant folk clubs. When he was 16 he joined a band his father put together for a television talent show called *Someone New.* Another member of the band was Bill Lee, father of future director Spike Lee. Bibb enrolled at Columbia

At a Glance . . .

Born August 16, 1951, in New York, NY; son of Leon Bibb (actor and singer). *Education:* Attended Columbia University.

Career: Musician, 1950s–.

Addresses: *Office*—Earthbeat Records, P.O. Box 1460, Redway, CA 95560.

University in New York but music still had the strongest pull on his energy. At age 19, on a trip to Paris, Bibb met rhythm-and-blues guitarist Mickey Baker and began to focus seriously on the blues.

At the same time, Bibb became disillusioned with the United States and its involvement in the Vietnam War. He saw a better chance to pursue his peace-loving philosophies in Europe than he could envision back home in bitterly divided America, with what he called (as quoted by the *Irish Times*) its "tribal strife." "What I see when I look around the world is basically local versions of the same type of frictions between groups, whether they're black or white, whatever religion, Middle East or Northern Ireland—it's basically brother against brother, when it comes down to it," he told the Irish newspaper.

Moved to Sweden

Invited to Stockholm, Sweden for a short visit, Bibb decided to stay on there. Though people of African descent were rare in Sweden, and Bibb found that he was treated as something of an exotic attraction, he liked the country's open and liberal attitudes. He delved deeper into American acoustic blues, finding places to play and Swedish musicians who wanted to work with him. As well, he began to encounter music from other parts of the world. Irish, Greek, and African sounds would all find their ways into his music at various times.

In 1980 Bibb returned to the United States, settling in New York and taking a shot at starting an American acoustic music career. The competitive atmosphere of 1980s America discouraged him, however, and he found the music scene much changed from what he had known in 1960s Greenwich Village. "Even the folkies were stepping over each other to make it—that really turned me off," he told the *Irish Times*. Bibb went back to Sweden. Between gigs he made a living as a school music teacher and, for a time, as a staff songwriter for the BMG music conglomerate. He translated children's books from Swedish into English on the side; one of them was called *The Clay Flute*.

Although he was a popular attraction in Sweden, Bibb's own music remained unrecorded for many years. Finally, in 1994, he released his *Spirit and the Blues* album on Sweden's Opus 3 label. The timing was fortunate, for a host of similarly oriented musicians were beginning their careers in the United States around the same time. Music buyers started showing a strong interest in contemporary extensions of roots traditions, and Bibb began finding audiences in Britain, Ireland, and Australia as well as in Sweden. In 1996 he appeared at the London Blues Festival with American bluesmen Corey Harris and Keb' Mo', and his sophomore release, 1997's *Good Stuff,* was picked up by the U.S. label Earthbeat.

Influenced by Taj Mahal

Bibb recorded mostly for the British Code Blue and Manhaton labels as his career picked up steam, and several recordings he made in Sweden were re-released in the United States. The electric-blues *Me to You* (1998) featured a pair of Bibb's idols, soul singers Pops and Mavis Staples, and such albums as *Home to Me* (1999) and *Roadworks* (2000) showed the influence of an older bluesman who had experimented with world music and tried to draw connections between the blues and the wider musical world—Taj Mahal. The 2001 album *Needed Time* took its name from Bibb's backing band.

More often than not, Bibb avoided the melancholy tone traditionally associated with the blues; many of his original songs (and he performed mostly originals) had a warm, positive outlook with spiritual overtones. Bibb pointed out that he personally wasn't a melancholy person and that historically, the blues served as dance music and as entertainment as often as it expressed sorrow and pain. And the traditional image of the blues, he argued in an *Irish Times* interview, was partly "the produce of the way it was marketed by people who had it in their vested interest to see the performers, these black musicians, as unidimensional, pitiable persons." Bibb's versatility served him well on the Grammy-nominated collaborative children's album *Shakin' a Tailfeather.*

Toured with Robert Cray

Bibb reached a new level with his *Painting Signs* CD (2001), which featured songs on social themes and world affairs, including a rousing cover of the Pops Staples composition "Hope in a Hopeless World." He finally became better known in the United States, touring with fellow modern bluesman Robert Cray in 2001 and 2002 and opening for the legendary Ray Charles in 2002. Bibb seemed to become more prolific as a musician as his fortunes improved, and he quickly followed up *Painting Signs* with two more albums, the more personal *Natural Light* and *A Family Affair,* an album pairing Bibb with his 80-year-old father Leon–who had also left the United States for the Canadian city of Vancouver. The folk music magazine *Sing Out!* termed *A Family Affair* "a very inspiring album."

A Family Affair wasn't released in the United States until 2003, and by that time Bibb had several more albums in the works or on the streets. Bibb moved from Sweden to London, England in 2003, telling the *Independent* that he had felt at home during his frequent tours in the United Kingdom and that "I was also very impressed by the way British society in recent years has been dealing with the whole issue of multiculturalism." His 2004 album *Friends* seemed to signal a point where Bibb reached the top tier of the blues world: it featured collaborations between Bibb and a diverse group of guest musicians that included Taj Mahal, guitarist Guy Davis, vocalist Ruthie Foster, Malian guitarist Djelimady Tounkara, and Odetta, who had been one of the artists that inspired Bibb as he soaked up the creative spirit of Greenwich Village in the 1950s and 1960s.

Selected discography

Spirit and the Blues, Opus 3, 1994.
Good Stuff, Opus 3/Earthbeat, 1997.
(With Taj Mahal and Linda Tillery) *Shakin' a Tail-feather,* 1997.
Me to You, Code Blue, 1998.
Home to Me, Manhaton, 1999.
Roadworks, Manhaton, 2000.
Needed Time, Opus 3, 2001.
Painting Signs, Manhaton, 2001.
Just Like Love, Opus 3, 2001.
A Family Affair, Manhaton, 2001.
Natural Light, Earthbeat, 2003.
Friends, Earthbeat, 2004.

Sources

Periodicals

Australian, September 5, 2003, p. 15.
Independent (London, England), February 21, 2003, p. 20.
Irish Times, May 15, 1998, p. 14.
New York Times, October 28, 1990, section 7, p. 32.
Sing Out!, Winter 2004, p. 157.
Sunday Herald Sun (Melbourne, Australia), April 8, 2001, p. 86; August 31, 2003, p. 115.
Times (London, England), November 20, 1998, Features section.

On-line

Eric Bibb, www.ericbibb.com (November 30, 2004).
"Eric Bibb," *All Music Guide,* www.allmusic.com (November 30, 2004).

—James M. Manheim

Gwendolyn E. Boyd

1955—

Engineer, activist

As the 22nd national president of Delta Sigma Theta Sorority, Inc., the nation's largest black sorority, in her career as an engineer at Johns Hopkins University's Applied Physics Laboratory, and in her dedicated community service, Gwendolyn E. Boyd has been a prominent advocate for women's equality and for the recruitment of black Americans into science and engineering.

Became an Engineer

Born on December 27, 1955, in Montgomery, Alabama, Gwendolyn Elizabeth Boyd was the daughter of Dora Lee McClain, a single parent and domestic worker. Attending public schools in Montgomery, Boyd enjoyed math and science. She began to think that she might become an engineer, although she had no role models or knowledge of what engineers did. However while attending Alabama State University on a four-year scholarship, Boyd realized that engineering was a profession in which she could apply her interests in mathematics and science to practical problems. In 1977 she graduated summa cum laude with a Bachelor of Science degree in mathematics and a double minor in physics and music.

A graduate fellowship enabled Boyd to enter the Yale University School of Engineering where she was the only woman and the only black among her program's 25 students. Specializing in acoustics, Boyd earned her master's degree in mechanical engineering in 1979 and went to work for IBM in Kingston, New York.

The following year Boyd joined the Johns Hopkins University (JHU) Applied Physics Laboratory (APL) as a team engineer. For almost two decades in APL's Strategic Systems Department, Boyd used her background in acoustics to test and evaluate submarine navigation systems for the Department of the Navy. Most of her research work remained classified.

Joined the APL Administration

In 1998 Boyd combined her scientific background with her administrative skills—garnered through years of community service—to become the APL Assistant for Development Programs. In this role she served as liaison for APL's external programs, including research programs at other universities.

Boyd helped develop the Atlas Scholars Program—the APL Technology Leaders Summer Internship Program for Historically Black Colleges and Universities (HBCUs), Hispanic-Serving Institutions, and Minority Institutions. ATLAS provides paid summer internships for qualified college seniors majoring in electrical engineering and computer science.

The president of JHU appointed Boyd to the JHU Diversity Leadership Council, which worked to expand diversity among the university's faculty, staff, and student body. Boyd served as chair of the Council between 2003 and 2005. In 2004 Boyd became executive assistant to the APL chief of staff.

At a Glance . . .

Born Gwendolyn Elizabeth Boyd on December 27, 1955, in Montgomery, AL. *Education:* Alabama State University, BA, mathematics, 1977; Yale University, MS, mechanical engineering, 1979. *Religion:* African Methodist Episcopal.

Career: John Hopkins University Applied Physics Laboratory, engineer, 1980-98, assistant for development programs, 1998-2004, executive assistant to the chief of staff, 2004–.

Selected memberships: Society of Women Engineers, 1980–; The Links, Inc., 1983–, area parliamentarian, 1993-2002; United Way of the National Capital Area, board of directors 1984–, chair 1997-2001; Children's National Medical Center-Children's Hospital, board of directors, 1996–, Parent's Board and Children's Research Institute Board, 1998–; Delta Sigma Theta, national first vice president, 1996-2000, national president, 2000-2004, immediate past national president, 2004–.

Selected awards: Black Engineer of the Year, Outstanding Alumnus Achievement, 2000; Black AIDS Institute, "Heroes in the Struggle," 2004; Johns Hopkins University Women's Network, Women's Leadership Award, 2004; U. S. Secretary of Energy, Special Recognition Award, 2004; Lincoln University, honorary doctorate of humane letters, 2005.

Addresses: *Office—* John Hopkins University Applied Physics Laboratory, 11100 Johns Hopkins Road, Laurel, MD 20723.

Led Delta Sigma Theta

Delta Sigma Theta (DST) was founded in 1913 at Howard University. DST membership included more than 250,000 college-educated black American women by 2004. With more than 950 chapters throughout the United States, as well as in Japan, Korea, Germany, and elsewhere, DST is the country's largest organization of black women. As a private non-profit organization, DST's programs and services are concentrated in five areas: economic development, educational development, international awareness and involvement, physical and mental health, and political awareness and involvement.

In September of 2000, at the 45th annual DST convention in Chicago, 15,000 members elected Boyd as their national president. Boyd told Denise Barnes of the *Washington Times* on March 8, 2002: "Our organization was founded by women who were activists and those who led change in their day, and the Deltas continue through our 89 years of existence. As we see issues affecting the growth and development of community and family, we must speak out."

Boyd was true to her convictions. On March 9, 2002, DST held a national day of service to increase awareness of HIV/AIDS among black Americans. That same year, Boyd was able to present Howard University with $1 million that had been raised by Deltas.

Drawing on her experiences at APL, Boyd oversaw the 2003 launch of the Delta SEE Connection, a five-year initiative promoting "Science and Everyday Experiences." In conjunction with the American Association for the Advancement of Science and funding from the National Science Foundation, SEE was a component of a broader effort to encourage women and minorities to consider careers in science and engineering. Delta SEE radio programs, primarily distributed to HBCU and other stations with large black audiences, featured interviews with black scientists, mathematicians, and engineers. In conjunction with the Delta Research and Education Foundation, the SEE program also produced websites and various print materials, including science pages for children and their families in black newspapers. Individual Delta chapters functioned as informal scientific resources.

That same year Boyd introduced the Delta Homeownership Initiative, a partnership between DST and GE Mortgage Insurance designed to assist DST members and their families and friends with purchasing homes. *PR Newswire* quoted Boyd: "African Americans are missing out on a brighter financial future by not taking full advantage of one of the most powerful tools for wealth accumulation available to them. We're very happy to be teaming with GE Mortgage Insurance to help our sisters and others break the rental cycle and create a personal homeownership plan. We want to show them how the home they've dreamed of could become a reality."

Devoted Herself to Service

Boyd joined the board of directors of United Way of the National Capital Area in 1984. Between 1997 and 2001, a period during which questions arose concerning the finances and governance of the regional agency, Boyd served as board chair.

Boyd joined the board of directors of the APL Federal Credit Union in 1993, eventually serving as vice-chair and chair. As of 2004 she was immediate-past chair. She was the founding chair of the board of directors of the National Partnership for Community Leadership, based in Washington, D.C. Boyd also served as the Honorary Vice Chairperson for the Bethune Visionary Committee Bronze Statue Project. In 2004 she joined the ministerial staff of the Ebenezer African Methodist Episcopal (A.M.E.) Church in Fort Washington, Maryland. In 2005 Boyd joined the national board of the Alzheimer's Foundation.

Boyd told *Contemporary Black Biography* in November of 2004 that she was particularly proud of her work since 1994 as a mentor with the Meyerhoff Scholars Program at the University of Maryland Baltimore County. Record numbers of minority students from this program have gone on to pursue doctoral research in mathematics, science, engineering, and technology.

In addition, Boyd served on the Thurgood Marshall Scholarship Foundation Board, on the Advisory Council of the College of Engineering, Architecture, and Physical Science at Tuskegee University, and as a member of the Metropolitan Area Network of Minority Women in Science. In 2005 Boyd joined the Bennett College for Women Board of Visitors.

Recognized for Her Achievements

Boyd has been the recipient of the "Find the Good and Praise It" Service Award from Phi Beta Sigma Fraternity and the 1996 Black Engineer of the Year Public Service Award. A member of the Leadership Washington class of 1996, she served on the board of directors from 1996 until 1999 and received their Outstanding Alumnus Award. Her many other awards include the Outstanding Service Award from the Howard County National Association for the Advancement of Colored People (NAACP) and the Community Service Award of the United Way, both in 1998, and the National Trio Achievers Award of the National Council of Educational Opportunity Associations. Boyd has received congressional citations and acknowledgements in the Congressional Record and has been presented with keys from more than 20 cities, for of which have declared "Gwendolyn E. Boyd Days."

Ebony named Boyd among the "100+ Organization Leaders" in 2001 and 2002 and among the "100+ Most Influential Black Americans" in 2003 and 2004. In 2003 she was recognized by *US Black Engineer*

magazine as one of the nation's "Most Distinguished Black College and University Graduates."

As a sought-after lecturer, Boyd frequently addressed groups ranging from small classrooms to international conferences. In addition to technical presentations, her subjects have included non-profit board development, leadership development, black American history and women's history, as well as inspirational and motivational topics.

In March of 2004, as reported in *America's Intelligence Wire*, Boyd spoke at the U. S. Department of Energy's Office of Economic Impact and Diversity celebration of National Women's History and National African American Months: "Women are everywhere and doing everything.... We need to make sure that we celebrate those women who challenged the debate, those who have been part of making the change, those who know that education is the key, and that knowledge is powerful."

Sources

Periodicals

America's Intelligence Wire, March 24, 2004.
Jet, September 11, 2000.
PR Newswire, September 9, 2003.
Science, June 27, 2003, pp. 2050-51.
Washington Times, March 8, 2002, p. B04.

On-line

"APL Minority Initiatives," *JHU Applied Physics Laboratory,* www.jhuapl.edu/education/minority/minorityinit.html (December 1, 2004).
"Biographical Statement for Gwendolyn E. Boyd," *Black AIDS Institute,* www.blackaids.org/gwen%20boyd%20bio.doc (December 1, 2004).

Other

Additional information for this profile was obtained through an interview with Gwendolyn Boyd on November 20, 2004.

—Margaret Alic

William Brower

1916-2004

Journalist

The career of journalist William Brower spanned vast developments in African-American life, and he chronicled them all. When he was hired by the *Blade* newspaper of Toledo, Ohio, in 1946, he was one of just a handful of African-American journalists employed by white-owned newspapers. Over the next 50 years he never stopped perfecting his craft, and by the time he retired he had received a host of honors for his reporting and writings. Among those honors was a designation as one of the most influential black journalists of the twentieth century by the National Association of Black Journalists (NABJ).

Brower was born on October 8, 1916, in McColl, South Carolina. One of eight children of a barber who was sometimes active as a traveling preacher in the A.M.E. church, he grew up under the full weight of Southern segregation. "Clearly it shaped his consciousness," his son William Brower, Jr. told the *Blade*. "People want to know about his epiphany. He didn't need one. It was his life; it was everything that defined his existence." The family moved to High Point, North Carolina when Brower was young, and it was a high school principal there who pointed him toward a better life by suggesting that he go on to college at Wilberforce University, a historically black school in Xenia, Ohio.

Although he applied and was admitted, Brower showed up at Wilberforce with no money to pay his tuition; his total assets on arriving in Ohio amounted to $17 plus some extra stamps and socks. But he quickly landed a job and managed to pay his own way through school, earning a degree in 1939. He then returned to North Carolina for several years, teaching adult classes and also breaking into journalism as a correspondent for a small-town paper. At first he worked as a sportswriter.

That job led to a reporter position in 1943 with the black-oriented Washington *Tribune,* and six months later to a similar post with the Baltimore *Afro-American,* one of the oldest and best-established black-owned newspapers in the United States. At the time, the *Afro-American* published editions in Richmond, Virginia and in Philadelphia, and Brower became the editor of each in turn. In Philadelphia he met his wife Louise, a teacher and later a Toledo school administrator; their son William was the couple's only child.

In 1946 Brower applied for an open position at the *Blade.* He was unsure he wanted to make the move, but after being told that the paper had no plans to relegate him to coverage of the black community, Brower replied (according to the *Blade*), "That's the kind of a job I want. When do I go to work?" Brower was hired as a general assignment reporter, covering the crime beat along with the education scene and other daily happenings. Even after he became well-known for his writings on African-American life, Brower continued to cover other topics such as the efforts of Toledo prosecutors to rein in the activities of the city's notorious Licavoli organized crime syndicate.

As Brower gained experience, the paper began to send him out on more extended assignments. In 1949 he traveled to New York City to cover a trial of 11 members of the Communist Party, and two years later

At a Glance . . .

Born on October 8, 1916, in McColl, SC; father was a barber and minister; moved with family to High Point, NC. *Education:* Wilberforce University, Xenia, OH, 1939. *Religion:* Episcopal.

Career: High Point, NC, teacher, early 1940s; *Washington Tribune,* reporter, 1942; *Afro-American,* Baltimore, and Richmond and Philadelphia branches, reporter, 1942; Toledo (OH) *Blade,* reporter, 1946-57, rewrite editor, 1957-63, assistant city editor, 1963-67, wire desk editor, 1967-68, news editor, 1968-71, assistant managing editor, 1971-76, associate editor, senior editor, and columnist, 1976-96.

Selected awards: Named one of the most influential African-American journalists of the twentieth century, National Association of Black Journalists.

he had the chance to undertake a project of national scope: a 16-part *Blade* series entitled "Fifteen Million Americans", based on information gathered on travels through 20 states, that surveyed the living conditions of African Americans in a still largely segregated country. In 1951, the civil rights movement was still several years in the future, and journalistic exposés like Brower's were rare. The series was nominated for a Pulitzer Prize, the first time a *Blade* story had been so honored. "The more the conscience of the American people is pricked by the shame of racial violence, the more such outrages will decline," Brower wrote.

Although Brower had a stellar career at the *Blade,* his life was touched by housing discrimination in Toledo. Fellow *Blade* reporter Seymour Rothman recalled that when a group of writers worked through the night on a story at the home of a white reporter and emerged in the morning, Brower noticed neighbors in the segregated white area coming out of their houses as well. He turned to the reporter who owned the house where they had been working, shook his hand, and said, "Thank you very much for letting me see your home. It's pretty much what we want. We'll give it some serious thought."

Brower rose through the ranks at the *Blade,* becoming rewrite editor in 1957, assistant city editor in 1963, a wire desk editor in 1967, news editor in 1968, assistant managing editor in 1971, associate editor in 1976, and finally to senior editor. In 1972 he returned to many of the sites he had visited for his 1951 series

in order to assess the progress of race relations in the interim. His new series, "Black America: 20 Years Later," was again honored, this time with a citation from the Robert F. Kennedy Memorial Foundation's journalism awards. Brower took time off from his work at the *Blade* to teach at Ohio's Defiance College in 1974 and 1975, at Central State University in 1978 and 1979, and at Temple University in Philadelphia in 1979 and 1980.

As his influence grew, he served as a mentor to younger black journalists like Greg Moore, who worked for Brower at the *Blade* for five years. Moore, in a speech quoted on the website of the American Society of Newspaper Editors, recalled Brower as "a hell raiser and an inside player. He taught me the importance of staying connected to one's roots, that my strength and my base—the place where I could always find stories—would be the African-American community."

Brower wrote a three-times-a-week column for the *Blade* from 1976 to 1996, when he finally retired. One of his last projects was a third survey of black life nationwide, "America in Black & White," written with Eddie B. Allen and once again an award winner, this time for best minority issues coverage by the Ohio Society of Professional Journalists. He was a member of Ohio's state library board in the 1990s, and when he retired, a bridge was named after him by the Toledo city council. Suffering from various health problems in his later years, Brower moved with his wife to Washington, D.C., where his son's family resided. He died in Washington on May 28, 2004.

Numerous awards garlanded Brower's career toward the end of his life. Of particular note is his NABJ citation as one of the twentieth century's most influential black journalists followed upon a Lifetime Achievement Award given to Brower in 1996. Seymour Rothman called him "the most courageous, most determined, and possibly the most hated reporter in the *Blade*'s post-World War II history." He had done much to advance equality in American life and to blaze the way for African-American journalists.

Sources

Periodicals

Blade (Toledo, Ohio), May 31, 2004.
NABJ Journal, October 31, 1999, p. 10.

On-line

"Greg Moore Delivers the Inaugural Robert McGruder Lecture at Kent State University," *American Society of Newspaper Editors,* www.asne.org (November 22, 2004).

—James M. Manheim

Byrd R. Brown

1930-2001

Attorney, civil rights activist

In Pittsburgh, Pennsylvania, Byrd Brown is considered a local hero. As a courageous and articulate civil rights activist, he fought prejudice and inequality during a time in history when progressive political leadership was crucial in America, thus giving voice to those who had no access to power. "Byrd Brown was an African American who stood in the front lines of the civil rights movement and faced down enormous hatred and prejudice. It takes a rare kind of courage to be able to do that," said Pittsburgh's mayor Tom Murphy in the *Post Gazette.*

Brown was also an attorney who was known for his great success in court as well as his willingness to give his services free of charge to those who couldn't afford it. "Pro bono was his middle name," said former NAACP president Harvey Adams in the *Post Gazette.* "He did a thorough job whether the client had a nickel or nothing." Brown's passion for fairness and equality, his charismatic leadership abilities, and dynamic and warm personality made him a powerful influence in the Pittsburgh African-American community.

Born in 1930, Byrd Rowlett Brown was destined for success. As the only child of the prominent Homer S. and Wilhelmina Byrd Brown, Byrd saw firsthand the character qualities needed to become an influential leader. Homer Brown, Allegheny County's first black judge, set an example for his son as a civil rights activist as well as a generous and energetic contributor to the Pittsburgh community. As the father of the Pennsylvania state Fair Employment Practices Act, Homer Brown is known to have also created one of the first pieces of Pennsylvania legislation that prohibited dis-

crimination in public places. Byrd's mother is also known as a talented civil rights activist who dedicated 50 years of her life to pubic service. His grandfather, the Reverend William Roderick Brown, was a well-known Pittsburgh North Side preacher.

Byrd graduated from Schenley High School in 1947 and then earned a bachelor of arts degree and a law degree from Yale University. Some of his contemporaries at Yale were George H. W. Bush, William F. Buckley, and Pat Robertson. Brown married Marilyn Parker and was later divorced. At the time of his death in 2001, he was survived by his wife Barbara and two daughters, Cortlyn Wilhelmina Brown and Patricia Brown Stephens.

Although born into a prominent and wealthy family, Byrd did not live above the black community, but for them. In spite of his success—revealed in his sports cars, property holdings, and Caribbean trips—Byrd strove to improve life for his fellow man. He was known to share his success with his community by donating generously to college scholarships and non-profit organizations that assisted the poor and less fortunate. For example, in the 1970s, when Warner Cable came to Pittsburgh, Brown arranged for company stock to be donated to several local charities. According to the Reverend Leroy Patrick, pastor emeritus of Bethesda Presbyterian Church, when Warner Cable was later bought out, his church received $300,000 for its stock.

Brown was also a contemporary of the Rev. Dr. Martin Luther King Jr. In the 1960s Brown helped to organize

At a Glance . . .

Born Byrd Rowlett Brown in 1930 in Pittsburgh, PA; died of emphysema, May 3, 2001, in Pittsburgh, PA; married Marilyn Parker (divorced); married wife, Barbara; children: Cortlyn, Patricia. *Education*: Yale University, New Haven, CT, BA, JD.

Career: Attorney, c. 1955–2001.

Memberships: NAACP, Pittsburgh chapter, president, 1958-71; Pittsburgh Foundation, board member; Freedom Unlimited, chair; Health Advisory Council of Community Action Pittsburgh (CAP), chair.

Awards: Drum Major for Justice Award, Homer S. Brown Law Association, 2000.

rallies at Forbes Field where King spoke, and in 1963 he helped lead a train convoy to the March on Washington. According to the *Post Gazette*, he stayed for some time listening to speeches and was about to leave when King began his most famous "I Have a Dream" speech. "All of us just somehow turned around and crowded back to the podium. And by the time he was finished I was crying like a baby," Brown said in a ceremony held in his honor by the Homer S. Brown Law Association in 2000. The ceremony was meant to honor Brown for his civil rights activism, and those who attended recalled how in 1967 Brown organized a downtown march of 5,000 people to seek better jobs for blacks at the company Duquesne Light.

Brown also organized marches against Mine Safety Appliances, Gimbels, Kaufmann's, Hornes, the Board of Education, Sears Roebuck, and the University of Pittsburgh. He picketed construction sites to push for more black jobs in construction. During one violent police confrontation, Brown suffered beatings and was sprayed with mace. His efforts, along with those of other civil rights activists, produced the Pittsburgh Plan, which was considered a national model for training blacks for construction jobs.

"I thought he symbolized all the things that we should aspire to be," said Louis "Hop" Kendrick in the *Post Gazette*. Kendrick knew Brown during his boyhood in the affluent neighborhood called Sugar Top, in the Hill District of Pittsburgh, and later marched with him to desegregate Pittsburgh public schools. "He was above reproach. He was always accessible. He had a sense of commitment.... He was financially independent. They

couldn't buy him off. They couldn't offer him a job. They couldn't offer him a check."

Byrd was thought of as one of the best trial lawyers that the Commonwealth of Pennsylvania has ever produced. Commonwealth Court Judge Doris Smith, who practiced law with Brown from 1972 to 1987, claimed that his sharp litigation skills, his learning in the law, his compassion, sensitivity, and his toughness made him one of the best lawyers in Pittsburgh history. He was also known as a tremendous mentor and teacher. U.S. District Judge Gary Lancaster, who worked for Brown from 1981 to 1987, said that Brown was committed to first class work, and did not tolerate sloppy work or poor excuses.

In 1970 Brown ran for Congress, and in 1989 he ran for mayor of Pittsburgh. "Byrd is the word," was the slogan for his mayoral candidacy, which was kicked off from the pulpit of Central Baptist Church in the Hill District. Although he did not win either election, he continued to be a spokesman for fairness and equality in the arena of civic and business leadership. Brown served as president of the Pittsburgh NAACP from 1958 to 1971. His father, the founder and first president of the Pittsburgh NAACP, served in the same capacity for 24 years. Under their combined leadership, the NAACP experienced unparalleled local success.

Byrd Brown died on May 3, 2001, of emphysema and complications from a lung transplant. He died on the day of the annual Pittsburgh human-rights dinner his mother helped found more than 40 years earlier. A 2001 editorial about Brown in the *Post-Gazette* said, "emphysema finally took his life, but the spirit that animated countless battles for equality lives on."

Sources

On-line

"Byrd Brown Feted by Peers," *Post Gazette* (January 18, 2000), www.post-gazette.com/businessnews/20000118brown3.asp (November 22, 2004).

"Byrd Brown: The Lawyer and Activist Took the Harder Road," *Post Gazette* (May 8, 2001), www.post-gazette.com/forum/2001050edbyrd5.asp (November 22, 2004).

Glasco, Laurence. "The Civil Rights Movement in Pittsburgh: To Make This City Some Place Special," *Freedom Corner,* www.freedomcorner.org/downloads/glasco.pdf (December 4, 2004).

"Lawyer Byrd Brown Dies; Giant in Civil Rights Struggle," *Post Gazette* (May 4, 2001), www.post-gazette.com/obituaries/20010504brown2.asp (November 22, 2004).

—Cheryl Dudley

Leroy Carr

1905-1935

Blues singer and pianist

In the late 1920s and early 1930s, among the African-American audiences that nurtured the blues, there was hardly a better-known performer than Leroy Carr. He made over a hundred recordings, the first of which, 1928's "How Long, How Long Blues," made him a star who could fill large theaters around the Midwest and South. After Carr's death in 1935, tribute songs were put on record by other blues performers, and later giants of the genre paid tributes of their own by covering Carr's songs repeatedly.

Yet in the decades after his death, Carr was almost forgotten. An LP compilation of Carr's music issued in the early 1960s by the Columbia label sold poorly, while a similar set devoted to Delta bluesman Robert Johnson became a nearly essential part of a rock-era record collection. Historians have offered several explanations for this comparative neglect of Carr's legacy.

One had to do with the fact that Carr lived in Indianapolis, somewhat apart from the major center of blues development on Chicago's South Side. Another was that Carr's music was low-key, conversational, and rather wry. He mightily influenced black musicians who followed him, and the sound he created with guitarist Scrapper Blackwell set a pattern for countless blues records to come. But the extreme guitar heroics prized by Eric Clapton and other rock musicians had little place in Carr's music. And finally, Carr didn't fit the image of a blues performer that the genre's audiences, predominantly white later in the twentieth century, expected. He wasn't a sharecropper but a musician born and raised in the city; he didn't speak in a mysterious, obscure dialect but rather in a precise, linear, carefully detailed English. And he wore the fanciest suits he could find.

Carr was a native of Nashville, Tennessee, born on March 27, 1905. The family lived on the city's north side, not far from Fisk University, and his father John Carr worked as a porter at nearby Vanderbilt University. Accounts of Carr's early life disagree with one another in many respects, but at some point after his parents separated he left Nashville with his mother for Louisville, Kentucky, and then for Indianapolis, Indiana, a growing city that was a center for automobile-industry jobs until Henry Ford's innovations shifted the focus of black migration to Detroit, Michigan. Carr taught himself to play the piano. He may have dropped out of high school, but he had more formal education than most country blues players of the same time.

Joined Circus

After a restless period that included a stint in a traveling circus and another in the U.S. Army in the early 1920s, Carr returned to Indianapolis and got married in 1922. He had one daughter. For a while, Carr worked in a meat-packing plant, but by the mid-1920s he was gravitating toward the city's Indiana Avenue nightclub strip, a rowdy area with abundant musical opportunities and also many bootleg liquor outlets, a temptation that snared Carr both as a drinker and as a bootlegger himself. It wasn't long before Carr's name became well known among black Indianapolis families looking for musicians to play at house parties or "rent

At a Glance . . .

Born on March 27, 1905, in Nashville, TN; son of a porter at Vanderbilt University; died of complications of alcohol abuse, Indianapolis, April 29, 1935. *Military Service:* Served in U.S. Army, early 1920s.

Career: Musician, 1920s-35.

Addresses: none.

parties" held to raise money when the bills came due. He found work in the notoriously wide-open city of Covington, Kentucky, in the mid-1920s and traveled to other cities as well.

It may have been through involvement in the liquor underworld that Carr met Scrapper Blackwell (1906-1962), a guitarist whose real name, according to Samuel Charters, was Francis Black. Blackwell made several recordings before joining with Carr on record, and some historians have stated that they were brought together by a talent scout from the Vocalion label in 1928. But others point out that even their very first recordings together show the uncanny mutual awareness that was to be one of their trademarks, suggesting that Carr and Blackwell had probably performed together along Indiana Avenue for several years.

"How Long, How Long Blues," the very first recording Carr and Blackwell made, was a hit from the start. Outwardly there was nothing very extraordinary about it; its theme of a man watching a train carry his lover away from town had been repeated in numerous blues lyrics, and although Carr and Blackwell were both solid, infectious instrumentalists, neither was a brilliant virtuoso. Yet "How Long, How Long," in the words of blues historian Elijah Wald (writing in the *New York Times*), "had an effect as revolutionary as Bing Crosby's pop crooning, and for similar reasons." Carr seemed a singer born to the microphone. While country blues singers, performing in the street or in a noisy rural juke joint, projected their voices with powerful, deep-in-the-lungs shouts, Carr, Wald wrote, "sounded like a cool city dude carrying on a conversation with a few close friends."

Carr and Blackwell would remake "How Long, How Long" six times between 1928 and 1935, with Carr tinkering with the lyrics each time. Within a few weeks of its release, Carr was being advertised as an "exclusive Vocalion artist who is fast becoming the greatest blues singer in the land," and Vocalion had rushed a follow-up, "Broken Spoke Blues," into stores. Carr recorded prolifically over his short career. Even the Great Depression of the early 1930s didn't keep him out of the studio as it did other artists, although it did slow his recorded output.

Toured with Guitarist Blackwell

Gaining fame far beyond Indiana, Carr and Blackwell appeared in various cities. They played a succession of clubs in St. Louis and appeared at the Booker T. Washington Theater. The year 1932 saw them both penetrating the Deep South and making a trip to New York City to record a fresh set of sides for Vocalion. "Naptown Blues" (named for Indianapolis) and "Corn Licker Blues" were two of the hits they brought to Chicago to compete with another early urban blues performer of the day, Tampa Red.

In a genre that was virtually defined by borrowing from a fund of traditional lyrics and ideas, Carr recorded almost exclusively original material. Occasionally he co-wrote songs with Blackwell, and once in a while he covered another blues of the time like Lucille Bogan's "Sloppy Drunk Blues": "I'd rather be sloppy drunk // Than anything I know," Carr sang cheerfully in 1930. But most of his texts were his own. Often he managed to restate common blues ideas in new language. His well-known "Midnight Hour Blues" expressed an ordinary blues theme of sleeplessness. But Carr sang: "My heart's in trouble // And my mind's thinkin' deep"—an idea original to Carr, not one that adapted a traditional blues line.

"Midnight Hour Blues" was one of many Carr songs that expressed a feeling of reflective melancholy, often lightened by a wry observation or a touch of wit. But he was also a gifted writer of comic songs. In "Papa Wants a Cookie" (1930) Carr takes up the common blues use of food as a symbol for sexual activity or favors. But instead of a simple double meaning he constructs an entire dialogue between a man and a woman (reported by the male protagonist of the song) in which the subject shifts quickly from cooking to attempted seduction and then back again, leaving the listener unsure as to what is really being talked about. Carr's "Carried Water for the Elephants" is a funny song about a boy who gets into a circus without paying by agreeing to bring water to the giant beasts. The song contains an impressive string of animal imitations from Carr.

These examples suggest that Carr often functioned as an entertainer, while the country blues of solo singer-guitarists like Robert Johnson gave the impression that the events and feelings they described had actually happened to the people singing them. In a way, Carr's music resembled the "classic" blues of singers like Bessie Smith who performed with small jazz groups, even though he never appeared with any musician other than Blackwell. Sometimes, though, Carr's songs seemed more personal.

"Straight Alky Blues" (1929) was a long composition that covered both sides of a 78 rpm record. It describes an individual on a spree, drinking undiluted alcohol. "My eyes saw double // They could not steer my feet," Carr sings. Then the mood darkens—"Oh, this alcohol is killing me"—only to change direction once again and deliver a series of metaphors of the sexual dysfunction alcohol brings. The song contains especially fine examples of cooperation between Carr and Blackwell, as the guitarist shifts several times from the usual blues triple division of the beat into an even double division, effectively depicting the staggering of a drunk man.

Suffered Effects of Alcoholism

By 1935, the effects of years of alcohol abuse had taken their toll on Carr's slight frame. His final recording session, held in Chicago in February of that year, contained several grim songs, including "Six Cold Feet in the Ground," in which he seemed to forecast his own imminent death. He died of alcohol-related kidney failure in Indianapolis on April 29, 1935, and was buried in the city's Floral Park cemetery. Years later a group of Indiana blues enthusiasts, including Mishawaka bluesman Duke Tumatoe, marketed a comedy CD to raise money so that a headstone could be purchased for his previously unmarked grave.

Carr's popularity was amply demonstrated by his influence on the next generation of blues performers. T-Bone Walker covered "How Long," and fabled Delta-to-Chicago transplant Muddy Waters said it was the first blues song he had ever heard. Even Robert Johnson, the intense Mississippi Delta bluesman who was in many ways Carr's polar opposite, may have modeled his "Stones in My Passway" on Carr's "Rocks in My Bed." The restrained, detailed piano blues of the young Ray Charles, in particular, seem barely removed from Carr's music.

After many years during which his recordings were available only on the original 78 rpm records and on a few scattered LP re-releases, Carr's music began to awaken the interest of blues enthusiasts once again in the 1980s and 1990s. Austria's Document label released his complete recordings on a set of six CDs, and in 2004 the Columbia label released a two-disc set of Carr songs entitled *Whiskey Is My Habit, Women Is All I Crave.* Carr's place in American musical history

was being emphasized anew by writers like Elijah Wald, who argued in the *New York Times* that "like rap, [blues] had deep, traditional roots but also a dynamic, modern sensibility that revolutionized American music. And Leroy Carr led that revolution, smooth voice, piano, fine suits, and all."

Selected discography

Naptown Blues, Yazoo, 1988.
Complete Recorded Works (7 vols.), Document, 1992-96.
American Blues Legend, Charly, 1999.
Essential Leroy Carr, Classic Blues, 2003.
Whiskey Is My Habit, Women Is All I Crave, Columbia Legacy, 2004.

Sources

Books

Charters, Samuel, *The Country Blues,* Da Capo, 1959.
Davis, Francis, *History of the Blues,* Hyperion, 1995.
Harris, Sheldon, *Blues Who's Who,* Arlington House, 1979.
Herzhaft, Gérard, *Encyclopedia of the Blues,* 2nd ed., trans. Brigitte Debord, University of Arkansas Press, 1997.
Palmer, Robert, *Deep Blues,* Penguin, 1982.

Periodicals

Down Beat, September 2004, p. 68.
New York Times, July 18, 2004, section 2, p. 22.

On-line

"Leroy Carr," All Music Guide, http://www.allmusic.com (November 30, 2004).
"Leroy Carr (1905-1935)," http://www.io.com/~tbone1/blues/bios/carr.html (November 30, 2004).

—James M. Manheim

Martin Carter

1927-1997

Poet

One of the most important poets to come out of the Caribbean, Martin Carter has been compared to literary lions such as W.B. Yeats and Pablo Neruda. His most famous work was fueled by the political turmoil that gripped his native Guyana in the 1950s and 1960s. He told fellow Guyanese writer Bill Carr in an interview for the Guyanese magazine *Release* that politics and poetry were inseparable. "[If] politics is a part of life, we shall become involved in politics, if death is a part of life we shall become involved with death, like the butterfly who is not afraid to be ephemeral." Unfortunately, because of the fame of his politically-charged poems Carter was often pigeon-holed as a revolutionary poet. But as Guyana's *Stabroek News* wrote, "there were other voices in Martin Carter, strains of tenderness, love poems of moving fervour, agonies expressed that have nothing to do with politics, insights into all of human nature."

During his life, Carter received limited recognition outside of Guyana, mainly because he refused to abandon his country. A friend of his told the *Guyana Chronicle,* "Exile for him was not going overseas like so many of the Caribbean's best writers, but exiled within his own country; in his own way, and fighting the fight at home." As he fought that fight, he wrought words of defiance, beauty, pain, and hope, leaving a literary legacy that, finally, in the 21st century is receiving worldwide critical respect.

Developed Early Passion for Poetry

Martin Wylde Carter was born on June 7, 1927 in Georgetown, Guyana (then British Guiana) to Victor and Violet Carter. His parents were of African, Indian, and European ancestry and held secure positions in Guyana's middle class, thanks both to their mixed blood and to Victor's civil service job. They were also avid readers and instilled in Carter a love of literature and letters. In 1944, after graduating from Queen's College, a prestigious boys school in Georgetown, Carter also took a job with the civil service. He worked first for the post office, and then as the secretary to the superintendent of prisons. In 1953 he married his childhood friend Phyllis. "We knew each other for a long time," Mrs. Carter told the *Guyana Chronicle.* "We were married when I was about 21, he was about 26." Their marriage lasted 47 years and produced four children.

Even as he held down his daytime job, Carter was passionate about producing poetry. Mrs. Carter recalled to the *Guyana Chronicle* that Carter would wake in the middle of the night and go to his desk. When she called out after him, he would reply, "I just got a word I wanted. I coming back." He was also known to spend long car journeys scribbling on the insides of cigarette packs, leaving the driving to his wife.

In the 1950s, Guyana was still a British colony. Though Carter was a product of British education and worked for the colonial government, he was not sympathetic to their rule. Like many Guyanese at the time, he longed for self-governance. He joined the anti-colonialist People's Progressive Party (PPP) and in 1950 published his first poems in the party's magazine, *Thunder*. How-

At a Glance . . .

Born on June 7, 1927, in Georgetown, Guyana; died on December 13, 1997; married Phyllis Carter, 1953; children: four. *Education:* Queens College, Georgetown, 1939-44.

Career: Poet; British Guiana Civil Service, secretary to superintendent of prisons, 1945-53; teacher, 1954-59; Booker Group of Companies, chief information officer, 1959-66; United Nations, Guyana representative, 1966-67; Republic of Guyana, minister of information, 1967-71; Essex University, England, lecturer, 1975-76; University of Guyana, Georgetown, writer-in-residence, 1977-81; University of Guyana, Georgetown, senior research fellow, 1981-??.

ever, in order to protect his civil service job, he published the most politically radical of his work under the pseudonym M. Black.

Published First Poems of Protest

Carter's first collection of poetry, *The Hill of Fire Glows Red*, was published in 1951 in Guyana. Literary critic Selwyn R. Cudjoe in *Dictionary of Literary Biography* wrote of the collection, "readers begin to see his characteristic preoccupation with the freedom of his country, his use of certain potent symbols of resistance, and a hint of the kind of consciousness with which his poetry has come to be associated." In 1952 Carter published two more volumes of work in Guyana, *The Kind Eagle (Poems of Prison)* and *The Hidden Man (Other Poems of Prison)*. Again the poems dealt with dreams of freedom. A line from "The Kind Eagle" reads, "I dance on the wall of prison! // It is not easy to be free and bold!" *The Literary Encyclopedia* noted that with the poems, Carter also "cultivates a poetics of social realism, meticulously documenting the concrete details of oppression." Despite his middle-class background, Carter related to the oppression and despair his hard-working countrymen dealt with daily as they toiled under the Caribbean sun and the dark shadow of colonialism.

In 1953 the British allowed Guyana to hold elections for self-governance. The PPP won and set about building a post-colonial society. However, inauguration ceremonies were barely over when the British, alarmed by the PPP's leftist leanings, sent in troops to re-assume control of Guyana. Demonstrations against the British broke out over the country and Carter was arrested for his involvement. "The soldiers came and they were outside the house," Mrs. Carter recalled to

the *Guyana Chronicle,* "they were lined up all at the gate." Carter was interred at a local air base for three months. He was arrested and briefly held a second time in 1954.

Found Fame with Prison Poetry

Carter's time in prison was a turning point in his life. It not only influenced his poetry, but also cemented his international reputation as a poet. In 1954 Carter's *Poems of Resistance from British Guiana* was published by a socialist press in London to critical acclaim. In *Release,* critic Paul Singh wrote that Carter was "jailed into poetic eminence" as a result of the collection. The poems brimmed with the anxiety of the times—oppression, fear, bloodshed. In one of his most famous poems, "This Is the Dark Time My Love," Carter wrote, "It is the season of oppression, dark metal, and tears. // It is the festival of guns, the carnival of misery. // Everywhere the faces of men are strained and anxious." Yet, in "I Come From the Nigger Yard," he revealed an optimistic belief in the future, writing "From the nigger yard of yesterday I come with my burden. // To the world of tomorrow I turn with my strength."

Not only did *Poems of Resistance* reflect the tragedy and hope of 1950s Guyana, but it also revealed Carter's skill as a poet. "I Come From the Nigger Yard" in particular has been hailed as one of his most emblematic works. Cudjoe wrote that through the poem, "readers discover Carter's capacity for sustaining and developing a complex emotional response in poetry. The subtle blend of aesthetic control and political content embodies the best of his work."

After the release of *Poems of Resistance,* Carter worked as a teacher for several years. In 1959 he joined the British sugar manufacturing giant Booker as their chief information officer. He also edited the company's newsletter. Meanwhile Guyana continued to struggle fitfully towards independence. In 1955 the PPP had split into two parties, with the PPP being led by a Guyanese of Indian descent and the People's National Congress (PNC) by a Guyanese of African descent. Carter shifted his loyalties to the PNC partly because of the racism he felt the PPP was promoting. The island had long been divided by two racial groups—East Indians and Africans. Though the PPP had formed as a multi-racial party, by the mid-1950s it was promoting its own interests by emphasizing racial divisions. In reaction to this Carter wrote the pessimistic series *Poems of Shape and Motion.*

Disillusioned by Guyana's New Government

In 1961 the PPP once again assumed power in Guyana. The following year, they instituted a series of harsh economic reforms that led to nationwide strikes. Carter participated, his fists held high in defiance, fueled again by a hope for change. The strikes turned into violent clashes, often racially based. British troops were called in to restore order. Carter reacted by writing *Jail Me Quickly,* a series of five poems. The poems did not shy from the brutality of what he had seen, yet with characteristic optimism they also shivered with hope. In "Black Friday 1962" he wrote, "And I have seen some creatures rise from holes, // and claw a triumph like a citizen, // and reign until the tide!"

Guyana received full independence from Britain in 1966 and the PNC won the new country's first elections. Carter joined the government as a representative to the United Nations from 1966 to 1967. He next became the nation's Minister of Information. During this time, Martin's poetry became less defiant, less hopeful, less alive. Many critics have contributed this change to the disillusionment he felt with Guyana's new government. He saw racism, hypocrisy, and corruption flourish where he had once hoped for equality, truth, and freedom. In 1970 he published a poem with the lines, "the mouth is muzzled // by the food it eats to live." To keep his role in the government, he would have to turn his back on the corruption he saw. As a chronicler of Guyanese life and a true believer in the human spirit, he would not do it. He resigned from his government post that same year.

Became the Poems Man of the People

Carter began to give literary readings and hold informal rap sessions with writers and intellectuals in Georgetown. In 1975 England's University of Essex hired him to be a writer-in-residence for a year. It was his longest period away from Guyana. When he returned home he became writer-in-residence at the University of Guyana. In 1977 *Poems of Succession* was published. Three years later, *Poems of Affinity* appeared. *The Literary Encyclopedia* wrote that both volumes, "express world-weariness and disillusionment at the nation's growing racial tensions and rampant political corruption." That made sense as in the 1970s, Carter's political ideals had been shattered yet again. In 1978 he had joined the Working People's Alliance (WPA), a socialist party formed in response to the corrupt authoritarianism of the PNC. Soon after he took to the streets in protest against the PNC and was beaten up by thugs on the PNC payroll. The following year he was at another WPA-led march when he witnessed the stabbing of Father Drake, a Catholic priest and political activist. The leader of the WPA was also eventually murdered.

Carter found refuge from the bitter disappointment of his political hopes by doing the things he loved best—writing poetry and being with friends. "He liked his drink and he always had friends because of that," his wife told *Guyana Chronicle.* "Anybody, anywhere, anytime, he would bring them here." Carter was a poet of the people, a fact he relished. He often joyfully recounted an encounter he had had with a 12-year-old girl deep in the interior of the country. Carter was walking towards a bridge when the girl came running towards him calling out 'Look! Look! The poems man!' He was touched that someone so young, in a place so remote, knew who he was. "That says something for the kind of popularity he enjoyed; that he related to the people and they to him," wrote the *Guyana Chronicle.*

Carter died on December 13, 1997. He was buried in the Place of Heroes, a site previously reserved for heads of state. He belonged there more than any politician ever did. It was he who had given words to the Guyanese people. He provided them a voice when they had been rendered mute by political manipulations from both the British and Guyanese governments. As the *Guyana Chronicle* wrote, "His words echo over and over again both within our private lives and our unfolding history."

Selected writings

Books

The Hill of Fire Glows Red, Miniature Poets, 1951.
The Kind Eagle, privately printed, 1952.
The Hidden Man, privately printed, 1952.
Poems of Resistance from British Guiana, Lawrence and Gishart, 1954.
Poems of Shape and Motion, privately printed, 1955.
Jail Me Quickly, privately printed, 1963.
Poems of Succession, New Beacon, 1977.
Poems of Affinity, Release, 1980.
Selected Poems, Demerara, 1989.

Sources

Books

Cudjoe, Selwyn R., "Martin Wylde Carter," *Dictionary of Literary Biography, Volume 117: Twentieth-Century Caribbean and Black African Writers, First Series,* The Gale Group, 1992.

Periodicals

Release, First Quarter 1978; First Quarter 1979.
World Literature Today, Winter 2001.

On-line

"Anniversary of Martin Carter's Death," *Stabroek News,* www.landofsixpeoples.com/gynewsjs.htm (October 27, 2004).
Johnson, Ruel, "Phyllis Carter Recalls Life with 'the poems man,'" *Guyana Chronicle,* www.landofsix peoples.com/gynewsjs.htm (October 27, 2004).
"Martin Wylde Carter," Peepal Tree Press, www.peep altreepress.com/author_display.asp?au_id=11 (October 27, 2004).

Patterson, Anita, "Carter, Martin Wylde (1927 - 1997)," *The Literary Encyclopedia,* www.litencyc. com/php/speople.php?rec=true&UID=762 (October 27, 2004).

Rutherford, Linda, "Honouring 'The Poems Man,'" *Guyana Chronicle,* www.landofsixpeoples.com/gy newsjs.htm (October 27, 2004).

—Candace LaBalle

Debra Martin Chase

1956(?)—

Entertainment executive

Film producer Debra Martin Chase is one of just a handful of minority women who wield power among the back offices at the major Hollywood studios. Chase's job entails overseeing the production of new movies on their way to the multiplex, and she scored her first genuine hit in 2001 with *The Princess Diaries*. This former corporate attorney had always dreamed of being a Hollywood player, she recalled in a 1997 *Essence* interview. "I'm the kid who was in the movie theater every Saturday," she told journalist Audrey Edwards. "I've been a movie fanatic since I was a child, and my images of the world were shaped by what I saw on the screen. I want to do my part to see that Blacks are not only represented in film but also enhance it."

Chase, Debra Martin, photograph. Frederick M. Brown/Getty Images.

Born in the mid-1950s, Chase hails from Illinois, but moved around with her family during her youth. They lived in the Northeast as well as in Pasadena, a suburb of Los Angeles. For college Chase headed east again to attend Mount Holyoke, a prestigious Massachusetts college. After earning her undergraduate degree in 1977, she entered law school at Harvard University. At Harvard, she met her future husband. The couple relocated to Houston, Texas, after graduation day in 1981. Taking an entry-level associate job with a law firm there, Chase realized that she had erred in her choice of career. "I hated every minute practicing law," she admitted to *Essence* in 2003.

Chase bounced around during the 1980s. She worked as a legal consultant, a freelance writer, and for the 1988 presidential campaign of Democratic Party nominee Michael Dukakis. When her marriage ended in the late 1980s, Chase decided to try to get a job in the film business, and headed to Los Angeles. She knew someone at Columbia Pictures, and won a spot in its executive-training program. One day in 1990, she was introduced to a top executive with the studio, and a few days later convinced him to hire her as his executive assistant.

Never starstruck, Chase admitted that she wavered for a second when she spotted actor Denzel Washington one day in the Columbia studio offices, and worked up the courage to introduce herself. Impressed by her moxie, Washington suggested that they set up a meeting. Even more impressed after their meeting, Washington hired Chase to run his production company, Mundy Lane Entertainment. Chase had attained, in a few short years, the production job she'd longed for. Film—and television—producing involves finding material for possible movie projects. Sometimes the material comes from original ideas in scripts passed around Hollywood, while in other cases books, magazine articles, or even old movies provide the basis for a new story idea. Producers then interest top names in the project, which helps land a deal with a studio to cover the massive cost of filming, marketing, and distributing a film.

Working with the Oscar-nominated Washington, fresh from his success as the lead in *Malcolm X,* was the lucky break that Chase needed to become a Hollywood dealmaker. "I learned a lot from Denzel," she told *Essence.* "One of his mantras is 'Let the work speak for you.' He said that if I did good work, I'd be one of the top producers. Period." Chase worked on a number of Mundy Lane projects, including the adaptation of Walter Mosley's crime-novel *Devil in a Blue Dress* and the 1995 television movie *Hank Aaron: Chasing the Dream.* She was also executive producer for the 1996 Washington-Meg Ryan military drama, *Courage Under Fire.*

In the late 1990s, Chase left Mundy Lane in order to run pop diva Whitney Houston's production company. Under Chase's leadership, the company scored a major coup in late 1997 with a television remake of the *Cinderella* story, which starred Houston, Brandy, and Whoopi Goldberg. The musical scored major ratings, with some 60 million viewers tuning in, as well as seven Emmy nominations. Because of her involvement in the updated rags-to-riches tale, Chase was targeted by an agent for a young-adult author who'd written a Cinderella-type novel. Chase agreed to read Meg Cabot's book, *The Princess Diaries*—about a California teen who learns she has inherited the throne of a tiny European principality thanks to the late father she barely knew—and loved it.

Chase sold the *Princess Diaries* idea to Disney, and the movie became one of the top-grossing films of 2001, starring Anne Hathaway as the unlikely royal and Julie Andrews as her formidable grandmother. It grossed $109 million at American box offices alone, with the foreign and DVD rights adding even more to its profitability. Chase was thrilled by the success. "It's been amazing and gratifying to see how *Princess Diaries* spoke to girls everywhere," she told Dinah Eng of *USA Today.* "When the first film came out in 2001, the conventional wisdom was that if you made movies for boys, the girls would come, but there was no market for girl movies."

Chase also knew that she had finally hit her stride as a producer, she explained to *Daily News* writer Bob Strauss. Most producers work in a specific niche, she noted, and hers was "these female wish-fulfillment/empowerment movies. I love stories that reinforce...that we each have the power to be whatever we want to be, that we are only limited by our own vision." In her own Cinderella-like career twist, Chase was able to form her own company, located on the Disney lot. She still worked closely with Houston, however, on such projects as *The Cheetah Girls* television movie in 2003.

Chase produced *Princess Diaries 2: Royal Engagement,* released in 2004, and was also working on a film adaptation of the Ann Brashares book, *Sisterhood of the Traveling Pants.* Ideas for future projects include a television series based on Barbara Neely's detective novels featuring an African-American maid-turned-crimesolver, Blanche White. Chase admitted that although *The Princess Diaries* had made a small fortune at the box office and her future in Hollywood would seem assured after that, it was still a high-stakes game getting any studio to sign on to any project. "People don't want to give up a piece of the pie to anyone," she commented to Hines in *Essence.* "If you're different—or doubly different as a Black woman—it makes it easier for them to exclude you. They think, We don't know you and don't have to know you."

Home for Chase is the Hollywood Hills, where she has spent more time since cutting back on her once-tough work schedule after surviving a serious car accident and a thyroid condition. She hoped to some day fulfill her dream of moving to Italy in order to write. The future is never far from Chase's mind because she understands how quickly life, especially in her business, changes. "This is a mercurial business," she reflected in *Essence.* "Too many people think it's going to go on forever. Then they wake up, and not only has it changed, they're not prepared for it."

Selected works

Films as producer

(Executive producer) *Hank Aaron: Chasing the Dream,* 1995.
(Executive producer) *Courage under Fire,* 1996.
(Co-producer) *The Preacher's Wife,* 1996.
(Executive producer) *Cinderella,* 1997.
The Princess Diaries, 2001.
The Princess Diaries 2: Royal Engagement, 2004.

Sources

Daily News (Los Angeles, CA), August 16, 2001, p. L5.
Essence, September 1997, p. 108; April 2003, p. 138.
USA Today, August 11, 2004.
Variety, May 3, 2001.

—Carol Brennan

Vince Cullers

1924(?)-2003

Advertising executive

When Vince Cullers began knocking on the doors of advertising agencies in the late 1940s, he had a thick portfolio, experience as an artist, and training from the prestigious Art Institute of Chicago. He was young, eager, and talented. He was also black. "He made the rounds of the ad agencies in Chicago, and what he ran into was that they did not hire blacks," his wife Marian Cullers told *Essence*. By 1956 Cullers had had enough and launched his own firm. Vince Cullers Advertising, Inc. was the first black-owned advertising agency in the United States and the first to actively target the African-American market. It changed the face of advertising. "There were rarely any blacks to be seen in advertisements up until that point," Tom Burrell, CEO of Burrell Communications Group, told the *Chicago Tribune*. "He established the template for targeted marketing in this country."

Inspired by Civil Rights Movement

Vincent T. Cullers was born around 1924 in Chicago to Samuel and Letitia Cullers. His mother was a deeply spiritual woman who inspired in Cullers a commitment to leaving the world better than he found it. After graduating from DuSable High School, where he played football and ran track, Cullers studied art at the Art Institute of Chicago. When the United States entered World War II, Cullers signed on with the Marines and became a combat artist in the South Pacific. While in the service another soldier showed Cullers a photo of his cousin, Marian Barnett, of Champaign, Illinois. Cullers was smitten. Upon returning to Illinois he sought Marian out, wooed her, and

eventually married her. They had two sons, Vincent Jr. and Jeffery.

By the time Cullers married Marian, he had developed an impressive portfolio. He started sending it to various advertising agencies in Chicago and New York, hoping to get work as an illustrator. The agencies would see it and offer him a position but "when he showed up and the interviewer saw the color of his skin, he suddenly didn't have a job," Cullers' son Jeffery recounted to the *Chicago Sun-Times*. "In those days, no African Americans were working in advertising," Burrell told the *Chicago Tribune*. "They not only couldn't get in the door, they didn't go beyond the lobby." Cullers resorted to freelance art work. Finally, in 1953 he landed a position as a promotional art director for *Ebony* magazine.

At the time, the Civil Rights Movement was gaining momentum. In 1954 the Supreme Court ruled in *Brown v. the Board of Education* that racially segregated education was unconstitutional. A year later Rosa Parks's refusal to give up her bus seat prompted the Montgomery Bus Boycott. The Rev. Dr. Martin Luther King, Jr. rose to national prominence. Black students faced furious mobs to attend school. Others endured insults and threats to take seats at whites-only lunch counters. As the fight for civil rights was slowly, painfully won, an image of Black Power rose up.

Founded First African-American Ad Agency

In Chicago, Cullers saw all of this and reacted in the

way he could best—through advertising. In 1956 he founded Vince Cullers Advertising. He would handle the art, his wife Marian the administration. His goal was two-fold: to open up the advertising world to African Americans, and to change the way African Americans were targeted in ads.

"For years, our agency actually functioned as a training ground for many young students seeking their first exposure to the ad industry," Cullers told *The Black Collegian*. African Americans were new to the industry and Cullers had no choice but to be both employer and mentor. In doing so, he not only brought black talent to advertising, but he also inspired other black agencies to form and flourish. "It's my sense from looking at the figures that one of the things that [Cullers] did was spark the formation of other African-American agencies, some of which have gone on to become far bigger than his ever was," an editor at *Advertising Age* told *Black Enterprise*.

With his agency, Cullers also changed the way advertising was targeted to blacks. "What was fantastic about what Vince did was that he approached corporate America with the idea that rather than integrating black people into a white concept of advertising, advertisers needed to buy into the idea of creating messages that resonated only with black people," Ken Smikle, presi-

dent of *Target Market News* told *Black Enterprise*. Until that time, no agency had exclusively targeted a specific market segment. Burell told *Advertising Age*, "targeted marketing has found its way into the mainstream…. It all started with Vince Cullers, and we should not forget that."

Broke Color Barriers in Advertisements

Cullers's billings for 1956 barely topped $10,000. His ideas, however, were breaking barriers and by 1968 his company landed its first major contract. "We were contacted by Lorillard, Inc., which makes Newport, True and Kent cigarettes," Marian told *Essence*. Cullers refused to create a standard advertising campaign, appealing to what he called a "black white person," as noted in *Target Market News*. Instead he created a campaign that featured a dashiki-clad African American. At the time, Black Power was at its apex, and blacks across the country had adopted the dashiki—a traditional African outfit—as a symbol of their unity. Johnson Products came calling next and hired Cullers to advertise Afro-Sheen, a line of black hair care products. Cullers filled the ads with attractive, proud African Americans and the tag line "Watu Wazuri," Swahili for "beautiful people." "The target audience was clearly black. But the message didn't have to be as black as Vince made it," Smikle told *Black Enterprise*. "It was a bold move on his part."

Business grew quickly and Cullers's client roster soon read like a *Forbes* who's who list—Ameritech, Amoco, Kellogg's, Pizza Hut, Sears & Roebuck. In 1973 billings had risen to $2.5 million. By 1990 that figure was $20 million. However, it was not an easy growth. "When we began, white clients were reluctant to spend money on the black market. They didn't understand it. Some didn't even believe it existed," Cullers told *The Black Collegian*. "We spent a lot of frustrating years knowing we had the knowledge to get a job done that others didn't even realize needed to be done." To help him get that job done, Cullers brought in his family. Wife Marian became vice president, and his sons and daughter-in-law Carmelita took key roles in the organization. They shared with Cullers the conviction that the black market held immense potential.

Meeting their objectives was not always easy for the Cullers family. "The ethnic agencies still seldom have the budgets the general market agencies receive," Cullers told *The Black Collegian*. Yet, with characteristic optimism he clarified, "but that doesn't mean we produce ads of lower quality. In fact, we are forced to be more innovative because we have less to work with. In the final analysis, it's not the money that produces excellent advertising for clients—it's talent." Cullers's talent earned the agency a slew of awards including two Clios, the advertising world's version of the Oscar.

Left Advertising Legacy for African Americans

In 1997 Cullers restructured the firm, overhauling staff and management. He dubbed the refurbished agency, "the oldest, newest African-American ad agency." Nonetheless, other black agencies such as Burrell Communications and Uniworld Group dominated the market. Ironically, their success was a direct result of Cullers's vision. "Vince was one of the true pioneers because he created an advertising agency for African Americans in the mid-1960s before affirmative action," Byron Lewis, CEO of Uniworld, told *Black Enterprise*. "I just felt that in my own mind if Vince could do it when times were really difficult, then the opportunities for those of us who came afterward were far easier."

In 2002 Cullers retired from his namesake agency and let his son Jeffery take over. On October 4, 2003, Cullers died of congestive heart failure. He was 79. True to his lifelong commitment to help integrate advertising, his family set up a fund in his memory. The Cullers Cornerstones Foundation provides scholarships for minority advertising students. In the face of shut doors and repeated rejections, pervasive racism and skeptical clients, Cullers forged a path for African Americans in advertising, both behind the scenes and splayed out on billboards. He considered it a job well done. "It has been a long and difficult journey but if I could begin my career over again, I'd choose to become an ad man," he told *The Black Collegian* in 2001. "Despite the many hardships, I would do it all over again."

Sources

Periodicals

Advertising Age, October 13, 2003.
Black Enterprise, December 2003.
Chicago Sun-Times, October 10, 2003.
Chicago Tribune, October 10, 2003.
Essence, January 1, 1990.
Jet, October 27, 2003.

On-line

"Reflections on Success: Vincent T. Cullers," *Black Collegian,* www.black-collegian.com/issues/30th Ann/reflectvcullers2001-30th.shtml (October 25, 2004).

"Remembering an Advertising Pioneer," *Black Enterprise,* www.blackenterprise.com/ExclusivesEKOpen .asp?id=534 (October 25, 2004).

"Vince Cullers, Founder of Nation's First Black-Owned Ad Agency, Dies in Chicago," *Target Market News,* www.targetmarketnews.com/peoplenews.htm (October 25, 2004).

—Candace LaBalle

Margaret Esse Danner

1915-1986

Poet

Poet Margaret Esse Danner's vivid imagery and uplifting poetic voice most often focused on Africa. Although she wrote on a wide range of themes, it is likely that her African poems will be the most enduring of her work. Author of four compilations and contributor to numerous anthologies, Danner published the bulk of her poetry during the Black Arts Movements of the 1960s.

Developed Poetic Voice

Margaret Esse Danner was born in Pryorsburg, Kentucky, on January 12, 1915. Soon thereafter her parents, Caleb and Naomi Danner, moved the family to Chicago, where she spent most of her childhood. Danner won her first poetry prize in eighth grade for her poem titled "The Violin," which uses the famous Stradivarius and Guarnerius violins as its central images.

After graduating from Englewood High School in Chicago, Danner pursued her studies at numerous universities, including Chicago's YMCA College, Loyola University, Roosevelt College (now University), and Northwestern University, where she studied under poets Karl Shapiro and Paul Engle. Although she continued to develop her poetic voice during these years, Danner did not receive any public recognition until 1945 when she won second place at the Poetry Workshop of the Midwestern Writers Conference held at Northwestern.

In 1951 Danner became an editorial assistant for *Poetry: The Magazine of Verse*, a publication known for introducing talented poets to the public. In that same year, *Poetry* published Danner's "Far From Africa," a series of four poems. These poems would later appear in numerous anthologies and earned Danner the John Hay Whitney Fellowship. This fellowship provided funding for Danner to travel to Africa, but Danner postponed the trip until 1966. In 1956 Danner became the first African American to be promoted to assistant editor at *Poetry*, a position she held until 1957.

Began Publishing Poetry

Danner's first collection of poems, *Impressions of African Art Forms*, first published by the Contemporary Studies of Miles Poetry Association of Wayne State University in Detroit in 1960, was republished in 1961 by Dudley Randall's Broadside Press. The poems of *Impressions*, which earned critical acclaim, focused on Danner's understanding of Africa as a land and as a state of her being. Unlike other African American poets who voiced frustration in their incomplete identity and unity with Africa, Danner finds inspiration and fulfillment in her poems such as "Her Blood, Drifting Through Me, Sings." In "The Convert" she celebrates self-discovery: "I became a hurricane // of elation, a convert, undaunted who wanted to flaunt // her discovery, flourish her fair-figured-find." In her 1993 study of Danner's poetry, Claire Taft noted in *The Langston Hughes Review*, "*Impressions of African Art Forms* glories in the beauty, nobility, and knowledge Danner

At a Glance . . .

Born on January 12, 1915, in Pryorsburg, Kentucky; died on January 1, 1984, in Chicago, IL; daughter of Caleb and Naomi Danner; married Cordell Strickland (divorced); married Otto Cunningham; children (first marriage): Naomi. *Education:* Attended YMCA College, Chicago, IL, Loyola University, Roosevelt University, and Northwestern University. *Religion:* Bahá'í.

Career: *Poetry* magazine, Chicago, IL, editorial assistant, 1951-55, assistant editor, 1956-57; Wayne State University, Detroit, MI, poet in residence, 1961-62; touring poet, Bahá'í Teaching Committee, 1964-66; Whitney fellow, Senegal, Africa, and Paris, France, 1966; Virginia Union University, Richmond, VA, poet in residence, 1968-69; LeMoyne-Owen College, Memphis, TN, poet in residence, 1970-75.

Selected memberships: Society of Afro-American Culture, member; Contemporary Artists, member; National Council of Teachers of English, member; Boone House, director; Nologonyu's, Chicago Southside Community Art Center, life member.

Selected awards: John Hay Whitney Fellowship, 1951; African Studies Association Award, 1961; Harriet Tubman Award, 1965; Poets in Concert Award, 1968.

During the early 1960s Danner became active in the Bahá'í faith, which she shared with Robert Hayden. According to Bahá'í teachings, the world is moving toward a unity characterized by peace and harmony, free from prejudice, extremes of wealth and poverty, and inequality. Danner wrote a number of poems through which her Bahá'í faith is revealed, and from 1964 to 1966, she served as a touring poet under the sponsorship of the Bahá'í Teaching Committee.

Influenced by Trip to Africa

In 1966 Danner finally took her Whitney Fellowship trip to Africa. She traveled to Dakar, Senegal, where she read some of her poems at the World Exposition of Negro Arts. She also spent part of the year in Paris, staying long enough to peruse an exhibit of African art. Africa had long been a major theme of Danner's poetry, and her influential trip simply served to reinforce her preponderance on the land of her ancestors.

The bulk of Danner's work was published during the 1960s, as the Black Arts Movement emerged. She produced three other compilations of her poetry during that decade: *To Flower* in 1963, *Poem Counterpoem* in 1966, and *Iron Lace* in 1968. She also edited two anthologies, *Brass Horses* in 1968 and *Regroup* in 1969, and her poems appeared in numerous literary publications. In *Poem Counterpoem* she partnered with Dudley Randall to produce a volume of twenty poems, ten by each poet. The poems on the same topics are paired on opposite pages as a dialogue between the two poets. In 1964 Danner recorded readings with Langston Hughes as part of *Black Forum* series. Although the recording was not released until 1970 and did not receive significant attention, Danner appreciated Hughes's help in increasing her recognition in the literary community.

Danner, who appeared at a variety of writers conferences and poetry festivals, spent the remaining years of her professional life as a poet in residence, first at the historically black Virginia Union University from 1968 to 1969 and then at LeMoyne-Owen College in Memphis, Tennessee, from 1970 to 1975.

In 1976 Danner published her final major work, *The Down of a Thistle*, which she dedicated to Robert Hayden. As in her other works, Africa is the central theme of much of the poetry. Richard K. Barksdale noted in *Praisesong of Survival*, "In the poetry of Margaret Danner...there is no questions nor doubts about a broad cultural highway from black America to black Africa, and her firm belief irradiates her work." Several other poems offered homage to Langston Hughes, who also displayed a strong connection to his African heritage in his writing and had inspired and influenced Danner throughout her life. In "The Rhetoric of Langston Hughes," she writes, "Langston Hughes (in his traveling) // has sung to so many for so long // and from so very Black a Power // that we

finds in her quest of understanding the identity of her ancestors. The vivid pictures of her journey involve her readers, helping them respect Africa."

Having gained exposure and recognition for her work at *Poetry* and her publication of *Impressions of African Art Forms*, in 1961 Danner was invited to serve as the poet in residence at Wayne State University in Detroit. During her stay in Detroit, Danner became involved in the community. Wishing to create an arts center, she enlisted other poets, including Robert Hayden, to help and convinced the minister of Detroit's King Solomon Church to allow her to use an uninhabited parish house. Boone Center, named after Dr. Boone, the minister of the church, became a community arts center, with numerous activities focused on reaching out to children. Danner honored the center in her poem "Boone House," which appeared in the *Negro History Bulletin* in 1962. Later, Danner would also found Nologonyu's, another such center for the arts in Chicago's Southside.

have clearly seen the 'angles' and dedicated ourselves // to the unraveling."

Sketchy Details of Personal Life

The available details of Danner's personal life are not complete. She was married to Cordell Strickland, with whom she had one daughter, Naomi. The couple divorced, and Danner married Otto Cunningham. Danner's grandson, Sterling Washington, Jr., became the inspiration for a number of Danner's later poems. Referred to as "the Muffin poems" by Danner, these poems cover a range of issues and include "Black Power Language" and "Muffin, His Baba and the Boneman."

Although Danner was not the most widely acclaimed poet of her time, she earned the respect of her peers as an artistic voice for those who wished to find meaning and inspiration in the relationship between black Africa and black America. Her message was one of hope but she did not trivialize the difficulty of being black in America. In her introduction to her poems that appeared in *The Forerunners: Black Poets in America*, Danner wrote, "As for my poetry: I believe that my dharma is to prove that the Force of Good takes precedence over the force for evil in mankind. To the extent that my poetry adheres to this purpose it will endure." Danner died in Chicago on January 1, 1984.

Selected writings

Poetry

Impressions of African Art Forms, Wayne State University, 1960.
To Flower, Hemphill Press, 1963.
(With Dudley Randall) *Poem Counterpoem,* Broadside Press, 1966.
Iron Lace, Kriya Press, 1968.
The Down of a Thistle: Selected Poems, Prose, and Songs, Country Beautiful, 1976.

Contributions to Anthologies

Beyond the Blues: New Poems by American Negroes, Hand and Flower Press, 1962.
American Negro Poetry, Hill and Wang, 1963.
For Malcolm: Poems on the Life and the Death of Malcolm X, Broadside, 1967.
(Editor) *Brass Horses,* Virginia Union University, 1968.
(Editor) *Regroup,* Virginia Union University, 1969.

To Gwen With Love, Johnson Publishing Company, 1971.
The Black Poets, Bantam, 1971.
Afro-American Literature: An Introduction, Harcourt Brace Jovanovich, 1971.
Black Writers of America: A Comprehensive Anthology, Macmillan, 1972.
The Poetry of Black America: Anthology of the 20th Century, Harper & Row, 1973.
Understanding the New Black Poetry, Morrow, 1973.
Black Sister: Poetry by Black American Women, 1746-1980, Indiana University Press, 1981.

Recordings

(With Langston Hughes) *Writers of the Revolution,* Black Forum, 1970.

Sources

Books

Bailey, Leaonead Pack, ed., *Broadside Authors and Artists,* Broadside Press, 1974.
Barksdale, Richard, *Praisesong of Survival: Lectures and Essays, 1957-89,* University of Illinois Press, 1992.
King, Woodie, Jr., ed., *The Forerunners: Black Poets in America,* Howard University Press, 1975.
Lee, Don I., *Dynamite Voices I: Black Poets of the 1960s,* Broadside Press, 1971.
Notable Black American Women, Gale Group, 2004.
Redmond, Eugene B., *Drumvoices: The Mission of Afro-American Poetry,* Anchor Books, 1976.
Stetson, Erlene, "Dialectic Voices in the Poetry of Margaret Esse Danner," in *Black American Poets Between Worlds, 1940-1960,* edited by R. Baxter Miller, University of Tennessee Press, 1986.

Periodicals

Booklist, November 15, 1976.
The Langston Hughes Review, Spring 1984, pp. 7-9; Fall 1993, pp. 45-49.
School Library Journal, January 1977.

On-line

"Margaret Danner," *Contemporary Authors Online,* www.galenet.galegroup.com/servlet/BioRC -(December 3, 2004).

—Kari Bethel

Idris Elba

1972—

Actor

Elba, Idris, photograph. © Zack Seckler/Corbis.

British actor Idris Elba is one of a number of foreign-born thespians who have begun landing impressive roles on American screens both large and small. Elba has made a name for himself in the United States for his compelling performance on the HBO series *The Wire,* which began its third season in 2004. He plays Stringer Bell, a drug kingpin, on the Baltimore-set drama, who dreams of becoming a legitimate business tycoon.

Born in 1972 in England, Elba gravitated toward a career in the entertainment business at an early age. He began helping an uncle with his wedding-DJ business at age 14, and within a year had started his own DJ company with some friends. He was working in nightclubs by the age of 19, but began auditioning for television parts in his early twenties. In 1995 he landed his first role on a British series called *Bramwell,* a medical drama set in 1890s England. That same year he also appeared in an episode of the notorious comedy series *Absolutely Fabulous,* seen regularly in reruns on the BBC America cable channel. He took parts in a few television movies before winning the role of handsome heartthrob Tim Webster on the British nighttime soap

opera *Family Affairs* in 1997. The show was set in Kent, England, and earned terrible ratings during the first season, but managed to revive its fortunes by having one entire family killed off in a barge accident. Elba was only on the show for its first year, but the exposure boosted his career immensely.

Elba went on to appear in a more established British television series, *Dangerfield,* in 1999 as a forensic scientist. Soon, however, he decided to move to New York City. "England is home, and I love it," he told *Essence*'s Esther Armah about why he decided to move. "But England couldn't house my ambition." At first, roles for the British actor with a Cockney accent were hard to win, and he took work spinning records in clubs in the East Village and Alphabet City to make ends meet. He returned to England occasionally for a job, such as a part in one of the *Inspector Lynley Mysteries,* a top-rated British crime series.

Elba's break in American television came when he landed a part on one of the top-rated American crime series, *Law and Order,* in 2001. He also appeared on the New York stage in the Shakespeare classic *Troilus*

At a Glance . . .

Born on September 6, 1972, in England; children: one daughter.

Career: DJ, 1986–; actor, 1995–.

Addresses: *Office*—HBO–Home Box Office, 1100 Avenue of the Americas, New York, NY 10036.

and Cressida that same year. The drama of ancient Greece is set during the Trojan War, and Elba was cast as Achilles, the once-powerful warrior now fallen from favor. "Elba, as Achilles, with an ever-present wine goblet in his hand and a controlling arm often around his doting companion, Patroclus, does have the swagger to convey both his physical prowess and his graceless egomania," noted a *New York Times* review of the play from Bruce Weber.

HBO producers then cast Elba in *The Wire,* a new series that debuted in 2002. The show was created by David Simon, a former Baltimore crime-beat reporter, and was marked by a gritty realism in its portrayal of the criminal underworld and the cops who fight it—and are sometimes lured into it by their own vices as well. Elba was cast as Russell "Stringer" Bell, an ambitious but ruthless drug dealer. Elba's character strives to make his mark when he emerges as the second-in-command for a local drug racketeer who is sent to prison. His on-screen nemesis is Dominic West as the conflicted Baltimore police detective Jimmy McNulty. Interestingly, West also hails from Britain and had to work to cover his accent with the appropriate Baltimore one, like Elba.

In an interview that appeared on HBO's official Web site for *The Wire,* Elba answered questions from viewers, including one about why he took the part of Bell. "Here was a chance to play a mountain of different roles molded into one," he reflected. "As a boy you dream of playing a gangster character who has all that power. Stringer is the embodiment of the powerful character who has successfully and charismatically eluded the police." Critics loved the dichotomies presented by the show's writers, some of whom were successful crime-novel writers before they joined *The Wire* team, such as *Clockers'* Richard Price and Dennis Lehane, author of *Mystic River.* The *New York Times* critic Caryn James asserted as third season began that though the cops-and-robbers game may seem like an overdone genre, since its onset *The Wire* has consistently proved a cut above. "With its frank attention to race and class, its moral ambiguity and its unabashedly confusing plots that challenge viewers to keep up, *The Wire* has become one of the smartest, most ambitious shows on television," she noted. Ken

Tucker, writing in *Entertainment Weekly,* also gave the show high marks, calling it a "hypnotically dense drama without pat answers."

Elba has appeared in a few feature films, among them *Buffalo Soldiers* in 2001 alongside Joaquin Phoenix. The film's negative depiction of American soldiers stationed in Germany just before the fall of the Berlin Wall in 1989 was deemed too politically insensitive, and it vanished quickly from theaters. Elba can also be seen in the occasional music video, including those from Fat Joe and Angie Stone, and still DJs under the name Big Dris. "I consider myself a blend DJ more than anything," he told the MTV Web site Mixtape Monday. "Like my mixtapes, the way I want to see them grow, I basically want to see if I can get my mixtapes to showcase new talent."

Elba has a young daughter, and cites Robert De Niro as his professional role model, especially in the 1983 dark farce, *The King of Comedy.* He was also slated to appear in a 2004 television movie about the 1994 genocide in Rwanda,...*Sometimes in April.* He admitted that it seemed easier to win roles in American television, he said in the HBO.com interview, noting that in Britain "rarely do producers take a chance on unknown actors and I think it's for mostly economical reasons. When 25 [percent] of TV viewers are black and rest are white, they don't feel they need to write for black characters. The black audience in England is so much smaller than here so they don't think they'll get the big financial return with a black show."

Selected works

Films

Belle Maman, 1999.
Sorted, 2000.
Buffalo Soldiers, 2001.
Johnny Was, 2005.

Television

Bramwell, 1995.
Family Affairs, 1997.
Law and Order, 2001.
The Wire, 2002.

Sources

Periodicals

Daily Variety, February 4, 2004, p. 24.
Entertainment Weekly, August 15, 2003, p. 14.
Essence, December 2003, p. 146; April 2004.
Mirror (London, England), May 9, 1997, p. 7.
New York Newsday, October 24, 2004.
New York Times, April 16, 2001; September 19, 2004, p. AR19.

On-line

"HBO—The Wire: Interview," *HBO.com,* www.hbo. com/thewire/interviews/idris_elba.shtml (October 28, 2004).

"Mixtape Monday," *MTV.com*, www.mtv.com/bands/ m/mixtape_monday/092704/ (October 28, 2004).

—Carol Brennan

Kirk Franklin

1970(?)—

Gospel singer

Franklin, Kirk, photograph. AP/Wide World Photos. Reproduced by permission.

"My message is simple and plain," Kirk Franklin insisted in the *Los Angeles Times*. "I'm trying to change the way people look at gospel music. It's not corny, and it's not hokey. We're not just running around here with some choir robes on, yelling and screaming. It's not about that anymore, kid." The charismatic Franklin has achieved mainstream success thanks to a fusion of hip-hop-flavored style and hardcore religious content. Where other gospel acts had replaced "Jesus" and "God" with "Him" and "You" in hopes of winning over pop listeners, Franklin has never blunted his proselytizing. At the same time, the recordings and concerts by the singer and his gospel group, The Family, have achieved sales that would be respectable even by secular standards and won a bevy of honors. Despite his rise to stardom, Franklin has kept his eye on the real prize. "When I try to reach people, it's by any means necessary," he told the *Tri-State Defender*. "The purpose is to win them. I spread the word of God through my music, and that's how souls are won—regardless of where it's heard."

Franklin's own soul underwent considerable turmoil in his youth. Born in Fort Worth, Texas, to a teenage mother, he never knew his father and was adopted at the age of three by the only mother he ever really knew—his great-aunt Gertrude—who raised him vigilantly. "She taught me everything," the singer told Cheo Hodari Coker of the *Los Angeles Times*. "She taught me how to respect people and respect myself, and that's something I'll never forget." A devout Baptist, Gertrude recognized and encouraged the boy's profound musical gifts; money she and Kirk made from recycling cans and newspapers paid for his piano lessons. His obvious talent for church singing led to an offer of a record contract by the time he was seven, but Gertrude refused to consider such an offer, considering Kirk's age. His precociousness could not be kept under wraps forever, though, and by age 11 he was leading the adult choir at Mt. Rose Baptist Church. "It was scary," he recalled to Coker. "I was [in charge of] people 60 and older. Could you imagine someone that young telling their elders they were singing wrong?"

Despite his immersion in a religious environment, Franklin was not immune to the call of street life. "I was always a moody child," he reflected in *Texas Monthly*. "In the house it was just me and an older woman. When

At a Glance . . .

Born Kirk Smith in 1970(?) in Forth Worth, TX; raised by aunt, Gertrude Franklin; married Tammy Renee Collins, 1996; children: four.

Career: Mt. Rose Baptist Church, Fort Worth, TX, choir director, 1981(?); singer, songwriter, arranger and producer, 1991–. Fo Yo Soul production company, founder, 199(?)–.

Awards: Dove Award, 1994, 1997, 1998, 1999, 2002, and 2003; Grammy Award, 1996, 1997, 1998; Stellar Award, 1996. *BMI* Christian Songwriter of the Year, three-way tie, 2003; NAACP Image Award, Outstanding Album, for *The Rebirth of Kirk Franklin,* Outstanding Song, for "Brighter Day," and Outstanding Gospel Artist, 2003.

Addresses: *Label*—Gospo-Centric Records, 417 E. Regent St., Inglewood, CA 90301.

I got around my peers, I was just buck wild, because I wanted to be a kid, you know?" Fear of being called a "church boy," he has noted in numerous interviews, motivated his acting out. "I was more of a perpetrator than a hardcore G[angster]," he asserted to *Gannett News Service.* "I was always one of the brothers trying to be a gangster with all the other kids because I didn't want them to think I was soft, although I was." Though his behavior was hardly extreme by street standards, he hung around pool halls, smoked marijuana and got into fights; it was only when, at 15, he saw a friend die of an accidental shooting that he decided to change his life. "I didn't think anyone could die so young," Franklin recollected to Coker of the *Los Angeles Times.* "I knew what I was doing was wrong. That was a major trip for me."

The incident had profound implications for the singer's path in life. "It woke me up," he told Gannett. "At 15 I had been in church all my life, but it wasn't in me." Further hardship ensued when he and his girlfriend had a child out of wedlock; she was left to care for the baby, Kerrion, for several years. "What I had done was wrong," he reflected in *Texas Monthly,* "but God forgave me, so I was able to forgive myself." Ultimately Franklin managed to place all his focus on his calling. Noted producer Milton Biggham heard a home demo tape Franklin had made and invited him to write material for a gospel album by the Dallas-Fort Worth (DFW) Mass Choir. Franklin fulfilled this request on the Choir's 1991 release *I Will Let Nothing Separate Me* and on 1993's *Another Chance.* He performed simi-

lar duties for the GMWA National Mass Choir's recording *Live in Indianapolis.*

But the vocalist wanted to perform his own material; to that end, he put together a 17-member singing group, the Family, culled in part from the DFW Mass Choir. "I called my group the Family because it was the extended family that I never had and the sense of family I always wanted," he proclaimed to Coker. After turning down a deal with Savoy Records, they signed a recording contract with Gospo Centric—a label run by gospel music industry veteran Vicki Mack-Lataillade—and released their debut, *Kirk Franklin and the Family,* in 1993. Recorded at Grace Temple Church in Forth Worth, the album scored with such songs as "Why We Sing" and "He Can Handle It." The *Los Angeles Sentinel* cited Mack-Lataillade's advice to Franklin: "I told him I didn't want gospel music to remain status quo; I wanted to make it for everybody," she pointed out.

Franklin's uplifting, modern take on gospel refused to omit "Jesus" and "the Lord" from the lyrics—as many gospel artists seeking mainstream fame have done—but at the same time pursued hip-hop fans with its up-to-date grooves and vocalizing. Though some purists objected to the appropriation of secular styles, Franklin brushed their qualms aside. "We're doing it our way," he asserted in the *Los Angeles Sentinel.* "If it's different, well, get used to it, because it's music inspired by God and it's here to stay."

Initially, the debut album sold respectably for a gospel record. But over a year and half after its release, Drew Dawson—an urban-radio deejay in Virginia—began playing "Why We Sing" regularly on his program; as a result, other secular radio stations began picking it up. Speaking to the *Tri-State Defender,* Dawson compared Franklin to multi-faceted R&B figure Babyface, another writer-performer-producer- arranger. "Because [Franklin]'s so talented as a songwriter and musician and because there's no one around in gospel music that is doing it all, his stuff stands out," Dawson insisted. It stood out so much, in fact, that Franklin soon became a sensation in the pop music world, becoming the first gospel debut to sell a million copies. "When my album started blowing up—I mean when God started blessing me—I started to go a lot of places," the singer related in *USA Today,* "but it was like a giving a diamond to a 4-year-old kid."

And Franklin had to deal with the consequences of challenging an entrenched form, in this case an approach to gospel that drew firm distinctions between secular and sacred music. "Gospel needs an edge," he asserted in the *Michigan Chronicle,* "so that it will receive the same type of respect that other types of music get. For so long gospel didn't get much respect from the industry." What's more, he pointed out in the same interview, his funky, contemporary approach drew in younger listeners. "A lot of Christian young people are saying, 'Man, this music that we like to listen to on the urban stations is real funky and it's jammin' but a lot of the songs are so nasty,'" Franklin reported. "'Can y'all give us something we can play in our Jeeps and ride down the street and pump to but it's talking about Jesus?'" Franklin and the Family did just that, incorporating references to secular rap and hip-hop hits, but reworking the lyrics to address religious themes. His explosive approach appeared in Family concerts as well. "Franklin came to us and said, 'We want lights, we want big sound, we want special effects,'" tour promoter Al Wash told the *Los Angeles Sentinel*, "and now we're putting on a show like no one else in gospel ever has."

Franklin further scandalized gospel's old guard by entering a production deal through Mack-Lataillade's new company, B-Rite Records, which was distributed by the controversial Interscope Records—home of the notorious rap label Death Row and such rock acts as Nine Inch Nails. Interscope co-founder Jimmy Iovine told the *Los Angeles Times* he considered Franklin "an innovative artist with a long career ahead of him. He's going to create a lot of avenues for artists in the genre that they don't have right now," continued the famed music executive. "I think the spirit of gospel will expand and be an even more important factor in the pop world." Mack-Lataillade asserted in the same article that Franklin provided a corrective to the kind of music for which Interscope had become infamous. "We're on a mission," she proclaimed, adding, "We want to show people that there's another way to go with the music. When Kirk's music stops, people don't feel violent, and today that's worth something."

Franklin and the Family followed up their debut with a Christmas album, but it was *Whatcha Lookin' 4*, a continuation of the pumped-up R&B-styled gospel that had made the first album a sensation, that was considered the true follow-up. The album hit the pop charts running and scored on both the gospel and R&B charts. Franklin—who played a pastor in the touring play *He Say, She Say But What Does God Say?*—told Janice Malone of the *Tennessee Tribune* that he was untroubled by the high expectations that greeted the album. "I just stayed focused and recognized that it had nothing to do with me," he insisted. "I don't know about other artists, but it's a lot different for me because I write all of my own material. By doing so it makes me more sensitive to the final outcome, song per song. Whenever I do a project, I don't pick out just one particular song. When God gives me the music, he also gives me the words to the song all together, so that was one worry, I didn't really have."

In early 1996, the singer married Tammy Renee Collins, a former member of the R&B group Ashanti; "She's wonderful," he exclaimed in *USA Today*. "She's my soul mate." He added, "I hate the single life. Even though my music has a lot of urban appeal, I'm still a church boy. I'm not supposed to be seen with three or four different women. I want to represent not just the music but the lifestyle." He further insisted, in

CCM, that his decision to marry Tammy was strengthened by Divine guidance. "God told me," he claimed. "When I was in my prayer time in Birmingham, Alabama, God spoke to me and told me He was pleased [about his plan to marry Collins]. And that He was pleased that she and I had waited [to be intimate]…[Marriage] is making me think and feel like a man. For so long, I was a boy. I know I'm a better man now that I'm married." He brought his son into the marriage, and she her 7-year-old daughter; the two later had a child together.

His spouse would prove an additional pillar of strength when Franklin suffered a serious accident. In late 1996 he fell from the stage of North Hall Auditorium in Memphis after introducing opening act Yolanda Adams, landing in the orchestra pit and sustaining head injuries. After a hospital stay brightened by "tens of thousands of postcards and phone calls from well-wishers," as *Jet* reported, Franklin convalesced and resumed his "Tour of Life." His experience, he told Steve Jones of *USA Today*, deepened his appreciation for his wife. "I started looking at her differently and started holding her hand differently," he related. "It was like I was falling in love all over again." Franklin's desire to attend gospel's Stellar Awards was so strong, his wife recalled, was strong even during the thick of his recovery. "When he was in the hospital he was telling us he was going," she recalled to Jones. "And we kept telling him, 'You're not going anywhere.' But he was like, 'Yes I am. Yes I am.' So finally, when the doctors said it would be OK, we said all right."

Franklin's appearance at the Stellar Awards—a mere month after his fall—was something of a valedictory. *Billboard*'s Lisa Collins reported that the singer "was the night's big winner, thrilling the crowd with a performance and testimony that brought the crowd to its feet." Though he took home five awards, including artist of the year, Franklin expressed a larger goal to Collins. "I wanted to make a fool out of the devil," he said. "You're not going to try to take my life and think I'm not going to praise God. I'm a living testimony."

Nearly a decade later, Franklin continued his mission. His music had generated an even bigger buzz in the music industry. Franklin made gospel music cool, opening the doors of churches to share their music over the airwaves and on television. He combined gospel with R&B, pop, rock, hip-hop, and even African and Latin music. Franklin was credited by his peers as helping to make gospel music into a multi-million dollar industry. VH1 offered viewers several concert shows in the early 2000s, and mainstream musicians—such as Bono, Mary J. Blige, and R. Kelly—partnered with Franklin in the studio. Franklin was hailed as a "visionary" of gospel music, and he knew all that label implied, telling *CNN* that gospel music's new popularity was "an opportunity to reach more people with the message—especially a generation that isn't into organized religion, God, the Jesus thing."

Selected discography

Kirk Franklin and the Family, Gospo-Centric, 1993.
Christmas, Gospo-Centric, 1995.
Whatcha Lookin' 4, Gospo-Centric, 1996.
God's Property, Gospo-Centric, 1997.
Nu Nation Project, Gospo-Centric, 1998.
One Nation Crew, Gospo-Centric, 2000.
The Rebirth of Kirk Franklin, Gospo-Centric, 2002.

Sources

Periodicals

Billboard, December 28, 1996, p. 16; February 15, 1997, p. 38.
CCM, August 1996.
Fort Worth Star-Telegram, June 6, 1996.
Gannett News Service, June 21, 1996.
Jet, November 25, 1996, p. 33.
Los Angeles Times, July 7, 1996, p. 7.
Los Angeles Sentinel, November 21, 1996.

Michigan Chronicle, November 7, 1995.
Philadelphia Tribune, May 9, 1995.
Tennessee Tribune, December 4, 1996.
Texas Monthly, 1996.
Time, January 22, 1996.
Tri-State Defender, November 29, 1995.
USA Today, October 17, 1996; December 10, 1996; December 11, 1996.
Washington Afro-American, February 18, 1995.

On-line

"Franklin Pushes New Gospel Boundaries with 'Nu Nation Project,'" *CNN,* http://archives.cnn.com/2000/SHOWBIZ/Music/01/31/wb.kirk.franklin/ (accessed January 20, 2005).
"Kirk Franklin," *Nu Nation,* www.nunation.com (accessed January 20, 2005).
"New Gospel Reaching Out to Next Generation," *CNN,* www.cnn.com/SHOWBIZ/Music/9901/07/franklin.gospel/ (accessed January 20, 2005).

—Simon Glickman and Sara Pendergast

Grant Fuhr

1962—

Hockey player, coach

The Edmonton Oilers dominated the National Hockey League (NHL) throughout the 1980s, in no small part due to the goaltending talents of Grant Fuhr. Fuhr was an indispensable component of a team that won five Stanley Cups in seven years, a sometimes brilliant defender who was particularly effective in playoff games. In 1988 Ralph Wiley called Fuhr—who was then 25—"the best goalie in the NHL. The best on earth."

Fuhr's once stellar reputation was tarnished by injuries and the admission of substance abuse. Suspended from the Oilers in 1990 for drug use that occurred during the team's glory years, Fuhr staged a comeback and continued as a successful keeper for several teams through the 1990s, most notably in a four-year run with the St. Louis Blues from 1995 to 1999. Just a few years after his retirement in 2000 Fuhr was named to the Hockey Hall of Fame, the first person of African descent to be so honored. He is now a goalkeeper coach for the Phoenix Coyotes of the NHL.

Hockey is nothing less than an obsession for most Canadians. Children learn to skate at an early age and dream of the NHL the way American boys dream of playing professional football. Grant Fuhr was no exception to this rule. At the age of seven he announced that he was going to become a goaltender in the NHL, and he made good on his promise. Fuhr was born in Edmonton in the autumn of 1962 to teenage parents who gave him up for adoption. Even though he considers himself black—or at least of mixed race—he was placed with a white family. Initially his adoptive parents were reluctant to accept him, fearing that they

would not be able to instill in him a sense of racial pride. They found that most people accepted their unorthodox family, however, and they were able to deal honestly with their son and his concerns. "We were always honest with Grant," Betty Fuhr told *Sports Illustrated*. "We asked him to be fair in his judgments, to not judge a person—or himself—on social or economic standing, but on their honesty and integrity."

Fuhr's father was an insurance salesman who was fond of both golf and hockey. He allowed his son to turn the family basement into a makeshift rink and bought the boy a pair of skates when he was four. Grant skated constantly, developing coordination far beyond the norm for one of his tender age. In school he excelled at other sports as well, but hockey remained his favorite. In 1979, when he was 16, he turned down a chance to play catcher with the Pittsburgh Pirates' baseball farm team because "hockey was in." Needless to say, this fascination with sports left little time for formal studies. Fuhr dropped out of high school at 16 and joined the Victoria Cougars of Canada's Western Hockey League. Wiley described the young athlete as "5 ft. 9 in., with strong legs, good eyes, and hands that defied description. He was…different."

Fuhr was also black, and he was attempting to make the majors in a sport that is still almost exclusively white. Bob White, a coach in Montreal, told *Sports Illustrated* that Fuhr might have been steered away from hockey had he grown up in eastern Canada. "If Fuhr had been born in Quebec, he might not have made it to the NHL," White said. "You can be recruited with a [goalie] mask on, like Grant Fuhr. He was lucky

At a Glance . . .

Born Grant Scott Fuhr on September 28, 1962, in Spruce Grove, Alberta, Canada; adopted son of Robert (an insurance salesman) and Betty Fuhr; married three times. *Education*: Attended Composite High School, Spruce Grove, Alberta.

Career: Goalkeeper, Edmonton Oilers, 1981-91; goalkeeper, Toronto Maple Leafs, 1991-92; goalkeeper, Buffalo Sabres, 1992-94; goalkeeper, Los Angeles Kings, 1994-95; goalkeeper, St. Louis Blues, 1995–99; goalkeeper, Calgary Flames, 1999-2000. Goalkeeping consultant, Calgary Falmes, 2000-04; goalkeeper coach, Phoenix Coyotes, 2004–.

Selected Awards: Vezina Trophy for NHL's outstanding goaltender, 1988; William N. Jennings Trophy, NHL, 1993-94; named to NHL Hall of Fame, 2003; named to Alberta Sports Hall of Fame, 2004.

Addresses: *Office*—c/o Phoenix Coyotes Hockey Club, 5800 W. Glenn Drive, Suite 350, Glendale, AZ 85301.

he was out west…. And it's good he wears the mask." If this harsh judgment speaks to inherent racism in hockey's ranks, it also speaks to Fuhr's outstanding ability, mask or no mask. As a teenager, Fuhr showed such obvious potential that he was made a member of the Edmonton Oilers as a number one draft choice before his eighteenth birthday.

Ron Low, a former Oiler, remembered Fuhr's early years in a *Sports Illustrated* feature. "Grant never played in the minors," Low said. "We all knew he was great from the first day of camp. A natural. Yet he had no style. Or, rather, his style was all styles. He would come out 15 feet to challenge the shot on one offensive rush. The next time he would be back in his crease. He could read the game so well. He anticipated the game. Grant was just…different. Different from anyone I'd ever seen." Fuhr honed his skills by practicing against his high-scoring teammates such as Wayne Gretzky and Mark Messier, as formidable a pair of offensive players as can be found anywhere. Quickly Fuhr improved his reflexes and grasped every nuance of the game, becoming expert at both instinctive plays and strategic moves.

Fuhr helped the Oilers to advance to the playoffs in his rookie season as well as his sophomore year. By 1984 the seeds of the dominant Oilers team had been sown. In that Stanley Cup season, Fuhr turned in ten playoff wins. The following season he stunned the league by

earning 15 playoff victories as the Oilers won another Cup. In the 1985-86 season the team once again advanced to the playoffs, and Fuhr stood in the goal even though he had spent several sleepless nights by his adoptive father's deathbed. When Edmonton contended for the Stanley Cup again in the spring of 1987, Fuhr had an astounding goals-against average of 2.46 through nineteen games. He was universally feared as a cool hand in the game's most stressful position and was considered nearly unbeatable in the clutch. Barry Pederson of the Vancouver Canucks summed up the exceptional talents of Grant Fuhr in *Sports Illustrated*. "Bar none, Grant Fuhr is the best goalie in the league," Pederson said. "He has the fastest reflexes. Sometimes his concentration might drift during inconsequential games. But in the big-money games Fuhr is the best. He's the Cup goalie. It's sure not by luck."

A five-time All-Star, Fuhr was chosen to be the starting goalie in the 1987 Canada Cup games against the Soviet Union's national team. Although Team Canada's roster also featured star goalies Kelly Hrudey of the New York Islanders and Ron Hextall of the Philadelphia Flyers, Fuhr started all three games and helped the Canadians to beat the Soviets for the Cup. Wiley called Fuhr's performance in that series "breathtakingly effective." Fuhr then turned in yet another stellar season with Edmonton in 1988, earning the Vezina Trophy as the league's best goaltender.

With such success to his credit, Fuhr was allowed to go his own way off the ice, with little supervision. Perhaps not surprisingly, he ran into trouble, financial and otherwise. In the early years of his contract, Fuhr's salary was extremely modest by the standards of professional sports. He paid little attention as his extravagant ways led him into debt. In retrospect, Fuhr told *Sports Illustrated* that he was "a kid who did some dumb things." He added, for instance: "When my clothes were dirty, I just threw them in the closet and went out and bought something else." Fuhr now admits that overspending was only one of his problems. He fell in with a fast crowd and began to use cocaine—not to the point of addiction, but certainly to the point that it added to his financial woes.

In 1990 Fuhr came forward about his drug use after spending two weeks in a counseling center in Florida. He admitted that he used "a substance"—he did not say cocaine—for some seven years, or most of the period that the Oilers rested at the top of the NHL. Details of Fuhr's drug use were supplied by the player's ex-wife, Corrine, who told the press in Edmonton that she often found cocaine hidden in Fuhr's clothing and that she fielded numerous threatening telephone calls from drug dealers who had not been paid. These embarrassing details no doubt contributed to the one-year suspension handed down in September 1990 by NHL president John Ziegler, who called Fuhr's conduct "dishonorable and against the welfare of the league."

Many observers felt that the year-long suspension was too harsh. Fuhr had, after all, acknowledged the problem and had sought treatment for it. He had also tested free of drugs for a year before the suspension even began. In fact, Fuhr was reinstated 59 games later, and he led the Oilers to a 4-0 shutout of the New Jersey Devils on his first night back. Despite this initial success, the Oilers, who were starting on a rebuilding program, traded Fuhr to the Toronto Maple Leafs at the end of the 1990-91 season.

Many speculated the Fuhr's trade to the Maple Leafs marked the beginning of the end of his career. Age had slowed his reflexes somewhat, and injuries had begun to affect his play. After years of recurring tendonitis in his left shoulder, he underwent surgery and had the joint pinned during his suspension. He had 25 wins, 33 losses, and 5 ties in his first season with the Leafs, and had developed a winning record during the 1992-93 season when he was traded to the Buffalo Sabres. Fuhr had a successful 1993-94 season with the Sabres, sharing time in goal with Dominik Hasek, with whom he shared the NHL's William N. Jenning's Trophy for fewest goals allowed. Early the next season he was traded to the Los Angeles Kings, where he saw limited action.

Many assumed the Fuhr's career was winding downs in the mid-1990s, especially as he endured recurring knee injuries. But his trade to the St. Louis Blues at the start of the 1995-96 season saw Fuhr return to form. From 1995 through 1999, Fuhr had four successive seasons in which he posted a winning record, and his goals against average was under 3.0 each season. On reconstructed knees, Fuhr led the St. Louis Blues to the Stanley Cup playoffs in 1998-1999. Fuhr was traded to the Calgary Flames in 1999 and played just 23 games with the Flames before retiring in 2000.

Fuhr retired with a lifetime record of 403-295-114, with 25 shutouts. He was only the sixth goalkeeper in the NHL to earn 400 wins, just one of the statistics that earned him selection to the Hockey Hall of Fame in 2003. Fuhr discussed his honor with the *Philadelphia Enquirer*: "Being a black athlete going into the Hall of Fame is obviously a special honor also—especially in hockey, being the first one—but the reason you get into the Hall of Fame is for what you have accomplished on the ice, and I probably take the most pride in that." Following his retirement, Fuhr served as a goalkeeping consultant for the Calgary Flames before joining the staff of the Phoenix Coyotes as a goalkeeper coach in 2004. On the club's Web site, Fuhr said: "I am extremely excited because becoming a goalie coach in the National Hockey League is a great opportunity."

Sources

Periodicals

Los Angeles Times, September 1, 1990; September 28, 1990.
Philadelphia Inquirer, November 8, 2003.
St. Louis Post-Dispatch, April 23, 1998; April 21, 1999; April 27, 1999; May 18, 1999.
San Francisco Chronicle, May 21, 1990.
Sports Illustrated, January 11, 1988; September 10, 1990.

On-line

"Grant Fuhr," *Legends of Hockey*, www.legendsof-hockey.net/html/ind03fuhr.htm (January 31, 2005).
"One-on-One with Grant Fuhr," *Phoenix Coyotes*, www.phoenixcoyotes.com/news/story_details.php?op=details&ID=3647&SectionID=11 (January 31, 2005).

—Mark Kram and Tom Pendergast

Samuel L. Gravely, Jr.

1922-2004

Naval officer

Gravely, Samuel L., photograph. Getty Images.

At the peak of his career, Samuel L. Gravely, Jr. was the highest-ranking African American officer in the U.S. Navy, a three-star vice admiral. Even after his retirement, he maintained the commanding presence that he had honed during his 38 years in the military. Throughout his long career, Gravely was not only the first African American officer to become an admiral, but was also the first to serve on—and later command—a fighting ship. His many decorations, honors, and awards attest to his success.

Born in 1922 in Richmond, Virginia, Gravely came from a family committed to government service. His father, Samuel L. Gravely Sr., was a postal worker, and his siblings worked at various government posts with the Veterans Administration and the Internal Revenue Service. After a short stint at the post office himself, Gravely responded to the call to arms issued during the Second World War and joined the U.S. Navy.

Interrupting his education at Virginia Union University, Gravely enlisted in the U.S. Naval Reserve in 1942. He quickly rose to officer rank. After boot camp at the Great Lakes Naval Training Station in Illinois, he attended Officer Training Camp at the University of

California at Los Angeles, and then midshipman school at Columbia University. He was the first African American to reach the rank of captain, and when he boarded his first ship in May of 1945, he became its first black officer.

After serving as a communications, electronics, and personnel officer, Gravely left the navy in 1946 to get married and return to school; in 1948, he earned a degree in history from Virginia Union University. He had no immediate plans to return to the navy. After graduation, he told *Ebony*, "I planned to teach and coach, but took a job in the post office instead. I guess the urge for government service was just that overpowering." The same year he graduated, 1948, President Harry S. Truman issued an executive order to integrate the armed forces. The following year, the U.S. military stepped up recruitment of African Americans. In 1952, Gravely returned to active duty on board the USS *Iowa*.

Gravely's tenure in the naval service was tainted by the difficulties of racial discrimination. He learned early on that he was, as he told *Ebony* magazine, "saving America for democracy, but not allowed to participate in the goddamn thing." As a new recruit, he was

At a Glance . . .

Born Samuel Lee Gravely, Jr., on June 4, 1922, in Richmond, VA; died on October 22, 2004, in Bethesda, MD; son of Samuel L. (a postal worker) and Mary George Gravely; married Alma Bernice Clark, 1946; children: Robert (deceased), David, Tracy. *Education*: Attended Officer Training Camp at the University of California, Los Angeles, and midshipman school at Columbia University; Virginia Union University, BA, 1948.

Career: U.S. Navy, career military officer, 1942-80; became vice admiral; commander, USS *Falgout*, 1962; commander, Third Fleet, 1976-78; director of Defense Communications Agency, 1978-80; Armed Forces Communications and Electronics Associations (AFCEA), executive director of education and training, 1984-87.

Awards: Named Distinguished Virginian by Governor Holton, 1972; Communications Award from the Los Angeles Chapter of the National Association of Media Women, 1972; Major Richard R. Wright Award of Excellence, Savanna State College, 1974; Prince Hall Founding Fathers Military Commanders Award, Scottish Rite Prince Hall Masonic Bodies of Maryland, 1975; San Diego Press Club Military Headliner of the Year, 1975. Military awards: Legion of Merit with Gold Star, Bronze Star Medal, Meritorious Service Medal, Joint Services Commendation Medal, Navy Commendation Medal, World War II Victory Medal, Naval Reserve Medal for 10 years of service in the U.S. Naval Reserve, American Campaign Medal, Korean Presidential Unit Citation, National Defense Medal with one bronze star, China Service Medal, Korean Service Medal with two bronze stars, United Nations Service Medal, Armed Forces Expeditionary Medal, Vietnam Service Medal with six bronze stars, and the Antarctic Service Medal.

members. Long after Truman's executive order, the unofficial policy in the navy was to have as few blacks as possible on any ship. Furthermore, African-American officers were limited to work on large ships.

Gravely had received a very friendly reception when he reported for duty aboard the battleship USS *Iowa* in 1952, but he later found a letter from the Bureau of Naval Personnel to the *Iowa* 's commanding officer, instructing the commander to brief the ship's personnel before Gravely's arrival. Gravely knew that the briefing pertained to his race, and he later told *Ebony*: "I gave the letter to my roommate and suggested that it be returned to the ship's office. When he saw that I had read the letter, he immediately began to tell me about the briefing, how delighted everyone was with my being assigned, and how I must have been a fine guy to have earned a commission. He added: 'There was one problem. No one wanted to live with you, so I volunteered.'"

Gravely survived the indignities of racial prejudice and displayed unquestionable competence as a naval officer. He eventually earned a reputation as an expert in naval communications. Early in his career, Gravely served with distinction as a radio specialist aboard the *Iowa*, where the ship's communications officer was more interested in his qualifications than his color: "I don't care if he's black, white, or green, all I want is a radio officer!" the senior officer once declared, according to *Ebony*. (This man later became godfather to Gravely's eldest child.) Several years later, on board the USS *Seminole*, a visitor to the ship remarked that Gravely, then working as operations officer, was "colored." *Ebony* reported that the ship's captain replied with a completely straight face: "Is that right? What color is he?"

In 1961 Gravely became temporary skipper of the USS *Theodore E. Chandler*, making him the first black naval officer to command a ship. A few months later, in January of 1962—having achieved the rank of lieutenant commander—he was assigned to the USS *Falgout*, the first fighting ship to be commanded by an African American officer. As a full commander, he again made naval history in 1966 as the first black commander to lead a ship—the USS *Taussig*— into direct offensive action.

The crew of the *Taussig* was skeptical at first. "I think," Gravely told *Ebony* magazine, that "initially they [were] interested in two things: can the Old Man take the ship out, and can he get it back in port." After proving himself, he was accepted by his staff. In fact, they quickly grew to like his style of command, because he gave officers more responsibility than they were usually allowed. One crew member noted in *Ebony*, "It makes a big difference in morale. There is a much freer atmosphere when junior officers can perform certain tasks. If junior officers never get a chance to run the ship, pretty soon they are senior officers and they still

trained in a segregated unit; as an officer, he was barred from living in the Bachelor's Officers' Quarters. As far back as 1945, when his first ship reached its berth in Key West Florida, he was specifically forbidden entry into the Officers' Club on the base. President Truman's executive order prohibited segregation, but it could not eliminate racism and hypocrisy among military staff

don't know how." Gravely said in the same article, "You have to have faith in your executive officers and department heads, and they have to have it in their junior officers."

Gravely also demanded very high standards from his crew. In a 1977 address to navy officers, as quoted in *Ebony*, he stated: "We must improve our individual understanding of our fundamental warfare skills. We must improve the performance and productivity of our people. And we must continue to stress the very rudiments of our profession—smartness, appearance, seamanship, and most importantly, pride. Pride in ourselves! Pride in our ships! And pride in our Navy!"

In 1976 Gravely became the commander of the entire third fleet. He was in charge of over 100 ships, 60,000 officers, and oversaw more than 50 million square miles of ocean, or about one-fourth of the earth's surface. His 32 official duties included protecting the western sea approaches to the United States, guarding merchant ships in the area, and providing emergency search and rescue aid. He also developed and improved fleet tactics, organized and scheduled ship movements and port visits, and conducted anti-submarine warfare operations. The stress of these responsibilities was inescapable, but he fought to relieve them through exercise when he had the time. He was also known to drink up to thirty cups of coffee a day and chain-smoke.

In 1978 Gravely became the director of the Defense Communications Agency and was able to move home to Virginia from his base in Hawaii. After his official retirement in 1980, he kept active as a military adviser and corporate consultant. Between 1984 and 1987, Gravely served as the executive director of education and training for the Armed Forces Communications and Electronics Associations (AFCEA). A year later, he became an adviser to Potomac Systems Engineering, and he continued to travel the world, speaking at conferences on leadership. "I still do things for the military," he told *Ebony* in 1990. "I still have great affection for the military. The military gave me an opportunity to do some things that I thoroughly enjoyed."

As a trailblazer for African Americans in the military arena, Gravely fought for equal rights quietly but effectively, letting his actions speak for him. After four decades of service in the U.S. Navy, he held no illusions about the status of race relations in the military but, according to *Ebony*, readily admitted: "I basically grew up in the military.... The military did a lot for me, and hopefully, I did some things for it." Gravely died on October 22, 2004, at the naval hospital in Bethesda, Maryland. In a fitting tribute, the obituary on the U.S. Department of Defense Web site quoted Gravely's formula for success: "My formula is simply education plus motivation plus perseverance."

Sources

Periodicals

Chicago Tribune, July 8, 1973.
Crisis, December 1973; March 1983.
Ebony, July 1966; September 1977; November 1985; December 1990; June 2, 1997.
Jet, February 5, 1970; June 5, 1975; August 28, 1980; November 8, 2004; November 15, 2004.

On-line

"Obituary," *United States Department of Defense,* www.defenselink.mil/releases/2004/nr20041022-1434.html (January 31, 2005).
"Vice-Admiral Samuel L. Gravely, Jr.," *Naval Historical Center,* www.history.navy.mil/bios/gravely.htm (January 31, 2005).

—Robin Armstrong and Tom Pendergast

F. Gary Gray

1969—

Film and video director

Gray, F. Gary, photograph. © Frank Trapper/Corbis.

"I'm single-minded," F. Gary Gray told *The Source* magazine. "When I'm working on a project all my attention is there." Gray has the been the object of a fair amount of attention himself, having earned more awards than perhaps any other video director for his work with smash acts like TLC, Coolio, and Ice Cube, as well as his feature film work. After breaking into music clips and making his way to the top of the video world, he directed a funky, low-budget comedy that earned ten times what it cost to make; his next venture, an action drama, saw him enter the Hollywood mainstream. Yet he refused to allow his newfound celebrity to change his focus. "These people will put you on a pedestal," he said of filmdom's star-makers, "and then knock your ass down."

F. Gary Gray was born in New York City, but did most of his growing up in South-Central Los Angeles. The lure of the street there was particularly strong, however, and during his teens he was sent to live in Highland Park, Illinois, with his father. "I went to a predominantly white, rich high school," he recollected in *The Source*, adding that the resources at this Midwestern institution "were much better than anything I had ever seen. I knew I had to take advantage of this situation."

"Taking advantage" in this case meant exploring video, learning how to direct and edit programming for the school's cable-access TV station. He demonstrated considerable ambition in his chosen field, and upon graduating, he came back to Los Angeles. There he pursued college studies in film and television. "From a young age, I knew I was going to be a filmmaker," he insisted in *The Source*. He landed camera-operator jobs for various television programs, including *Screen Scene* for the Black Entertainment Network (BET) and *Pump It Up* for Fox. At the Fox network, more importantly, he met rappers W.C. and the Maad Circle—which featured a then-unknown MC named Coolio—and talked them into letting him direct their video. "The first thing I did," he recalled, "was use my director's fee to shoot the video in 35 millimeter, like actual films are shot." The larger frame size—most videos are shot in the smaller 16 millimeter format—fit Gray's swelling ambitions.

Fortunately, Gray had talent to match those ambitions, and word of his directorial skill spread to other acts. Soon, he found himself directing clips for Mary J. Blige,

---

At a Glance . . .

Born in 1969(?) in New York, NY. *Education:*Attended L.A. City College and Golden State College.

Career: Video and film director, c. 1990s–. BET and Fox television networks, camera operator, early 1990s.

Awards: Best Rap Video and Best New Artist Rap Video for Coolio's "Fantastic Voyage," 1995 Billboard Music Video Awards; four awards, including Video of the Year for TLC's "Waterfalls" and Best Rap Video for Dr. Dre's "Keep Their Heads Ringin'," 1995 MTV Music Video Awards; African American Film Critics Association, special achievement award, 2003.

Addresses: *Home*—Los Angeles, CA. *Publicists*—Bragman Nyman Cafarelli, 9171 Wilshire Blvd., Penthouse Suite, Beverly Hills, CA 90210-5530.

Coolio, TLC, Ice Cube. and Dr. Dre, among others. The video for Ice Cube's "It Was a Good Day" was listed among *Rolling Stone*'s Top 100 Videos of All Time. Gray garnered multiple trophies at the 1995 MTV Video Music Awards, including four awards for the TLC clip "Waterfalls"—including Video of the Year—and the Best Rap Video honor for Dr. Dre's "Keep Their Heads Ringin'." A decade later, Gray's video-related honors had swelled to include more than four dozen awards and nominations.

Due to the success of Ice Cube's "It Was a Good Day," Gray earned his first opportunity to direct a feature film. Co-written by Cube, *Friday* is a broad comedy inspired by the pot-fueled antics of 1970s comedians like Cheech and Chong. The novice filmmaker was given a paltry $3 million budget to make it. "I've been doing videos for about four years now, and I've been wanting to direct a feature since I was about 17," Gray told *High Times* magazine. "I knew that I had to deliver something that was high-quality. There was a lot of pressure, because with making motional pictures, when you're a first-time filmmaker, if the dailies don't look good the first week, if the performances aren't good the first week, the director gets fired."

Any concerns Gray may have had regarding his abilities were unfounded. His instincts allowed him to plan the shoot and still leave room for improvisation. Co-stars John Witherspoon and Chris Tucker, Gray told *High Times,* "are so funny on the fly and right off the cuff that I didn't want to miss any of that, so I said, 'Stick to the script for the first two takes, and on the third take, do it how you want to do it.' When I got to editing, I used most of the third takes because they were so funny, especially Chris' facial expressions." Cube, meanwhile, "has a lot of discipline," Gray reported. "It helps me as a director for him to have that much discipline and be the star of the movie," he added, "because if everybody wanted to run wild, then it would just be a big babysitting session and you lose a lot of time. Cube doesn't play that whole 'I'm a star' trip."

Friday may not have been a favorite with critics—*Times* reviewer Peter Rainer was in the majority when he declared the film a "scattershot jokefest"—but its lean budget helped it go into the black quickly, and it eventually earned ten times what it cost to make, and turned out to be one of the most profitable releases of 1995. "These movies are a double edged sword," Gray reflected in the *Los Angeles Times.* "Though any other comedy would have three times the budget and twice as long to shoot, I appreciated New Line [Pictures] giving me a shot. How often does anyone write a check like that to an unproven 23-year-old?" Gray pointed out that after making such a splash directing rap and R&B videos, "I was besieged by hip-hop offers." After *Friday,* he explained in *Vibe,* "I didn't want to be pegged as an in-the-hood-type director. It's just too easy to get that title." He informed *USA Today* that he "was offered every regurgitated action comedy idea that Hollywood has done."

Instead, Gray took on a far more ambitious project: an urban heist thriller with four female protagonists. Though the hit film *Waiting to Exhale* had demonstrated the box-office potential of black women, the edgy *Set It Off* brought in action elements designed to woo male viewers. And, added Gray in *Vibe,* "these women are just exhaling all over the place." Co-starring rapper and television star Queen Latifah and budding star Jada Pinkett, *Set It Off* tells the story of a group of down-at-heels women who turn to armed robbery. Gray's conception for the film was, he asserted in *Newsday,* "dramatic smart action." He had already used many of the elements of action filmmaking—such as helicopters—in his videos, and wanted to reach beyond the usual trappings of the genre. "I didn't want to use the action gratuitously because then it has no weight," he claimed. "The sequences just become set pieces for action. It's not worth it." He had been looking, he said, for material with "something for the emotions."

In *Set It Off,* Gray found the right combination of elements. "It takes a lot for me to get passionate about something," he told Thulani Davis of *Newsday.* The film, he ventured in *Detour,* "has always been in me. But it was definitely a leap. I would shoot for 14 hours, then I would watch dailies for two, then I would rewrite and work on the script for three hours. If I got five hours of sleep it was like heaven: usually it was two or three." "Perhaps the biggest challenge of the film," Gray mused to Davis, was its female focus. "It's a male-dominated industry," he averred. "Stories are told from a male point of view. I wanted to create a women's perspective." He sat down with the cast members and talked about a range of issues; but he also took them to a firing range to make sure they looked natural using guns onscreen. "I would also create special rehearsals," the filmmaker told *Detour.* "Normally, you go straight for the script, but when you have characters who have a history with each other, you have to create that feeling, and it has to be as genuine as possible. So for the first week, I would take the actors out for meals and movies to create a camaraderie that comes second-nature." The results, he added, were "fantastic."

Critics didn't entirely agree, however. Kenneth Turan of the *Los Angeles Times* admired the production's style but complained of "genre contrivances that are the obstacles to [the film's] being taken seriously." The director received both praise and blame in Turan's review. "Though he is obviously talented," the critic wrote, "Gray is also 26 years old, and *Set It Off* is characterized by the youthful director tendency to be overambitious, to try to squeeze every possible movie moment into one finite film." *USA Today*'s Susan Wloszczyna, meanwhile—admitted that the film was "more fun to watch than it has any right to be"—but, nonetheless dubbed it "overlong, overdone, and over-wrought." Gray, she continued, "knows how to ignite high-octane action, but the dramatic passages drag like a rusted tailpipe."

Although he hasn't dwelt on it much in interviews, Gray's celebrity derives in part from his success in the mainstream as a black filmmaker. Yet he never claimed to have encountered adversity because of race. "The strong battles, the battles that re historical for blacks in Hollywood, I haven't experienced any of that," he pointed out in *Newsday.* "I've had the opportunity to make a film that I think is good." And in *USA Today,* Gray warned against pigeonholing audiences. "I know a lot of people who enjoy rap music who aren't black," he pointed out. "You can't just say it's black music. To segregate films the way Hollywood likes to segregate films, ultimately everyone loses." Gray's assessment of the present-day situation in Hollywood was mixed. "I can honestly say it's changing," he said. "I can see my colleagues getting opportunities they didn't have even five years ago. In the same breath, it still needs more of a major change. I think ultimately black filmmakers need more options and more support—everything from getting the best material to getting the best financial support to make it right."

Gray shared a bit of his creative method with *Detour.* Budget constraints, he allowed, forced him to "priori-tize" shots in order of importance. With that part of the process completed, "I'll sit back with a cigar and some classical music, and read the scene, start to envision it, and write it down shot for shot," he explained. "Some-times you can't come up with a shot to save your life, and sometimes shots come so fast that you start misspelling words because you're writing so fast." He added that his visual sense compels him to "put the camera where the story is, so I dissect a scene and think about it in the context of the whole movie and decide how I'm going to cover it." He discussed his strategy for overcoming a lack of creative flow in *Vibe,* "Sometimes I get slowed down by writer's block or visual block where I can't find the shot," he admitted. "But I don't worry. Creativity is a mansion. If you're empty in one room, all you have to do is go out into the hallway and enter another room that's full."

After the release of *Set It Off,* Gray's career itself began to resemble such a mansion. The *Los Angeles Times* deemed him a "face to watch in 1997," and he discussed his options with the paper. "I'm not afraid of a big studio film; I trust my instincts," he insisted. "But for me it's not really about the box office. It's about looking back on your work and not having to apologize for it. I'm trying to keep my blinders on and continue to perfect what I do, because I'm very young and I have a lot to learn." At the same time, Gray recognized that he brought something unique to the table. "I think the movie audience is starving right now for new material and fresh ideas," he noted. In *Detour,* he described directing as "a love it or leave it job," and confessed to feeling doubts at times. "Sometimes you think, Am I out of my mind for doing this?" he reflected. "But then you sit back—I just got back from the Boston Film Festival, and we had a standing ovation for [*Set It Off*]—you take really deep breath and you say, 'It was all worth it.'"

Gray used his up-and-coming notoriety to land several more high-profile films. In 1998 he directed Samuel L. Jackson and Kevin Spacey in *The Negotiator,* a film about a standoff between two top police negotiators. Critic Roger Ebert praised Gray in the *Chicago Sun Times,* for directing one of the year's "most successful thrillers." He wrote that the film, which "essentially consists of two men talking to one another…could have dragged." But "it doesn't" because "Gray makes us care about the characters …, to get involved in the delicate process of negotiations." Although his direc-tion of Vin Diesel in *A Man Apart* earned less praise, Gray rebounded in 2003 with a remake of Michael Caine's 1969 film, *The Italian Job.* In this story of a group of thieves who plot to steal back their money from another group of crooks, Gray's "direction never loses the dramatic thread in the slow scenes and never loses control in the chases," according to the *San Francisco Chronicle.* The African American Film Crit-ics Association honored Gray for demonstrating "strong growth and a solid command of the filmmaking process" with a special achievement award, according to *America's Intelligence Wire.* Gray was planning to direct a sequel to *The Italian Job* as well as the sequel to *Get Shorty* in early 2005.

Selected works

Films

Friday, 1995.
Set It Off, 1996.

The Negotiator, 1998.
A Man Apart, 2002.
The Italian Job, 2003.

Sources

Periodicals

America's Intelligence Wire, December 23, 2003.
Chicago Sun Times, January 29, 1998.
Detour, November 1996, p. 70.
High Times, June 1995.
Los Angeles Times, April 26, 1995, p. F2; April 23, 1996, p. F1; November 6, 1996, p. F1; January 5, 1997, (Calendar) pp. 6-7.

Newsday, November 3, 1996, p. C14.
Rolling Stone, April 4, 2003.
San Francisco Chronicle, October 10, 2003.
The Source, January 1996, p. 27.
USA Today, August 21, 1996, p. 7D; November 6, 1996, p. 8D.
Vibe, September 1996.

Other

Additional information was obtained from publicity materials provided by Bragman Nyman Cafarelli, 1996.

—Simon Glickman and Sara Pendergast

Warren J. Halliburton

1924—

Professor, writer, editor

Warren J. Halliburton was one of the first authors to provide access to African-American resources to the American public. Publishing from the 1970s through the early 1990s, Halliburton offered a wide array of materials to his readers, including simply worded biographies of famous black Americans and histories of significant achievement of black Americans aimed at school-aged children. He also contributed eight volumes to the reference-based Africa Today Series. Although Halliburton's writing never gained him much critical or public attention, his books were some of the very first on the shelves of many school libraries that addressed issues important to African Americans.

Halliburton was born on August 2, 1924, in New York, New York, to Richard H., a book shipping manager, and Blanche (Watson) Halliburton. He grew up in New York during the Great Depression, and following his graduation from high school, he served in the U.S. Army Air Forces during the last years of World War II, from 1943 to 1946. After leaving the military, he enrolled at New York University. He married his first wife, Marion Jones, on December 10, 1947. They had four children: Cheryl, Stephanie, Warren, Jr., and Jena.

During his time at New York University, Halliburton was an outstanding track and field athlete and an exceptional hurdler, and he carried his love for running and jogging with him throughout his lifetime. While working on his bachelor's degree, he was active in the Phi Alpha Fraternity and traveled in the same social circles as fellow academic and author Harry B. Dunbar.

After graduating with his undergraduate degree in 1949, Halliburton took a position as an instructor in English at the historically black Prairie View Agriculture and Mechanical College (now University) in Prairie View, Texas. In 1951 he moved his family to Dallas, Texas, where he was an instructor of English at the now-defunct Bishop College, another historically black school. In 1952 he left the classroom behind to become an associate for the Institute of International Education, the organization that, among other functions, administers the Fulbright Program.

Halliburton moved back to New York City in 1953 to work as a newspaper reporter and columnist for the *Recorder*. Five years later, he served as a junior high school teacher and dean in a school in the Bedford-Stuyvesant section of Brooklyn, a position he held from 1958 to 1960. From 1960 to 1965 he was an associate for the New York Department of Education, and in 1967 he became an editor for the publisher McGraw Hill, Inc.

On February 11, 1971, Halliburton married his second wife, Frances Fletcher, a teacher. In that same year he returned to academia as a visiting professor of English at the all-male Hamilton College and its sister school, the all-female Kirkland College, both in Clinton, New York (the two schools merged in 1978). Returning once more to New York City in 1972, Halliburton spent he next five years filling various roles at Columbia University Teachers College. He was an editor and research associate, served as the director of a scholarly journal, a government-sponsored program, and headed up the Ethnic Studies Center. In the late 1970s

At a Glance . . .

Born on August 2, 1924, in New York, NY; son of Richard H. and Blanche (Watson) Halliburton; married Marion Jones, December 20, 1947; married Frances Fletcher, February 11, 1971; children (first marriage): Cheryl, Stephanie, Warren, Jr., Jena. *Education:* New York University, BS, 1949; Columbia University, MEd, 1975, DEd, 1977. *Military Service:* U.S. Army Air Forces, 1943-46.

Career: Prairie View A&M College (now University), instructor in English, 1949; Bishop College, instructor in English, 1951; Institute of International Education, associate, 1952; *Recorder* (New York, NY, newspaper), reporter and columnist, 1953; high school in Brooklyn, teacher and dean, 1958-60; New York City Board of Education, coordinator, and New York State Department of Education, associate, 1960-65; McGraw Hill, Inc., editor, 1967; Hamilton-Kirkland Colleges, visiting professor of English, 1971-72; Columbia University, editor, research associate, and director of scholarly journal, government program, and Ethnic Studies Center, 1972-77; *Reader's Digest*, editor and writer; freelance editor and writer.

Addresses:*Home*—Wilton, CT.

Halliburton became an editor and writer for *Reader's Digest*, as well as a freelance editor and writer.

Halliburton has been an avid reader all his life and prolific writer since the 1960s. On his Web site *Dunbar on Books*, Harry B. Dunbar remembered: "I...recall, from being in a course with him at NYU more than 50 years ago, that he was even then voracious and rapid reader, and that he had absolutely no difficulty reading the torrent of books that the professor in a literature course that we took together would assign to us on the spur of the moment on any given day." Author of more than twenty books, nearly 100 short stories, and innumerable papers, monographs, reviews, workbooks, and teachers' guides, Halliburton's bibliography includes a wide range of writing styles and topics.

Serving as co-editor with Mauri E. Pelkonen, Halliburton's first published material was *New Worlds of Literature*. One of the earliest attempts to highlight cultural literature, the book was published in 1966 and with a revised second edition in 1970. In 1969, Halliburton published three novels: *The Heist*; *Cry, Baby!*; and *Some Things that Glitter*, all with the

McGraw imprint. This would be his only major attempt at full-length fiction, and the books received little attention. In 1970 Halliburton was the sole author of his first major work that featured nonfiction books by and about blacks. *America's Majorities and Minorities*, published by Ayer Company Publishers, served as an early canon of writings that were being produced by black intellectuals who were attempting to interpret the rapid social and racial changes that had happened within the United States during the 1960s.

Perhaps influenced by his experience as a junior high school teacher in a black community of Bedford-Stuyvesant area of Brooklyn, Halliburton turned his attention to the audience of black youth. In 1970 he authored *They Had a Dream*, with Laurence Swinburne and Steve Broudy, which recounted true stories about black Americans and their achievements. *The Picture Life of Jesse Jackson*, first published in 1972 with a second edition released in 1984, is aimed at second- to fourth-graders and provides a simple biography of Rev. Jesse Jackson, including numerous photos. The treatment of Jackson's life avoids most charged political issues and focuses on the details of his life rather than his political agenda.

Halliburton followed the publication of *The History of Black Americans*, published in 1973, with *Harlem: A History of Broken Dreams*, published in 1974. In his history of Harlem, Halliburton traces the development of this six-square mile section of Manhattan from a Dutch encampment to the home of over a half million black Americans. In that same year, Halliburton also published *Pathways to the World of English*. Along with his busy writing schedule, Halliburton also continued his education at Columbia University during the 1970s, earning his Master of Education in 1975 and his Doctor of Education in 1977.

In 1978 Halliburton published *The Fighting Redtails: America's First Black Airmen,* an illustrated history of the 332nd Fighter Group, a World War II all-black combat unit that gained recognition. The following year he authored a biography of Daniel James, Jr., the first black American to achieve the rank of a four-star general. His *The Picture Life of Michael Jackson*, published in 1984 and once again aimed at elementary school-aged children, is heavily dependent on photos, with brief text outlining the pop star's life to date.

Halliburton followed his recounting of the events surrounding Custer's last stand in *The Tragedy of Little Bighorn*, published in 1989, with another biography of a prominent black American, Supreme Court Justice Clarence Thomas, published in 1993. In 1992 and 1993 Halliburton published eight titles in the Africa Today Series, with topics ranging from wildlife to industries to city and village life. The series, which is aimed at fourth- to sixth-graders, attempts to make complex issues accessible to school-aged children. In his last publication, *Historic Speeches of African Americans*, Halliburton compiles speeches by such famous black Americans as W. E. B. DuBois, Booker T. Washington, Martin Luther King, and Malcolm X.

Although many of his books have gone out of print, Halliburton's prolific literary offerings marked an important place in the growth and development of a core of nonfiction writings focused on African and African-American topics.

Selected writings

(Editor, with Mauri E. Pelkonen) *New Worlds of Literature,* Harcourt, 1966.

The Heist (novel), McGraw, 1969.

Cry, Baby! (novel), McGraw, 1969.

Some Things that Glitter (novel), illustrated by Elzia Moon, McGraw, 1969.

(With William L. Katz) *American Majorities and Minorities: A Syllabus of United States History for Secondary Schools,* Arno, 1970.

(With Laurence Swinburne and Steve Broudy) *They Had a Dream,* Pyramid Publications, 1970.

(Editor and contributor) *America's Color Caravan,* four volumes, Singer Graflex, 1971.

The Picture Life of Jesse Jackson, F. Watts, 1972, 1984.

The History Black Americans, Harcourt, 1973.

(With Ernest Kraiser) *Harlem: A History of Broken Dreams,* Doubleday, 1974.

Pathways to the World of English, Globe, 1974.

The Fighting Redtails: America's First Black Airmen, illustrated by John Gampert, Contemporary Perspectives, 1978.

Flight to the Stars: The Life of Daniel James, Jr., Contemporary Perspectives, 1979.

The Picture Life of Michael Jackson, F. Watts, 1984.

The Tragedy of Little Bighorn, F. Watts, 1989.

Africa's Struggle for Independence, Africa Today Series, Crestwood, 1992.

African Wildlife, Africa Today Series, Crestwood, 1992.

Celebrations of African Heritage, Africa Today Series, Crestwood, 1992.

Nomads of the Sahara, Africa Today Series, Crestwood, 1992.

African Industries, Africa Today Series, Crestwood, 1993.

African Landscapes, Africa Today Series, Crestwood, 1993.

Africa's Struggle to Survive, Africa Today Series, Crestwood, 1993.

City and Village Life, Africa Today Series, Crestwood, 1993. *Clarence Thomas: Supreme Court Justice,* Enslow, 1993.

(Compiler and introduction) *Historic Speeches of African Americans,* F. Watts, 1993.

Sources

Periodicals

Booklist, March 1, 1993; April 15, 1993; June 1, 1993; April 1, 1994.

School Library Journal, July 1994; August 1984; February 1985; February 1993; May 1993; July 1993; September 1993.

On-line

Contemporary Authors Online, Gale Group, http://galenet.galegroup.com/servlet/BioRC (December 3, 2004).

"The Evolution of Black Nonfiction Books in the Twentieth Century," *Dunbar on Books: A Monthly Online Newsletter,* www.queenhyte.com/dobb/dobb_03/dobb_dec03.html (December 3, 2004).

"Spotlight on Warren J. Halliburton," *Dunbar on Books: A Monthly Online Newsletter,* www.queenhyte.com/dobb/dobb_archives/dobb_01/dec_01.htm (December 3, 2004).

—Kari Bethel

Larry Leon Hamlin

1948—

Actor, festival director

Hamlin, Larry Leon, photograph. Sebastian Artz/Getty Images.

In head to toe purple, Larry Leon Hamlin is a hurricane-strength force on the stage of black theater. He is the vision, the fury, and the power behind the National Black Theatre Festival, the world's largest gathering of black theater professionals. Every other summer, the festival draws thousands of actors, directors, producers, poets, filmmakers, and fans to Winston-Salem, North Carolina for a week of performance, practice, and parties. Hamlin said he started the festival to help revive and unify black theater. He succeeded. "I think that black theater needed me," Hamlin told *Contemporary Black Biography* (*CBB*). "Of course, I needed it as well."

Stepped on Stage at Age Five

Born on September 25, 1948, Larry Leon Hamlin was the second of four children of Annie and Charles Hamlin. He grew up in Reidsville, North Carolina, about 45 minutes from Winston-Salem, deep in tobacco country. His father worked for the American Tobacco Company, his mother was a housewife, and according to North Carolina's *The News & Record,* Hamlin was "the first generation off the factory floor."

He landed on the stage. Hamlin told *CBB* that he fell in love with the theater the moment he uttered his first line in a first-grade play. "Once I got back to class, I immediately wanted to be back on the stage, so I raised my hand and asked if I could go to the bathroom" he told *CBB*. Back in the auditorium Hamlin continued, "I saw the stage and was so happy. I ran down to the stage and put my arms around the footlights. They were hot, really hot, but I hugged them." He has embraced theater ever since.

"My mother really supported my acting when I was a child," Hamlin told *CBB*. "She would work with me on my lines and help with delivery." Hamlin acted throughout childhood but after high school, he gravitated north and ended up majoring in business at Rhode Island's Johnson & Wales University. "After graduation I had to think about what I wanted to do for the rest of my life," Hamlin told *CBB*. "I thought about it and went all the way back to that experience I had when I was five, and I said, 'Of course, acting. That's what I love.'" Hamlin promptly enrolled in theater classes at Brown University and joined the school's theater company. "I've been focusing on my acting ever since," he told *CBB*.

There were very few black theaters in the country in the mid-1970s. Hamlin, with characteristic vision and a heavy dose of self-confidence set about fixing that. He formed his first company, Star Theater Productions, while he was still in Rhode Island. However, the South was calling him back. "Eventually I had to go home so I came to Winston-Salem because my family had settled there," he told *CBB*. Again, he found that there was no local black theater. "In fact not in the whole state of North Carolina," he told *CBB*. So with $2,000, Hamlin founded the North Carolina Black Repertory Company in 1979. He served as the company's executive and artistic director—a post he still held into 2004. He also acted, directed, and wrote plays. Like all small theaters, the company struggled. Over the years, it produced several local shows, launched national tours, and even took performances to the Caribbean. Much of the company's success was due to Hamlin's electric personality. Whether standing onstage, speaking about the state of black theater, or asking for donations, Hamlin's personal style oozed a can-do attitude that made people want to say "yes."

Founded National Black Theatre Festival

In the mid-1980s Hamlin wrote an article about the state of black theater in the South. "As I was interviewing these different theater companies, I saw so much pain and frustration," he told *CBB*. "They didn't have money, didn't have good management, they couldn't put on the shows they wanted." He continued, "I began to wonder what was happening in the other parts of the country. And it was the same—pain, frustration. Then I looked around in New York and saw that black theaters were closing at such a rate that I figured by the millennium they'd disappear." Hamlin decided something had to be done. "I didn't see anyone else doing it," he told *CBB*. He came up with the idea of a national black theater conference. "There were some successful companies out there, and I thought if we could share our experiences, we could build a core of black theater companies that could work together and develop an agenda for all of us," Hamlin told *American Visions.*

With a budget of $500,000 the National Black Theatre Festival debuted in 1989. "The first one we decided not to call a conference," Hamlin told *CBB*. "Conference sounds so boring. So we called it a festival. That sounds like a party. A celebration." A chance meeting with Maya Angelou at an airport bar gave the festival a needed boost of celebrity. "Most of the people I talked to thought I was crazy," Hamlin told the *Winston-Salem Journal.* "She said she would support my dream, as it were." Angelou signed on as the festival's first chairperson and brought along friend Oprah Winfrey as a celebrity guest. The star power worked. Over 10,000 people showed up to see 30 performances by 17 of the country's top black theater companies. Theater professionals took part in workshops on topics from raising money to producing new works. *The New York Times* wrote, "The 1989 National Black Theatre Festival was one of the most historic and culturally significant events in the history of black theatre and American theatre in general." Hamlin had struck a long-neglected nerve and revealed a hidden cultural resource. "At first I thought there were only about 60 or 70 black companies in the country," Hamlin told *CBB*. "I found out there were over 250. We didn't know about each other. We had never had an occasion to get together."

Subsequent festivals, held every two years, grew exponentially on all fronts. In 1991 the number of performances jumped to 45 performances and the workshops doubled. Celebrities flocked to Winston-Salem to take part, including black theater royalty Ossie Davis and Ruby Dee, who signed on as that year's chairpersons. By 1993 performances were up to 76. In 1995 international troupes joined in the festivities, coming from Africa, the Caribbean, and Latin America. Over 20,000 guests endured the North Carolina heat to see them perform. The prestige of the festival also grew. 1997 saw the premier of renowned playwright August Wilson's play, *Jitney*. By 1999 corporate heavy hitters had signed on as sponsors including US Airways, Sara Lee Corporation, and R.J. Reynolds Tobacco Company. They were needed as the festival's budget had tripled to $1.5 million. The 2001 and 2003 festivals featured over 100 performances a piece and drew upwards of 50,000 guests each. By that time the festival had also added an awards gala, a film festival, poetry jams, a market, and true to its founding vision, dozens of workshops. "There's something going on morning, noon, and night," Hamlin told the *Winston-Salem Journal*.

Brought Black Theater Together

The theme of the 2001 was "Black Theater, Holy Ground," which nicely summed up the way the festival had come to be viewed by those in the black theater community. "It's one of the greatest things we have going," actor Bill Cobbs told the *Winston-Salem Journal*. "In terms of having an opportunity to network and interact with people in the world of theater, it is a great thing." "It is so culturally significant to all of us, whether you are a nationally respected artist or some little theater practicing in a church basement," producer Ernie McClintock added. "It's a focal point for black cultural expression." It is also a focal point for celebrities. People like Denzel Washington, Sidney Poitier, Cicely Tyson, Angela Bassett, Leslie Uggams, Malik Yoba, and Malcolm-Jamal Warner are regulars year after year.

The festival has also been a boon for the city of Winston-Salem, jam-packing hotels and restaurants and bringing in an estimated $11 million over a five-day period. "It obviously has a multimillion-dollar impact on the city," Gayle Anderson, the president of the Greater Winston-Salem Chamber of Commerce, told the *Winston-Salem Journal*. "But more important is the image we create of Winston-Salem as a cultural center. The fact that it is African-American theater is unique. We couldn't pay for all the publicity that this generates." Winston-Salem's mayor, Allen Joines, also hailed the importance of the festival, and gave direct credit to Hamlin. "This festival has brought international recognition to Winston-Salem, and I think Mr. Hamlin's work has really made it successful," Joines told the *Winston-Salem Journal* in 2002. "His personal perseverance has been key to the festival's success."

As the founder, artistic director, and producer of the festival, Hamlin's name has become synonymous with the National Black Theatre Festival. Dressed in his favorite color purple—which is also the official color of the festival—he has been the festival's number one promoter, cheerleader, and fundraiser. For each festival

he planned dozens of workshops, wooed hundreds of celebrities, screened thousands of plays, and raised hundreds of thousands of dollars. "I sleep very, very little," he told *CBB*. "For years I didn't sleep at all. Now I am starting to think that maybe I should get at least three hours a night." Ask anyone in black theater, anyone in Winston-Salem, and they will tell you his sleeplessness has paid off. The *Winston-Salem Journal* noted, "Hamlin has been praised as a visionary who built a nationally recognized black-theater festival in a Southern city that many New York and Los Angeles actors would never visit." However he has not been without critics who have claimed that his over-the-top personality has wreaked financial and logistical havoc. In 2001, on the eve of the seventh festival, Hamlin dismissed those critics. "If I did not know how to handle money this would have ended in 1989," he told the *Winston-Salem Journal*.

His Future Looked "Marvtastic"

Hamlin has been recognized for his work on behalf of black theater with dozens of awards, including a prestigious NAACP award for community service. However his biggest honor was an invitation to the White House from President and Mrs. Bill Clinton. "I wasn't even aware that he knew I existed," he told *CBB*.

As 2004 came to a close, Hamlin was intensely planning the 2005 festival, scheduled to be "marvtastic"—a word Hamlin coined. "It is marvelous and fantastic, but what it means to me is there is nothing greater than this," he told *CBB*. He continued to run the North Carolina Black Repertory Company, writing plays, and of course, acting. He also had another big idea brewing—the National Black Theatre Hall of Fame and Museum. "There is a major need for it," he told *CBB*. "And it doesn't look like anyone else will do it, so here I go again." If anyone can make it a reality, it is Hamlin. And if he does, he would more than qualify to become one of the museum's first honorees.

Sources

Periodicals

American Visions, April-May, 1995.
The Cincinnati Enquirer, August 19, 2001.
The News & Record, (Piedmont Triad, NC), August 31, 2001; August 24, 2003.
The New York Times, August 8, 2003.
Winston-Salem Journal (Winston-Salem, NC), August 1, 1999; June 12, 2001; July 29, 2001; August 1, 2001; August 7, 2001; May 18, 2002; July 1, 2003; August 12, 2003.

On-line

"Larry Leon Hamlin," *The National Black Theatre Festival,* www.nbtf.org/bio.htm (October 29, 2004).

Other

Additional information for this profile was obtained through an interview with Larry Leon Hamlin on November 9, 2004.

—Candace LaBalle

Illinois Jacquet

1922(?)-2004

Jazz saxophonist

Jacquet, Illinois, photograph. Frank Driggs Collection/Getty Images.

When 19-year-old Illinois Jacquet stepped to a Decca Records microphone in May of 1942 to take his solo on the Lionel Hampton Band's "Flying Home," he was a young saxophonist with tremendous ability but no clear identity. It was the first or second time he had made a recording, and he had recently switched from alto to tenor sax at Hampton's instruction. "I didn't know what I was going to play or what I was going to sound like, or who I was going to imitate," he told *Texas Monthly*. One of Hampton's sidemen told him to try to find his own style. And then Jacquet delivered one of the two or three most influential solos in all of jazz history, an 80-second masterpiece that began with a quotation of an obscure operatic melody, suddenly gathered energy, and climaxed in a screeching, honking, thrilling repetition of a single note.

Nearly every tenor player who followed made it a priority to learn that solo, note for note. But "Flying Home" marked neither the beginning nor the end of Jacquet's seven-decade career. He was one of jazz's great survivors, thought of as an outrageous musician when he was young but hailed as a classic figure in old age. He was as effective with romantic jazz ballads as

he was with the explosive performances with which he made his reputation.

Changed Name to Illinois

Of French-Creole ancestry on his father's side, Jean-Baptiste Jacquet (pronounced Ja-KETT) was born in Broussard, Louisiana, on October 31, 1922 (one researcher has argued for a 1919 date). He moved with his family to Houston when he was young and, finding that his French name caused difficulties for Texans, began to use the name Illinois instead. Jacquet's mother was a Native American of the Sioux tribe, and his two versions of how he came by the new name were both connected to her: he said variously that the name was derived from a Siouxan word "Illiniwek," meaning "superior men," and that he was named for a friend of his mother's who came from Chicago to help out when was born.

The family was a musical one; Jacquet's father and three older brothers were all musical professionals, and he made his debut at age three, singing on the radio in Galveston, Texas, to promote a stage show mounted by his brothers. He was a tap dancer at first, but he soon learned to play drums and the soprano and alto saxophones (he eventually mastered the bassoon, an unusual jazz instrument, as well). Jacquet was something of a prodigy, joining the Milton Larkin Orchestra at 15 and finding that he could keep up with the best players he encountered. "Every band that came through heard about this young guy and would want to jam with me," he told *Texas Monthly*. "It was inspiring because they weren't doing too much that I wasn't doing." But he became depressed by the realities of Southern segregation and set out for Los Angeles in 1939.

The talented teenager quickly made friends in the L.A. jazz community, and a young singer named Nat Cole steered him toward a big band being formed by the popular vibraphonist Lionel Hampton. Hampton hired Jacquet late in 1941 but insisted that he switch to tenor sax. The move proved a smart one on Hampton's part, for the more guttural sound of the tenor instrument fit Jacquet's style. The bandleader noticed that crowds responded strongly to Jacquet's solos when the new Lionel Hampton Band appeared live.

So Hampton took Jacquet with him into the studio in May of 1942 for the famed session that produced "Flying Home." Jacquet's solo was brilliantly structured, hovering and twisting around bent notes for much of its length, building up energy that was released in a torrent with the sequence of repeated notes at the end. The recording became a hit, covered even by country musicians. After Jacquet, exhausted by playing the solo night after night, quit Hampton's band in 1943, Hampton demanded that his replacements learn to reproduce it exactly, and Jacquet's solo eventually became part of every good saxophonist's advanced education.

Appeared at Jazz at the Philharmonic Concerts

Jacquet quickly signed on with bandleader Cab Calloway and appeared in several films, including *Stormy Weather* and a musical short subject called *Jammin' the Blues*. As promoter Norman Granz put together his Jazz at the Philharmonic concert in 1944 to raise money for Mexican men arrested after the Los Angeles "Zoot Suit riots," Jacquet was a natural choice. The opening concert at the city's Philharmonic Hall produced a live Jacquet recording, "Blues (Part 2)," on which the saxophonist bit his reed while playing to drive the instrument to the very top of its range. Jazz purists were cool to Jacquet's flamboyant style, with its screeches and honks, but what they missed was that Jacquet had forged a style that drew strongly on the blues music of his native Texas. Jacquet's playing influenced rhythm-and-blues and later rock saxophonists, and some writers have even claimed "Blues (Part 2)" as the first rock and roll recording.

After the end of World War II, Jacquet moved to New York and took the place of saxophonist Lester Young in the Count Basie Orchestra, with which he had already often appeared. He formed a sextet of his own in 1946 and continued to tour with various Jazz at the Philharmonic groups, recording for the small Aladdin and Apollo labels and later, more prolifically, for Granz's Clef label. As the large swing bands declined, Jacquet revealed other facets of his style in addition to the explosive aspect that had made him famous; he cultivated a smooth ballad style and sometimes took solos on the mellow-sounding and extraordinarily difficult-to-play bassoon.

The composer of several jazz standards, including "Blue Velvet," "Robbins Nest," and "Port of Rico," Jacquet occasionally reunited with bands led by Hampton and Basie. Recording more sporadically after a disagreement with Granz in 1958, and perhaps feeling trapped by the stylistic mold the concert-going public expected him to fit, Jacquet spent much of the 1960s and 1970s touring in Europe. A stint as artist-in-residence at Harvard University in 1983 (he was the first jazz musician to serve in that position) brought Jacquet back to the United States and stimulated a new burst of creativity in his career.

Re-formed Swing Band

"I made up my mind that if I could make students at Harvard sound that good, it was time for me to come back to New York and pick the best musicians I could find and form my own big band," Jacquet told *Jazz Times*. Full-sized swing bands were rare by the mid-1980s, but the Illinois Jacquet Big Band shattered attendance records at the prestigious Village Vanguard club. Jacquet moved into a house in Queens with companion Carol Scherick and took his place among

New York jazz royalty. The album *Jacquet's Got It!* documented this phase of the musician's career and was nominated for a Grammy award. The documentary film *Texas Tenor: The Illinois Jacquet Story* also lent new prominence to the saxophonist's work.

The nation as a whole was reminded of Jacquet's talents in 1993 when he shared the stage at the White House with President and fellow saxophonist Bill Clinton. Jacquet kept up a full concert schedule into his old age, receiving the Jazz at Lincoln Center Award for Artistic Excellence in 2000 and honorary doctorate from the Julliard School of Music in May of 2004. He played his last concert with his big band at New York's Lincoln Center on July 16, 2004, one week before his death from a heart attack at his home. A funeral at the city's Riverside Church was attended by dozens of jazz musicians who admired Illinois Jacquet and had been creatively shaped by his meaty, immensely influential music.

Selected discography

(With Lionel Hampton) "Flying Home," 1941.
Illinois Jacquet Jam Session, Atlantic, 1951.
Port of Rico, Clef, 1956.
The Blues: That's Me, Prestige/OJC, 1969.
Jacquet's Got It, Atlantic Jazz, 1988.
Flying Home (recorded 1947-67), Bluebird, 1991.
Flying Home: The Best of the Verve Years (1951-58), Verve, 1994.

Jazz at the Philharmonic, Verve, 1994.
Illinois Jacquet All-Stars 1945-47, Blue Moon, 1994.
The Complete Illinois Jacquet Sessions 1945-1950, Mosaic, 1996.

Sources

Books

Contemporary Musicians, vol. 17, Gale Research, 1996.

Periodicals

Boston Globe, July 23, 2004, p. 16.
Daily News (New York), July 26, 2004, p. 35.
Down Beat, October 2004, p. 24.
Houston Chronicle, July 30, 2004, p. A2.
Jazz Times, January 1985.
Jet, August 9, 2004, p. 61.
New York Times, July 23, 2004, p. A4.
Newsday (New York), July 24, 2004, p. A18; July 30, 2004, p. A17.
Pittsburgh Post-Gazette, July 25, 2004, p. B5.
Texas Monthly, November 2002, p. 142.
Times (London, England), July 26, 2004, p. Features-25.
Washington Post, July 24, 2004, p. B5.

—James M. Manheim

James Earl Jones

1931—

Actor

Some people know him as one of the nation's finest stage actors, an artist who tackles the works of such playwrights as William Shakespeare and Eugene O'Neill. Others know his sonorous bass voice as the most menacing aspect of the evil Darth Vader in the blockbuster film *Star Wars*. Still others recognize him as a television star who brings depths of humanity to clichéd character parts. James Earl Jones fits all these descriptions and more: for more than 40 years he has been one of the most esteemed actors in the United States.

Jones has worked steadily for decades in a market that supplies little hope to black performers. Having first established himself as a serious dramatic actor, he has never balked at the so-called "low brow" pursuits of television and popular film. His resume includes *Othello* as well as television episodes of *Tarzan*. He has received Tony, Emmy, and Obie awards, and yet he can be heard as the voice announcing "This is CNN" for Cable News Network. With film appearances ranging from the classic *Dr. Strangelove* to the forgettable *Conan, the Barbarian*, Jones admitted in the *Saturday Review* that he takes roles to surprise people— including himself. "Because I have a varied career, and I've not typecast myself, nobody knows what I'm going to do next. They don't know if I'm going to drop 20 pounds and play an athlete. They don't know whether I'm ready to be a good guy or a bad guy."

Whatever Jones plays—villain or hero—he infuses each role with "enormous talent, range, courage, taste, [and] sensitivity," wrote a *Newsweek* correspondent. During a career that began in the late 1950s, James

Earl Jones has struggled to define himself not as a black actor, but simply as an actor. In an effort to resist stereotypes, he has opted for maximum variety, but each new part bears his particular, memorable stamp. In *Newsweek*, Jack Kroll called Jones "the embodiment of the living paradox that informs all great acting: his powerful persona is at once intimate and apart, friendly and heroic. He's right there in the room with you, but he's also in your mind, an electrifying double presence that only the strongest actors can create."

The only child of Robert Earl and Ruth Connolly Jones, James Earl Jones was born on January 17, 1931, in Arkabutla, Mississippi, on his maternal grandfather's farm. Before his son's birth, James's father left the family to pursue a career as a prize fighter and later as an actor. Ruth Jones soon followed suit when she found tailoring work that kept her separated from her son for long periods of time. Born during the Great Depression, Jones remarked in *Newsweek* that he realizes economic circumstances forced his parents apart. Still, he said, the abandonment hurt him deeply. "No matter how old the character I play," he concluded, "those deep childhood memories, those furies, will come out. I understand this."

Living on his grandparents' farm, Jones was afforded a measure of security. As a youngster he hunted, fished, and performed various farm chores. He also attended church, where he watched his grandmother's emotional displays of holy rapture. "There was a strong evangelistic aspect to her religion, and when she went to church and felt the spirit, she ended up behaving like a holy roller," Jones recalled in the *Saturday Review*.

At a Glance . . .

Born on January 17, 1931, in Arkabutla, MS; son of Robert Earl (an actor) and Ruth (a tailor; maiden name, Williams) Jones; married Julienne Marie (an actress), 1967 (divorced); married Cecilia Hart (an actress), March 15, 1982; children: (second marriage) Flynn Earl. *Education*: University of Michigan, BA, 1953; received diploma from American Theatre Wing, New York City, 1957; studied acting with Lee Strasberg and Tad Danielewsky. *Military*: U.S. Army, 1953-55; became first lieutenant.

Career: Actor, 1957–.

Selected awards: Obie Awards for Off-Broadway work, 1962 and 1965; Tony Awards for best actor, 1969, for *The Great White Hope*, and 1987, for *Fences*; Academy Award nomination for best actor, 1970, for *The Great White Hope*; Emmy Award for best actor in a series, 1991, for *Gabriel's Fire*; Daytime Emmy, 2000, for *Summer's End*; Kennedy Center Honors honoree, 2002; DVDX Award, 2003, for *Finder's Fee*.

Addresses: *Agent*—c/o Horatio Productions Inc., PO Box 610, Pawling, NY 12564.

"There wasn't much touching in the family, but there was emotion."

Eventually Jones's grandparents formally adopted him, and took him north to rural Michigan. Jones acknowledged in *Newsweek* that the move north helped him to escape "a certain self-castration" common among Southern blacks at the time, but he did not adjust easily to his new surroundings. He developed a stutter and eventually found communication so difficult that at certain periods during grammar school he could talk only to himself or his immediate family. The problem followed him to high school, where one of his English teachers suggested he memorize speeches and enter oratorical contests. It seemed an unlikely way to cure a stutter, but it worked for Jones. Slowly, wrote Michelle Green in the *Saturday Review*, Jones "became such a skilled speaker that he began besting his voluble opponents."

Jones attended the University of Michigan on a full scholarship, intending to study medicine. At first he took acting classes simply as a sideline, but he soon switched his major to theater. When he was 21 years old, and a junior at Michigan, he traveled east to New York City to meet his father. They had only spoken briefly on the telephone several times. The relationship was strained by the long years without communication, but Jones's father encouraged him to pursue a career in theater; James graduated from Michigan in 1953 with a bachelor's degree in drama.

The U.S. Army, specifically the Reserve Officers' Training Corps (ROTC), recruited Jones in 1953 for two years of compulsory service. He spent much of his stint in a rigorous ranger-training program in the Colorado mountains and was set to reenlist in 1955 when his commanding officer suggested that he taste civilian life before making a long-term commitment to the armed services. So Jones moved to New York City and enrolled in further acting classes. Two things helped ease his decision: he knew he could return to the army if he did not find success as an actor, and his tuition at the American Theater Wing was paid for by the Army's G.I. Bill.

Jones lived with his father for a time, and the two supplemented their meager acting incomes by polishing floors in Off-Broadway theaters. In 1957 the younger Jones earned his first professional role in an Off-Broadway production of *Wedding in Japan*. He was rarely out of work after that, but his salary during the last years of the 1950s averaged $45 a week. He made ends meet by renting a cold-water flat on the Lower East Side. Even as a journeyman actor, Jones proved willing to try any role, no matter how small. In 1959 he began a long tenure with the New York Shakespeare Festival, carrying a spear in *Henry V*. Before long he was given more prominent roles, culminating in his 1963 performance as the lead in *Othello*—one of a staggering 13 plays he appeared in that year.

Othello ran for a year Off-Broadway with Jones in the lead. The actor also found time to do television spots and to make one film appearance—as the bombardier in Stanley Kubrick's dark comedy *Dr. Strangelove*. In the mid-1960s Jones began augmenting his theater work with television parts. He took cameo roles in shows such as *The Defenders* and *East Side/West Side*, and he became the first black man to take a continuing role on a daytime serial when he portrayed a doctor on *As The World Turns*. The big break for Jones, though, came during a period when he was touring Europe as the lead in Eugene O'Neill's *The Emperor Jones*.

A copy of a play titled *The Great White Hope* landed in Jones's lap in 1967. A dramatization of the life of boxing champion Jack Johnson, *The Great White Hope* was slated for a possible Broadway run. Jones wanted the part desperately. He began to train at gymnasiums in order to build his muscles, working with boxing managers and watching old footage of Johnson's fights. He was ultimately awarded the part, and the show opened on Broadway on October 3, 1968.

The Great White Hope was a success, and its reception propelled Jones to stardom. "Fourteen years of good hard acting work, including more Shakespeare than most British actors attempt, have gone into the making of James Earl Jones," wrote a Newsweek reviewer who also concluded that "only an actor with the bigness and power of Jones" could make such a play work. Jones won a Tony Award for his contribution to The Great White Hope, and he was nominated for an Academy Award in 1970 when the play was made into a motion picture.

The instant celebrity brought Jones a new awareness of his limitations. The actor told TV Guide that his work in The Great White Hope did not prove to be the career boost he thought it would. "I thought with the Oscar nomination that several projects would be waiting for me immediately," he continued in TV Guide. "But then projects—very viable ones close to getting go-aheads—caved in under racism's insanity." One of those projects was a life story of civil rights activist Malcolm X, a version of which was finally scheduled for release by filmmaker Spike Lee in 1992.

Jones returned to the stage, appearing in Hamlet in 1972, King Lear in 1973, and Of Mice and Men in 1974. He also performed in a series of minor films, including The Man and The Bingo Long Traveling All-Stars and Motor Kings. Jones's most notable movie role of the 1970s and early 1980s, though, was one in which only his voice was used. He gave a memorable level of malevolence to the half-man, half-machine villain Darth Vader in all three Star Wars films.

In 1982 Jones appeared on Broadway as Othello to standing ovations. He also portrayed the villain in the film Conan, the Barbarian. To critics who faulted him for taking roles in substandard films, Jones had a simple reply: movies and television pay well, theater does not. "I can't afford to take a vacation unless I do some commercials when I'm in New York," he pointed out in the Saturday Review. "Money goes fast, and you can't get along doing only stage work. I've never minded doing commercials.... Commercials can be very exciting." In 1991 Jones lent himself to a string of TV ads for the Bell Atlantic Yellow Pages, his first on-air product endorsement.

Jones's work in the late 1980s and early 1990s was as varied as his early career. He played an enigmatic writer in the 1990 hit film Field of Dreams, a CIA chief in the 1992 screen adaptation of Tom Clancy's novel Patriot Games, and an ex-convict private investigator in the award-winning television series Gabriel's Fire. Not neglecting his onstage work, he earned yet another Tony Award in 1988 for his portrayal of a disenchanted Negro League baseball player in August Wilson's play Fences. Jones explained in the Los Angeles Times that he has taken so many minor film roles and so much television work simply because he likes to work. "Just as, on stage, I waited years for a role like Jack [Johnson] in Great White Hope, or a role like Troy in Fences, you do the same thing in movies," he said. "Unless you are among that handful of exceptions, the stars who have projects lined up, you don't wait, at least I didn't want to wait.... I don't think I've done many films that counted. What I'm getting at, rather than waiting for that wonderful role in a movie, I take 'off' jobs."

To quote Los Angeles Times correspondent David Wallace, those "off jobs" are often "memorable only for [Jones's] commanding presence [or] for the brevity of his appearance." That situation would change, however; in 1990 Jones announced that his age and health were forcing him to curtail his work in live theater. "After six months in a play, the fatigue factor begins to affect the quality of a performance," the actor conceded in the Los Angeles Times. "The audiences might not know it, but I do. My thing is serious drama, and usually the lead character has a heavy load to carry. I find that after six months, if you get four out of eight shows a week that work perfectly the way you want, you're lucky."

Though he phased out most of his theatrical work, Jones continued to make occasional appearances in films and on television. Star Wars fans, for example, could count on Jones to return as the voice of Darth Vader in the latest installation in that film series, Revenge of the Sith, released in 2005. He wrote his biography, James Earl Jones: Voices and Silences, in 1993, and dedicated his voice and his stature to efforts to support literacy and education.

Despite a shelf full of awards and contributions to every sort of mass media, James Earl Jones remains a modest man with a sense of adventure about his career. He and his second wife, actress Cecilia Hart, have one son, and Jones told the Los Angeles Times that he guards against appearing heroic to his child. "When I go home nobody is saying, 'Hi, can I have your autograph?' I'm me, that's reality. I'm an actor. That's something you do, not something you are, and I want my son to have a sense of reality." Looking toward the future, Jones sees no lack of opportunities in show business. "There are lots of wonderful cameos and a lot of good lead roles out there," he concluded in the Los Angeles Times. "There are a lot of things I can do."

Selected works

Books

(With Penelope Niven) James Earl Jones: Voices and Silences, Scribner, 1993.

Films

Dr. Strangelove: Or, How I Learned to Stop Worrying and Love the Bomb, 1964.
The Great White Hope, 1970.

(Narrator), *Malcolm X*, 1972.
Deadly Hero, 1976.
The Bingo Long Traveling All-Stars and Motor Kings, 1976.
(Voice) *Star Wars*, 1977.
The Greatest, 1977.
(Voice) *The Empire Strikes Back,* 1980.
Conan the Barbarian, 1982.
(Voice) *Return of the Jedi*, 1983.
Gardens of Stone, 1987.
Matewan, 1987.
Field of Dreams, 1989.
The Hunt for Red October, 1990.
Sneakers, 1992.
Patriot Games, 1992.
(Voice) *The Lion King*, 1994.
Clear and Present Danger, 1994.
Jefferson in Paris, 1995.
Cry, the Beloved Country, 1995.
(Voice) *Primary Colors*, 1998.
The Annihilation of Fish, 1999.
Finder's Fee, 2001.
The Sandlot 2, 2005.
(Voice) *Star Wars, Episode III: Revenge of the Sith,* 2005.

Plays

The Blacks, 1961.
A Midsummer Night's Dream, 1961.
Othello, 1964, 1982.
The Emperor Jones, 1967.
The Great White Hope, 1968.
Of Mice and Men, 1974.
Master Harold...and the Boys, 1983.
Fences, 1987.

Television

The Defenders, 1962.
The Greatest Thing That Almost Happened, 1977.
Paul Robeson, 1978.
Paris, 1979.
Roots: The Next Generations, 1979.
Aladdin and His Wonderful Lamp, 1984.
The Atlanta Child Murders, 1984.
Heat Wave, 1989.
Last Flight Out, 1990.
Gabriel's Fire, 1990.
The JFK Conspiracy, 1992.
(Narrator) *Lincoln*, 1992.
(Host) *Twilight Zone: Rod Serling's Lost Classics*, 1994.
Merlin, 1998.
Summer's End, 1999.
Feast of All Saints, 2001.

Sources

Periodicals

Chicago Tribune, May 26, 1990; May 5, 1991.
Ebony, April 1965; June 1969.
Los Angeles Times, September 2, 1990; August 26, 1991; September 26, 1991.
Movieline, May 1999.
Newsweek, October 21, 1968; April 6, 1987.
Saturday Review, February 1982.
Time, April 6, 1987.
TV Guide, October 27, 1990.
Variety, September 23, 1991; December 5, 2002.

—Anne Janette Johnson and Tom Pendergast

Meb Keflezighi

1975—

Distance runner

The silver medal earned by Meb Keflezighi at the 2004 Olympic Games in Athens, Greece, represented a renaissance for distance running in the United States: Keflezghi's was the first American Olympic medal in the marathon since the silver medal earned by Frank Shorter in 1976. Keflezighi's medal was more than simply an American athletic triumph; it was also a demonstration of the resilience of the human spirit. Rising from a background of poverty and the violence of war, Keflezighi was a survivor in more ways than one. "I have

Keflezighi, Meb, photograph. AP/Wide World Photos. Reproduced by permission.

seen and dealt with a lot more than the average person," Keflezighi told the *San Diego Union Tribune.* "Does it make me tougher? To a point it does."

Mebrahtom Keflezighi—the first name means "let there be light" and the last name is pronounced Ka-FLEZ-ghee—was born in Eritrea, 15 miles from the city of Asmara, on May 5, 1975. One of 10 children, he grew up without electricity or running water. He ran away from the first car he saw as a child, and when he first encountered a television set he wondered how people could be fit into such a small box. His daily chores included caring for the family cattle herd and gathering

firewood. Keflezighi's grandfather could tell time by looking at the sun.

Pulled Corpses from Buildings

During his youth, Eritrea was in the midst of a long guerrilla war of independence from neighboring Ethiopia, and the fighting impinged severely on the lives of the Keflezighi family. Keflezighi's older brothers had to be on the lookout for Ethiopian army troops, who were known for kidnapping and conscripting teenage boys for military service. When they heard troops were on the way, the Keflezighis scattered and hid in nearby fields. In Asmara one day, Keflezighi, still a child, had to help remove corpses from a building after an explosion.

Facing these obstacles, Keflezighi's father decided to leave his homeland. He walked 600 miles to the nation of Sudan and worked there for a time. Then, with the help of a relative, he moved to Milan, Italy. The family joined him there and on October 12, 1987, when Keflezighi was 12, they moved on to San Diego, California, in search of better educational opportunities for the Keflezighi children. One of Keflezighi's sisters would go on to attend medical school at the University of California at Los Angeles (UCLA), and another sister went to law school there. Five siblings earned college degrees.

With little ability to speak English, Keflezighi was miserable at first. Classmates teased him about his unusual clothes. He and his brothers had learned to play soccer in Italy, and he dreamed of following in the footsteps of the Brazilian soccer superstar Pele. In a seventh-grade physical education class at San Diego's Roosevelt Middle School, however, he entered a running contest and ran a mile in an impressive 5 minutes, 20 seconds.

His teacher called a local high school coach who had guided a young runner to an Olympic appearance, and Keflezighi was given the chance to train seriously. Within two years he had shaved nearly a minute off his mile time and was winning local track titles. As a senior at San Diego High School, Keflezighi placed second in the nationwide Foot Locker National Cross-Country Championships.

Earned Track Scholarship

Moving on to UCLA in 1994 on a track and field scholarship, Keflezighi benefited from one of the top college track programs in the United States as he began working with coach Bob Larsen. Keflezighi became the winningest runner in UCLA history, notching a series of titles that began in his freshman year. As a junior in 1997, Keflezighi won the National Collegiate Athletic Association (NCAA) indoor 5,000-meter champion-

ship and went on to capture both the 5,000-meter and 10,000-meter outdoor crowns later that year.

The year 1998 was a landmark one for Keflezighi as he graduated from UCLA, became a U.S. citizen, and became the first winner of the annual Carl Lewis Award, given to the country's top male track and field athlete. He made his debut on the international running stage when he won the U.S. Olympic trials in 2000 at the 10,000-meter distance and went to Sydney, Australia, to represent his new country in the Olympics. Finishing in a personal-best 27 minutes and 53.63 seconds, he placed 12th despite coming down with the flu shortly before the race.

Keflezighi went on to set a new American record at 10,000 meters on May 4, 2001 at California's Stanford University, with a time of 27 minutes, 13.98 seconds. In order to take his career to the next stage he began working once again with Larsen, by then retired from his job at UCLA. Keflezighi took up residence at the U.S. Olympic Training Center in Chula Vista, California, close to San Diego. Part of his training involved running on trails on California's Mammoth Mountain, a hot, dry course of desert hills that would serve him well when he faced a similar environment in Athens.

Keflezighi took up mountain running on the advice of then-marathon world record-holder Haile Gebreselassie of Kenya, and he soon bought a home near Mammoth Mountain and split his time between there and Chula Vista. One of Keflezighi's training partners on Mammoth Mountain was 2004 Olympic women's marathon bronze medalist Deena Kastor. After his training sessions, Keflezighi would stand in a freezing cold stream that came down from higher in the mountains in order to reduce the inflammation in his leg muscles from the pounding they took on 20-mile training runs.

Ran in New York to Support City

While he was still in high school, Keflezighi had been told by a top San Diego marathon runner that he had natural ability at the 26.2-mile distance, but he had never followed up on the suggestion. As the 2002 New York Marathon approached, however, Keflezighi was looking to new challenges after winning national championships at the distances of 12,000 and 15,000 meters. He registered for the New York race, choosing it over the flatter and faster Chicago marathon partly to show support for his adopted country after the terrorist attacks of September 11, 2001. "I'm glad I'm an American," Keflezighi told the *San Diego Union-Tribune.* "I want to do what I can for New York."

Although he had never even run a half-marathon race, Keflezighi, in his first marathon on November 3, 2002, became the top U.S. finisher with a time of 2 hours, 12 minutes, and 35 seconds. He placed ninth overall, a fine showing for a first-timer. Although his first words after finishing (according to the *Marathon & Beyond* Web site) were "Well, that was my first and last marathon," he soon began looking toward the 2004 Olympics. But he took time off for a trip to Eritrea later in 2002, the first time he had been back there in 17 years.

He found himself a national celebrity as a crowd of 60,000 at a cycling race chanted his name as he jogged around the final lap of the course. Keflezighi met relatives who had been wounded in the long war against Ethiopia, and remembered some who had been killed. "Sometimes people ask me what it takes to be a No. 1 distance runner," Keflezighi told the *Union-Tribune*. "It's about a work ethic. Eritreans know about sacrifice." He had brought 50 T-shirts and about 15 pairs of shoes as souvenirs for family members. "But they were most delighted to see me," he recalled to the *Union-Tribune*. "It wasn't about the T-shirts."

Indeed, a lot of people enjoyed Meb Keflezighi's company. "Anybody who knows Meb loves him," Larsen told the *Marathon & Beyond* Web site. "He's one of the most likeable guys around." "Everyone in the family is like that," added teammate Deena Kastor, "and the credit goes to his parents. To have come from such extreme conditions and such a hostile environment, and to somehow be able to raise children as strong, independent, and educated as they are, is pretty incredible."

Keflezighi ran a blazing 2 hours, 10 minutes, and 3 seconds in the Chicago Marathon in October of 2003. Training for the 2004 Olympic Marathon trials in Birmingham, Alabama, Keflezighi faced a series of problems—possibly because he had taken a complete four-week break after the Chicago race. Plagued by tendinitis in both knees, he also suffered from a bout with the flu over the Christmas season. By the February 7 trials, however, Keflezighi was rested and ready. He finished second, five seconds behind winner Alan Culpepper. He returned to training on Mammoth Mountain, paced by cyclists and squads of freshly rested runners. He worked up to a schedule of 130 miles of running per week.

Arriving in Athens in August, Keflezighi shrugged off the hilly course, paralleling the route of the original marathon run by ancient Greek military messenger Pheidippides, that had intimidated other runners. "Those are not hills," he told Larsen (according to *Marathon & Beyond*). "From what you guys have prepared us for, those are not hills." Keflezighi began conservatively, bringing up the rear for the first mile of the race. But he shadowed the group of leaders throughout the race's midsection and found himself in fourth place with five miles to go. Unscathed by a bizarre incident in which Brazilian leader Vanderlei Lima was attacked by a spectator, Keflezighi made a move for the front.

Won Olympic Silver Medal

For a time, Keflezighi considered going for the gold, a risky move that might have led to no medal at all instead. He finished in 2 hours, 11 minutes, and 29 seconds, in second place, 34 seconds behind Italian winner Stefano Baldini. U.S. running fans were ecstatic after the long medal drought. "USA running is back!" Keflezighi exclaimed to the *Denver Post*. At the start of the race, 38 runners had notched faster personal-best marathon times than Keflezighi, and his silver medal was widely regarded as a stunner. "Was it a surprise? Maybe," the runner told the *San Diego Union-Tribune*. "But I don't think it was to me. My plan was to be in the top three."

That characteristic confidence showed through once again as Keflezighi entered the New York City Marathon in November of 2004, just three months after the Olympics; top runners usually rest for six months or so between major races. "Can Meb recover in 70 days?" Keflezighi (who often refers to himself in the third person) asked the *Union-Tribune*. "People say you can't do it. According to who? We will see." A hefty appearance bonus speculated to be in the low six figures, plus a shot at hundreds of thousands of dollars in prize money played a role in his decision, but so did the fact that the New York Road Runners Club, the race's sponsor, had supported his Olympic training efforts.

Keflezighi ended up duplicating his Olympic surprise, finishing second behind South African Hendrik Ramaala and notching a personal-best time of 2 hours, 9 minutes, and 53 seconds. He looked toward an eventual career as a motivational speaker, but what impressed many observers of the running scene was that he hadn't yet hit his peak as a distance runner. "I think he's going to be incredible in the next few years," Deena Kastor told the *Marathon & Beyond* site. "Each training period he goes through, he gets faster and stronger and looks more effortless." An Olympic gold medal seemed within reach of the former cattle hand from war-torn Eritrea.

Sources

Periodicals

Daily News (New York), October 31, 2002, p. 81.
Denver Post, August 30, 2004, p. D1.
New York Times, April 6, 2003, section 8, p. 10; March 28, 2004, section 8, p. 10; July 11, 2004, section 8, p. 7; November 8, 2004.
Palm Beach Post, November 8, 2004.
Runners World, August 2004.
San Diego Union-Tribune, May 5, 2001, p. D7; March 22, 2002, p. D2; November 2, 2002, p. D3; January 27, 2003, p. C1; February 6, 2004, p. D2; September 9, 2004, p. D10; November 5, 2004, p. D2; November 8, 2004, p. E1.
USA Today, May 9, 2001, p. C2.

On-line

"Rejoice. It's a Beautiful Day," *Marathon & Beyond,*
www.marathonandbeyond.com/choices/meb.html
(November 22, 2004).

—James M. Manheim

Simmie Knox

1935—

Portrait artist

When Simmie Knox's portrait of President Bill Clinton was unveiled at the White House in June of 2004, it marked the first time an African-American artist had painted an official presidential portrait. A great deal of prestige accrued to Knox after he was selected to create the Clinton portrait, as well as one of First Lady Hillary Rodham Clinton. Bill Clinton was not the first to appreciate Knox's talents, however; Knox built his career by painting portraits of various political and cultural figures, including comedian Bill Cosby. "You can't live in Washington, D.C., and not know Simmie Knox," Clinton administration energy secretary Hazel O'Leary told the *Christian Science Monitor* in 2001.

Knox was born on April 18, 1935, in Aliceville, Alabama. His father was a carpenter and mechanic. Knox's parents divorced when he was three, and he lived for a time with an aunt on a sharecropper farm in Leroy, Alabama, and later in Mobile. In that city he developed into quite a sandlot baseball player, able to hold his own with the neighborhood standout, future slugger Hank Aaron. Sometimes bottle tops and broom handles stood in for baseballs and bats in their games. "When you've played with bottle caps, baseballs are

Knox, Simmie, photograph. © Ron Sachs/Corbis.

like basketballs," Knox told the University of Delaware *Messenger.*

Hit by Baseball

Knox's promising baseball career came to an end when he was hit in the eye with a ball. It took him more than a year to recover from his injury, and during that time a doctor recommended that he be given things to do that would make him exercise his eyes by focusing closely. Catholic nuns at Mobile's Heart of Mary School steered him toward drawing, and they were impressed when the youngster produced a set of images of the Stations of the Cross. There was no such thing as an art class for a young black student in the segregated South of the early 1940s, so the nuns arranged for Knox to take drawing lessons from a neighborhood mailman.

He stuck with drawing and painting while he was attending Mobile's Central High School, but he didn't see a career in art as a possibility at the time. He joined the military in the 1950s and used the money he made to enroll in college after he finished his term of service. By 1961 he was attending Delaware State College and working in a nearby textile mill when he created his first

At a Glance . . .

Born April 18, 1935, in Aliceville, AL; married; three children. *Education:* Attended Delaware State College, early 1960s; University of Delaware, BA, 1967; Tyler School of Art, Temple University, Philadelphia, BFA, 1970, MFA, 1972. *Military Service:* Served in U.S. military, 1950s.

Career: Art instructor, various institutions including Duke Ellington School for the Arts, late 1960s-early 1980s; portrait artist, 1980–.

Address: *Studio*—Knox's Portraits and Fine Arts, 13801 Ivywood Lane, Silver Spring, MD 20901. *Web*—www.simmieknox.com.

full-scale painting, a self-portrait. The painting turned into a moment of self-revelation for Knox.

"You begin to realize, at that age in those times, that you were suffering for silly reasons," he told the *Washington Post,* referring to the system of segregation under which he had grown up. "Once in your life, at that one moment, you'll sit and you'll look at yourself. I mean really look at yourself and ask: Who am I? What am I? What kind of person do I want to be? I knew, deep within me, that I wanted to be an artist."

Switched Major to Art Education

That realization didn't translate immediately to a change in career direction. Moving on to the University of Delaware, Knox majored in biology. His grades were just fair, but an instructor noticed the detailed drawings of amoebas and other organisms that Knox included with the assignments he turned in. The instructor suggested that Knox take some art courses, and Knox soon changed his major to art education. He convinced a friend to pose for him while he drew his portrait over and over and over. His aim was to become an art teacher, and after graduating from Delaware in 1967 he did just that. For 18 years, Knox taught at a series of schools and colleges in Pennsylvania, Delaware, Maryland, and Washington, D.C., where he moved in 1972.

By that time, Knox had earned two more degrees by taking evening art classes: he received a Bachelor of Fine Arts degree from the Tyler School of Art at Philadelphia's Temple University in 1970 and went on for a master's degree there two years later. At the time, abstract art was the style that ruled the art world. Knox adopted the style with some success, participating in a group exhibition at Washington's Corcoran Gallery of Art with such top names as Roy Lichtenstein and Philip Pearlstein. Knox also worked for a time at Washington's Museum of African Art.

But Knox was still dissatisfied. "With abstract painting I didn't feel the challenge," he told the *New York Times.* "The face is the most complicated thing there is. The challenge is finding that thing that makes it different from another face." He did several portraits, one of African-American abolitionist writer Frederick Douglass, and another of a Milwaukee executive named Bill Gehl. After losing a job at the Duke Ellington School of the Arts in 1980, he began to focus more seriously on portraiture. Despite his extensive art education, Knox has sometimes described himself as self-taught. He pointed to the fact that he never took a course in portrait painting, which was considered old-fashioned by the critics and theorists who dictated the art trends of the time.

After several slow years of selling paintings at Washington's Eastern Market, Knox got a break when artist David Driskell introduced him to Bill Cosby in 1986. The comedian, then at the top of the entertainment universe, took a liking to Knox's work and decided to bankroll it. "He told me to just focus on my craft, and he'd make sure work came my way," Knox told the *New York Times.* "He gave me the opportunity I needed to practice, practice, practice." Knox did several portraits of Cosby family members, and soon his name became better known among prominent African Americans in the Washington area.

Intimidated by Thurgood Marshall Commission

Subjects who sat for Knox's portraits included boxer Muhammad Ali, Knox's childhood friend Hank Aaron, writer Alex Haley, musician Lou Rawls, and former U.S. Supreme Court justice Thurgood Marshall, whom he painted in 1989. Knox was a bit intimidated by the august jurist, but "Thurgood Marshall calmed me down," Knox recalled to the *Christian Science Monitor.* "He could tell I was nervous. He told jokes, he told stories about his life. I came away feeling so good about the man." Another Supreme Court justice who sat for Knox was Bill Clinton appointee Ruth Bader Ginsburg. She was one of just a few white clients he had at first. "Race has played quite a role in this country," Knox observed to the *Monitor.* "There are those who, no matter how good I am, will never let me paint their portrait."

But Ginsburg was pleased with her portrait and recommended Knox to President Clinton. Knox had first gone to the White House, portfolio in hand, in 1992. He got nowhere at the time, but now doors began to open. Clinton interviewed Knox several times in 2000 and selected him for the official portraits of himself and his wife Hillary shortly before leaving office in 2001. Clinton met with Knox to pick the pose he liked from a series of sketches Knox had made. "He liked the tie, the way I captured the hands," Knox told *Newsweek*. But the artist worked mostly from photographs.

The Clinton portraits took several years to finish, and Knox (as quoted by *Newsweek*) characterized the experience as "my personal Super Bowl." The portraits were unveiled on June 14, 2004, at a White House ceremony. "For three years, I've been extremely nervous," Knox told the *New York Times*. "But today, I put it to rest. I will sleep tonight." Knox came to feel a strong kinship with Clinton owing to their shared experience of growing up poor in the South. And, approaching age 70, he looked to new challenges. He was available for portrait commissions, with prices ranging from $9,500 to $60,000, and he told an interviewer from the *Milwaukee Journal Sentinel* that he hoped one day to paint anti-apartheid crusader and former South African president Nelson Mandela.

Sources

Periodicals

Christian Science Monitor, June 22, 2001, p. Arts & Leisure-13.
Daily News (New York), June 15, 2004, p. 8.
Messenger (University of Delaware), March 1996.
Milwaukee Journal Sentinel, June 16, 2004, p. A2.
New York Times, June 15, 2004, p. A20.
Newsweek, February 26, 2001, p. 9.
Washington Post, June 16, 2004, p. C1.

On-line

Simmie Knox, www.simmieknox.com (December 9, 2004).
"Simmie Knox, an Exceptional Portrait Artist," *African American Registry,* www.aaregistry.com/african_american_history/1642/Simmie_Knox_an_exceptional_portrait_artist (November 24, 2004).

—James M. Manheim

L.L. Cool J

1968—

Rap musician, actor

In the turbulent climate of rap music, careers are often brief moments of success crested atop long stretches of obscurity. For L.L. Cool J, this is not so, as he has helped lay down the groundwork for rap during the genre's early days and refine and reinvent it for over a decade. A veteran in a field with few veterans, Cool J has broken numerous commercial records, as well as artistic barriers by appealing to so-called "crossover" audiences and establishing himself as an actor. A working dynamo, the rapper sees his longevity as only just beginning. "I hate when people say 'still'," he was quoted on the Def Jam Web site. "Imagine asking a doctor, 'Yo man, you still a doctor?' It's not like I'm fighting to stay above water, I'm swimming and I got a shark fin going at 100 miles per hour."

L. L. Cool J, photograph. © Ron Sachs/Corbis

Growing up in the tough neighborhood of St. Alban's in Queens, New York immediately provided Cool J, born James Todd Smith in 1968, with the tenacity and experience that has shaped many rappers. However, unlike many of his "gangsta" contemporaries, Cool J later celebrated the strength gained from his youth, but not affiliations with gangs. "I did everything you could possibly name in the street," Cool J told Vibe maga-

zine. "I really came from that realness. I have that Queens experience on my mind, and it'll never leave me. The things I've been through…the gunshots fired at me because me and my friend put blanks inside snowballs and threw them on people's windshields. We was nuts to a certain extent, but for the most part, I'm glad I did everything I did because it helped mold me as a person."

Not only did the streets provide Cool J with life lessons, they also became the medium in which he became engaged in rapping, at a very young age. Experimenting from age nine, Cool J was fronting local rap crews at 11 years old, and in less than two years was tinkering with recording equipment. After his grandfather bought him a two-track recorder in lieu of a dirtbike, the precocious Cool J cut his first demo tapes when only thirteen, and soon began mailing them out. When the tapes captured the attention of producers Rick Rubin and Russell Simmons, founders of the budding label Def Jam, Cool J was almost immediately locked on a track for stardom.

In 1984, a time when rap music was only just gaining credibility with mass audiences, Def Jam was a gutsy venture to begin with. However, by releasing then

At a Glance . . .

Born James Todd Smith, on January 14, 1968, in St. Alban's, Queens, NY; married Simone, 1995; children: three.

Career: Singer, 1984–; actor, 1991–.

Awards: *Village Voice* Album of the Year Award, 1990; Artist of the Year, Album of the Year, Song of the Year in New York Music Awards, 1991; Grammy Award for *Mama Said Knock You Out*, 1991; Grammy Award nomination for *DEFinition*, 2005.

Addresses: *Record Label*—Def Jam Records, 652 Broadway, New York, NY, 10012.

16-year-old Cool J's "I Need A Beat" as their maiden single, Rubin and Simmons were taking a true risk. Their conviction of Cool J's talents were founded, and the single took off in popularity. A year later, Cool J recorded his debut album *Radio* for Def Jam, also their first long player, to the approval of many sectors. Called "the most engaging and original rap album of the year" by *Village Voice* music critic Robert Christgau, the album was a showcase of bass-driven favorites such as "Rock The Bells" as well as tender ballads, justifying his full moniker, Ladies Love Cool James. The album went platinum, as did all of Cool J's full-length releases from that point on.

Already a recording star, Cool J quickly proved to be a powerful live presence as well. He was invited to perform in the rap film *Krush Groove* to deliver a version of his song "I Can't Live Without My Radio." Within the next several years, Cool J would figure prominently in several major rap tours under the Def Jam banner–the Raising Hell Tour of 1986, featuring Run DMC and the Beastie Boys, and the Def Jam Tour a year after, whose roster included Public Enemy, Eric B. and Rakim, and Whodini. "See L.L. live," urged *Los Angeles Times* critic Robert Hilburn, "and it's easy to understand why he is emerging as a legitimate culture hero. His confidence and way with rhymes suggest a young Mohammed Ali, but some of his stage antics are reminiscent of Prince," he continued. With his low brimmed floppy cap and massive gold chains, Cool J's image neatly summed up all that was "old school" rap.

With the release of his second album in 1987, *Bigger and Deffer*, Cool J scored with audiences across the board, helping to broaden the barriers of rap listeners. The album's single "I Need Love" became the first rap song to top Billboard magazine's R&B chart, and proved that rap could embrace romantic modes, even while *Spin* magazine called *Bigger and Deffer* "argu-

ably the heaviest rock'n'roll record ever released on a major label". As the album joined Radio in platinum territory, Cool J's track "Going Back To Cali" for the film *Less Than Zero* help push that movie's soundtrack to gold sales.

By the end of the 1980s, Cool J began to show a genuine commitment to social issues. In November of 1988, he performed in Abidjan, the capital of the Ivory Coast as a benefit to a local hospital, and consequently was crowned honorary Chief Kwasi Achi-Brou by the elder council of the nearby village Gran-Bassan. In addition to later appearing in a pervasive set of drug awareness public service announcements for television, Cool J was approached by then First Lady Nancy Reagan to headline an anti-drug benefit concert at New York City's Radio City Music Hall. Just as the general public was developing uneasiness over a link between rap music, gang violence, and narcotic addiction, Cool J stood firm on the issue. "Kids come to my show to have fun, not to hear how bad the world is," he was quoted in the Def Jam homepage. "I don't promote violence and I don't promote drugs, simple as that."

Cool J continued to release platinum selling albums, as well as amassing awards and nominations for his recordings. Although the massive 18-track *Walking With A Panther*, released in 1989 was perhaps Cool J's low point among critics, it was still a commercial smash, and harbored at least one truly impressive single, "I'm That Type Of Guy." However, the 1990 follow up, *Mama Said Knock You Out*, was almost immediately accepted as Cool J's best album yet, through which he "reclaim[ed] his persona as the most articulated of homeboys, above uncluttered funk riffs assembled by the producer Marley Marl," as *New York Times* columnist Jon Pareles assessed. Indeed, while the album contained some of Cool J's smoothest compositions, such as the memorable "Around The Way Girl," yet another single which peaked on multiple charts, it was the bass thumping, confident drive of "The Boomin'System" and the album's title cut which gave *Mama Said Knock You Out* its appeal. As Cool J stated in an *America Online* interview, the title song was "a testament to the fact that no matter how rough times get and no matter how tough times get, you should never give up because that was the entire premise of that song. I was at a rough time in my life and I was inspired by my grandmother to get out there and knock them out!"

The onset of the 1990s saw Cool J explore the media of film and television, both as a musician and as an actor. On the big screen, he turned in an impressive performance as an undercover cop in the drama *The Hard Way* in 1991, which led to a part in director Barry Levinson's 1992 film *Toys*. For MTV, Cool J took part in two groundbreaking specials, both in 1991. In May, he performed acoustic versions of songs such as "Mama Said Knock You Out" and "Jingling Baby" for the popular series *Unplugged*, and was the first rap artist to do so. Shortly thereafter, he appeared in the music network's *History of Rap* documentary, discussing classic rap acts like Afrika Bambaata and The Sugarhill Gang, as rap began to get the recognition it deserved as a cultural phenomenon. In addition, Cool J took a leading support role on the television series, *In The House*, first shown on the NBC network in 1995, then switched to the UPN network, where it ran until 1999.

Rap had undergone a myriad of changes and upheavals, branching into countless factions and styles, by the 1990s and Cool J's next several albums proved that he was able to retain his vitality throughout. His 1993 album *14 Shots to The Dome* was memorable, and provided the rapper with yet another platinum-seller. *Mr. Smith*, released in 1995, rated as one of the artist's most successful fusions of hard-edged attitude and laid back eroticism. As *Rolling Stone* critic Cheo H. Coker noted, *Mr. Smith* did not always "deliver the haymaker punches of *Mama Said Knock You Out*, but it has enough force to prove that the king from Queens is no punk," with the highly sexual singles "Doin' It" and "Hey Lover" among the highlights. A year later, the retrospective album *All World Greatest Hits* hit record stores, which spanned a decade of Cool J's career, and in the process, ten years in the history of rap music.

Another decade later, Cool J continued to produce platinum-selling albums. Reminiscing about his music career, Cool J told the *St. Louis Post Dispatch* that "I don't have a favorite [album]. I feel as good about my music now as I did then." He enjoyed a great deal of success with his 2002 album *10,* which included his hit song "Love U Better," and with his 2004 album *DEFinition,* which earned him a Grammy nomination in 2005. When asked about his longevity in the music business, Cool J explained to the *St. Louis Post Dispatch* that he would not consider retirement "as long as I feel motivated and as long as I feel like I have something to say—as long as I can make a contribution to the language of hip-hop."

Reluctant to pick a favorite between music and acting, Cool J concentrated as much on his acting career as he did on his music at the start of the new millennium. He told the *St. Louis Post Disptach* that he loved "diving into different lives and exploring various emotions. It's pretty amazing." Although he had appeared in more

than a dozen films since his debut in 1991, including *Any Given Sunday* in 1999, *Charlie's Angels* in 2000, and *S.W.A.T.* in 2003, Cool J landed his first complex, leading role in the police drama, *Edison,* released in 2005. He told the *St. Louis Post Dispatch* that "I got to do the kind of work I've always dreamt of doing with the depth of this character." With his dual careers steaming ahead full throttle, Cool J added a new one: clothing design. His "James Todd Smith" clothing line appeared in malls in 2004. Indeed, after more than two decades in the limelight, Cool J seemed far from stepping off the stage.

Selected discography

Radio, Def Jam, 1985.
Bigger and Deffer, Def Jam, 1987.
Walking With A Panther, Def Jam, 1989.
Mama Said Knock You Out, Def Jam, 1990.
14 Shots to The Dome, Def Jam, 1993.
Mr. Smith, Def Jam, 1995.
All World Greatest Hits, Def Jam, 1996.
Phenomenon, 1997.
G.O.A.T., 2000.
10, 2002.
The DEFinition, 2004.

Sources

Periodicals

Los Angeles Times, July 19, 1987, p. C58.
New York Times, November 18, 1990, sec. 2, p.32.
Rolling Stone, February 8, 1996, pp. 49-50.
St. Louis Dispatch, September 16, 2004; September 23, 2004.
Vibe, March 1997.

On-line

"LL Cool J," *Def Jam Records,* www.defjam.com/llcoolj/home.las (January 31, 2005).
"LL Cool J," *MTV.com,* www.mtv.com/bands/az/ll_cool_j/artist.jhtml (January 31, 2005).

—Shaun Frentner and Sara Pendergast

Mance Lipscomb

1895-1976

Singer and guitarist

The music of Texan Mance Lipscomb opens a window on the musical culture of African Americans in the early twentieth century, before the blues became a dominant genre. Lipscomb sang and played the blues, but he rejected the label of blues musician in favor of "songster," which covered the much wider range of musical types that were part of his repertoire. Discovered by a wider audience during the folk revival of the 1960s, Lipscomb performed for large audiences nationwide until his death in 1976.

Bodyglin (or Bowdie Glenn) Lipscomb was born in Navasota, Texas, northwest of Houston, on April 9, 1895. His father had been a slave in Alabama, and he acquired the name Lipscomb when he was sold to a Texas family of that name. Lipscomb took the nickname Mance to honor a friend named Emancipation who had died. Music ran in Lipscomb's family, and after his mother bought him a guitar when he was 11, he began accompanying his fiddler father at local dances. Before long, Lipscomb was in demand for "Saturday Night Suppers" in and around Grimes County, Texas.

In addition to his family, Lipscomb picked up musical pointers from Texas blues singer Blind Lemon Jefferson. A traveling performer asked Lipscomb to go on tour in 1922, but Lipscomb said no, and until the 1960s he rarely left the area in which he was born. He married his wife Elnora around 1913 and the two stayed married for the rest of Lipscomb's life, raising one son, Mance Jr., three adopted children, and numerous grandchildren. He worked as a tenant farmer (he disliked the term "sharecropper") for various em-

ployers, and most of his musical appearances were at local functions. In contrast to the stereotype of the hard-living blues musician, he never gambled and rarely used alcohol.

Lipscomb did leave the Navasota area occasionally. He is known to have met Texas blues guitarist Sam "Lightnin'" Hopkins in Galveston in 1938. In 1956 Lipscomb hit a foreman who had mistreated his wife and mother; he had to leave town quickly and worked for several years in Houston, playing in bars and working in a lumberyard. The incident occurred on the farm of Tom Moore, and Lipscomb later recorded a ballad about the harsh conditions there, "Tom Moore's Farm." It was released anonymously, for Lipscomb's own protection. In *A Well-Spent Life,* a documentary about Lipscomb made by filmmaker Les Blank, the musician characterized the attitude of white farm owners this way: "Mule die, they buy another one; nigger die, they hire another one."

Things finally simmered down, and Lipscomb, with money saved from his work in Houston, bought land and built a house in Navasota. He got a job with a highway construction company, and one day in 1960 encountered music researchers Chris Strachwitz and Mack McCormick on a job site. They were looking for "Lightnin'" Hopkins, who had just left the area, but they agreed to listen to Lipscomb's music instead. Strachwitz was in the process of forming his California-based record company, Arhoolie, and a group of songs recorded around Lipscomb's kitchen table were put

---

At a Glance . . .

Born on April 9, 1895, in Navasota, TX; died on January 30, 1976, of heart disease in Navasota; married Elnora; children: Mance Jr., and three adopted children.

Career: Musician. Worked as tenant farmer, ca. 1910-1956; played for local dancers and suppers; worked in lumberyards and performed in clubs, 1956-58; worked in highway construction, 1958-early 1960s; recorded by producer Chris Strachwitz on the Arhoolie label, 1960-64.

---

together on the album *Mance Lipscomb: Texas Songster and Sharecropper,* Arhoolie's debut release.

Lipscomb's name quickly became well known among blues and folk music fans. He appeared at the Texas Heritage Festival in Houston in 1960 and 1961, then capitalized on his California connection and made appearances for three years running (1961-63) at the large Berkeley Folk Festival held at the University of California. In between festival appearances he appeared at folk coffeehouses in the San Francisco and Los Angeles areas, and he made several more recordings for Arhoolie.

What made Lipscomb stand out from the other Southern blues performers recorded during this period was the diversity of his repertory. His recordings provided examples of song and dance forms with both white and black roots—waltzes, two-steps, children's songs, jigs, reels, polkas, and a few others that Lipscomb named in his autobiography *I Say Me for a Parable* (the title meant "I give myself as an example"): the buzzard lope, cakewalk, slow drag, one-stop, wing-out, and ballin' the jack.

Many of these were African-American dance forms from early in the twentieth century, before the blues became popular among blacks and then turned into a nationwide craze. Perhaps Lipscomb's relative isolation in rural east Texas, far from the Mississippi River migration routes that shaped the blues, explained the preservation of these older forms in his music. For Lipscomb, the blues was only one type of music among many. It was a "true story song," he said in *I Say Me for a Parable,* "or nothin' but a cow huntin' for a calf.... Ya got ta be unsatisfied ta have the blues."

In the late 1960s, as interest in the blues mounted, Lipscomb experienced still greater success. He appeared at the Festival of American Folklife, held on the National Mall in Washington, D.C., in 1968 and 1970,

and he performed at other large festivals, including the Ann Arbor Blues Festival in 1970 and the Monterey Jazz Festival in California in 1973. Among the many musicians who became Lipscomb fans was vocalist Frank Sinatra, who issued a Lipscomb recording, *Trouble in Mind,* on his Reprise label in 1970. He appeared that year in Les Blank's film and two years later was featured in a French blues documentary, *Out of the Blacks into the Blues.*

Another fan was Texan-born Americana singer-songwriter Steve Earle, who was drawn to another aspect of Lipscomb's music: his intricate guitar work. In a *No Depression* article, Earle wrote that "as a finger-style guitarist, Mance had few peers (Mississippi John Hurt, Merle Watson, and Chet Atkins are the only names that come to mind), and any Lipscomb recording is a case study in how to get folks up out of their seats armed only with a single guitar.... The truth was, if you had Mance, you didn't need a band." Lipscomb preserved a sense of how individual entertainers managed to keep the attention of boisterous crowds of people at neighborhood functions.

Despite his success, Lipscomb avoided the trappings of luxury. He did, however, buy a set of dentures with a golden guitar stamped on the inside. Lipscomb suffered from heart trouble in the mid-1970s and gradually retired from the stage. *I Say Me for a Parable* was compiled by Texas author Glen Alyn from conversations with Lipscomb, which Lipscomb agreed to on condition that the two share any profits from the book equally. Alyn kept his end of the bargain, splitting the profits with Lipscomb's family after the musician's death in Navasota on January 30, 1976. *I Say Me for a Parable,* told entirely in Lipscomb's own voice and dialect without editing, later won a Music Book of the Year award from the ASCAP music licensing agency.

Selected works

Recordings

Mance Lipscomb: Texas Sharecropper & Songster, Arhoolie, 1961.
Texas Songster, Volume 2 to *Volume 6,* Arhoolie, 1961-64.
You'll Never Find Another Man Like Mance, Arhoolie, 1964.
Trouble in Mind, Reprise, 1970.

Books

(With A. Glenn Myers) *Out of the Bottoms and into the Big City,* Possum Heard Diversions, 1979.
(As told to and compiled by Glen Alyn) *I Say Me for a Parable: The Oral Autobiography of Mance Lipscomb, Texas Bluesman,* Norton, 1993.

Sources

Books

Harris, Sheldon, *Blues Who's Who,* Arlington House, 1979.

Herzhaft, Gérard, *Encyclopedia of the Blues,* Brigitte Debord, trans. University of Arkansas Press, 1997.

Myers, A. Glenn, *Mance and His Music: Mance Lipscomb Speaks for Himself,* Possum Heard Diversions, 1976.

Periodicals

Austin American-Statesman, January 31, 1990, p. B1.

Houston Chronicle, January 23, 1994, p. Zest-25.

Texas Monthly, April 1998, p. 224.

On-line

Earle, Steve, "Captain, Captain!: Navasota's Native Son—Mance Lipscomb," *Steve Earle,* www.steve-earle.net/biblio/nodepression-ml.php (December 1, 2004).

"Lipscomb, Mance," *Handbook of Texas Online,* www.tsha.utexas.edu/handbook/online/articles/view/LL/fli26.html (December 1, 2004).

Other

A Well-Spent Life (film), 1970.

—James M. Manheim

Roland S. Martin

1969(?)—

Journalist

One of the rising young stars of African-American journalism at the beginning of the twenty-first century, Roland S. Martin seemed like a whirlwind of activity as his career took off. He worked as a reporter for black-owned and white-owned newspapers; his voice was heard on radio news programs; he held editorial positions at a major magazine and a high-traffic black-oriented Web site; his syndicated column ran in newspapers nationwide; he was a frequent guest on radio and television talk shows of all political stripes; he ran a multimedia company of his own; and he wrote books. In 2004 Martin took on perhaps his greatest challenge: the revitalization of the once-mighty, but increasingly moribund, *Chicago Defender.*

Born around 1969 in Houston, Texas, Martin was inspired to follow a career in journalism by his father, an avid newspaper reader and fan of television news. In 1987 Martin graduated from Houston's Jack Yates High School in a magnet program devoted to communications. He went on to study journalism at Texas A&M University, graduating with a bachelor's degree in 1991. Martin landed a job at the *Austin American-Statesman* and started his journalism career at a basic level, covering county government and neighborhood news. In 1992 he covered the Republican National Convention for the paper and was sent to Louisiana to file reports from the area devastated by Hurricane Andrew.

Covered Branch Davidian Standoff

Moving on to the larger *Fort Worth Star-Telegram,*

Martin helped cover the fatal standoff mounted by the Branch Davidian religious sect in Waco, Texas, in 1993 and the 1995 right-wing terrorist bombing of the Oklahoma City, Oklahoma, federal building. His coverage of the Oklahoma City bombing earned him an award from the Managing Editors group of the Texas Associated Press, the first of more than 20 journalism awards he would receive. Martin covered Fort Worth's city hall and began to expand his range as a writer, contributing sports and news columns to the paper.

Martin worked as a morning reporter for all-news radio station KRLD in Dallas and then moved to black-oriented KKDA, where he served for three years, from 1995 to 1998, as news director and morning anchor. He also did sports reporting there, earning a 1997 award from the National Association of Black Journalists. While at KKDA, Martin broke a story involving drug possession charges being leveled against former Dallas Cowboys player Michael Irvin. Martin, KKDA general manager Chuck Smith told the *Chicago Tribune,* "was like a pit bull. He demanded a lot, but he mainly wanted to see other people succeed."

The chance to revitalize a publication and put his own stamp on it lured Martin back to the world of print journalism. He became managing editor of the black-oriented *Dallas Weekly* and led the paper's staff to local, state, and national journalism awards. Later Martin served in the same position at the *Houston Defender.* From there, Martin branched out into an impressive variety of journalistic activities; he seemed

Born in 1969(?) in Houston, TX; married Rev. Jacquie Hood Martin. *Education:* Texas A&M University, BS, journalism, 1991; Louisiana Baptist University.

Career: *Austin American-Statesman,* reporter, 1991-93; *Fort Worth Star-Telegram,* reporter, 1993-95; KRLD radio, Dallas, reporter, 1995; KKDA radio, Dallas, news editor and morning anchor, 1995-98; *BlackAmericaWeb,* founding editor; managing editor, late 1990s; *Dallas Weekly,* managing editor, late 1990s; *Houston Defender,* managing editor, late 1990s; *Savoy,* news editor, 2002-4(?); Creators Syndicate, syndicated columnist, 2002–; *Chicago Defender,* executive editor, 2004–.

Selected memberships: National Association of Black Journalists; Unity Journalists of Color, mentor to young journalists.

Selected awards: Regional Edward R. Murrow Award, Radio Television News Directors; National Association of Black Journalists, Salute to Excellence Award, for sports reporting, 1997.

Addresses: *Office—Chicago Defender,* 2400 S. Michigan Ave., Chicago, IL 60616. *Web—*www.rolandsmartin.com.

2003, Mississippi Senator Trent Lott attempted to save his job by espousing such goals as affirmative action after getting into hot water over comments lauding the past segregationist policies of onetime presidential candidate Strom Thurmond. "Who'd a thunkit?" Martin wrote in *Savoy.* "Black folks have been clamoring for a comprehensive legislative agenda in the wake of Democratic losses during the midterm election and Trent comes along to lead the charge. Move over, Jesse [Jackson] and Al [Sharpton]–Trent's going to carry black folks to the Promised Land. Can I get an amen?!"

This sort of wit made Martin attractive to hosts of all persuasions in the rapidly growing sphere of political talk. Martin became a familiar face and voice, not only within the sphere of African-American media like National Public Radio's Tavis Smiley Show, but also on the Cable News Network (CNN) and on Fox television's conservative-oriented *O'Reilly Factor.* In 2002, Martin began writing a column of his own; it was picked up by the nationally distributed Creators Syndicate ran in such major newspapers as the *Detroit News, Denver Post,* and *Indianapolis Star.* Martin also found time to write a book, *Speak, Brother! A Black Man's View of America.*

Married to a minister and author, the Rev. Jacquie Hood Martin, Martin had a strong interest in Christian issues himself. He pursued a master's degree at Louisiana Baptist University and made plans in 2004 to release *Yes, God! Listening to the Spirit Within,* a collection of his columns on religious themes. Martin experienced a rare taste of failure in 1993 as he purchased a small Christian newspaper in Dallas and tried to turn it around. The paper folded within a year, but Martin gained experience that would help him deal with a much larger turnaround project.

Hired to Revitalize Chicago Defender

In 2004, Martin was hired as a consultant by the *Chicago Defender,* a 99-year-old daily paper that had played a vital role in the civil rights revolution of the middle twentieth century. Many black Chicagoans remembered the newspaper's contributions positively, but its circulation, long unaudited, had dropped to less than a tenth of its peak of 250,000 and was centered mostly on the South Side's Bronzeville neighborhood. With a 90-day contract, Martin shook things up immediately. Several longtime employees departed, but the paper's owners noticed the *Defender*'s new look, with a focus on a single relevant story of the day. And they were impressed by Martin's streamlining of the paper's accounting practices.

So, at the end of August of 2004, Martin was hired as executive editor of the *Defender.* Though some doubted the paper's ability to survive as a daily, Martin,

to be trying to become black journalism's Renaissance man. He became a founding editor of radio personality Tom Joyner's *Black America Web* Web site, returned to radio himself as a news correspondent for the American Urban Radio Network and as a sports commentator on Washington, D.C., radio station WOL's "Fifth Quarter Program," and launched the ROMAR Media Group in Dallas as an umbrella company encompassing his various activities, which included marketing consultancies for various media organizations.

Became Editor at Savoy

In the early 2000s, Martin became news editor for the new *Savoy* magazine, a New York-based publication focusing on African-American lifestyles. That post gave Martin the chance to hone his individual style as a writer; a style that could be pointed and outspoken yet was marked by a twinkle-in-the-eye humor sometimes lacking in the writing of other black commentators. In

variously described (according to the *Chicago Tribune*) as "brazen, arrogant, and visionary," seemed the right person to give it a chance. Sometimes clad in red pants and a Texas A&M Aggies shirt, he injected a jolt of energy into the staid old paper. Laying plans to raise the *Defender*'s circulation of 18,000 to 60,000 by reaching the city's West Side and suburban black populations, Martin added auto and business sections and revived the paper's Web site. He continued to write prolifically, exhorting black Chicago parents to take an interest in their children's educations. "Whether you like it or not," he wrote in the *Defender*'s pages, "the lack of an education will likely result in your child being incarcerated."

"One of the things that he has is a very great interest in himself," KKDA's Chuck Smith told the *Tribune*. "That's what egotistical people do, and I don't mean that in a negative way. If you're going to change stuff, you have to have some sense that you're right and you have some higher cause." The higher cause of African-American journalism, it seemed, was being energetically served by the fast-rising Roland S. Martin.

Selected writings

Speak, Brother! A Black Man's View of America, ROMAR Media Group, 2002.

Sources

Periodicals

Chicago Defender, September 1, 2004, p. 3; September 7, 2004, p. 2.
Chicago Reader, September 17, 2004.
Chicago Sun-Times, July 29, 2004, p. 63.
Chicago Tribune, September 26, 2004, p. 1.
Crain's Chicago Business, November 1, 2004, p. 56.
Editor & Publisher, August 31, 2004.
Houston Chronicle, September 1, 2004, p. A2.
Savoy, February 2003, p. 82.

On-line

"Biography," http://www.rolandsmartin.com (November 24, 2004).

—James M. Manheim

Ruby Grant Martin

1933-2003

Government official

Ruby Grant Martin grew up surrounded by the pervasiveness of racism in the pre-Civil Rights era. She rode in the back of buses, was barred from restaurants, and could not go where she wanted, when she wanted. Yet she never let these obstacles stop her. She found her way around racist policies, beating the racists at their own game. "We were able to foil the system that tried to dehumanize us by making fun of it," Martin explained in "Reinventing Race Relations," a 1992 speech she gave in Richmond, Virginia. But Martin played smart too. She provided research for the Civil Rights Act of 1964. She oversaw desegregation in schools around the country. She advised governors, counseled Congress, and founded a law firm to help minorities and poor people. She did not just foil the system—she changed it.

Found Education and Racism in College

Ruby Grant was born in the rural town of Lake Village, Arkansas, on February 18, 1933. She lived there until her family moved to Cleveland, Ohio, when she was nine. Though most schools in the South were still segregated by race, many northern schools were not. Martin was thus educated alongside white children, mostly Eastern European immigrants. Her father insisted that Martin's grades be better than her classmates because her family could speak perfect English, while the parents of her schoolmates could not. Martin took her father's advice and excelled in school.

Though she had been spared the brunt of deep southern racism by her family's move north, she felt it keenly when she enrolled in Fisk University, a historically black college in Nashville, Tennessee. In "Reinventing Race Relations," Martin recalled, "I was subjected to all of the officially imposed racial separation and sanctions, as well as all of the instances of abuse and the indignation that were heaped upon me and my fellow classmates, simply because we were colored in a city of the deep south." Those sanctions included being forced to sit in the back seats of buses and to use "colored" facilities like restrooms, drinking fountains, and even fitting rooms in department stores. Martin got around the last indignity by bringing her blonde-haired, blue-eyed roommate to try on clothes for her.

Martin graduated from Fisk in 1956 and moved to Howard University, another historically black college in Washington, D.C. When she received a law degree from Howard in 1959 she had the highest academic average of her class. She was also the class president. Despite her impressive achievements on campus, as soon as she stepped onto the streets of Washington, D.C., she became a second-class citizen. "What made the situation in the nation's capitol so much more heartbreaking was that persons from the international community, even those whose skin was blacker than mine and whose hair was more kinky than mine, were allowed to dine in restaurants and patronize theaters whose doors I could not even darken, no pun intended," Martin continued in "Reinventing Race Relations." She and her fellow students got around the double-standards by borrowing clothing from African classmates, and walking proudly past "whites-only" signs dressed in traditional African garb.

At a Glance . . .

Born on February 18, 1933, in Lake Village, AR; died on May 8, 2003; married Henry S. Martin; three children. *Education:* Fisk University, BA, 1956; Howard University, LLB, law, 1959.

Career: U.S. Commission on Civil Rights, Washington, DC, staff attorney, 1960-65; Cleveland Community Relations Board, Cleveland, OH, investigator, 1959-60; Department of Health, Education, and Welfare (HEW), assistant, Washington, DC, 1965-67; Office of Civil Rights, HEW, Washington, DC, operations director, 1967-69; Washington Research Project, Washington, DC, co-director, 1969-72; House Committee on the District of Columbia, Washington, DC, counselor, 1972-78; lawyer in private practice, Richmond, VA, 1978-90; Commonwealth of Virginia, Richmond, VA, state secretary of administration, 1990-93.

Selected memberships: National Bar Association; Women Executives in State Government, treasurer; Children's Defense Fund, board of directors; Southern Regional Council, board of directors; Port of Richmond Commission, chairperson.

Selected awards: U.S. Civil Service Commission, Distinguished Federal Women's Award, 1968; Department of Health, Education, and Welfare, Distinguished Service Award, 1968; NAACP, Freedom Fund Award, 1991; NAACP, Public Service Award, 1992; Virginia Union University, Honorary Doctorate, 1993.

Helped Turn Civil Rights into Law

After graduating from Howard, Martin went home to Ohio and took a job with the Cleveland Community Relations Board. Within the year, however, she returned to the nation's capital. Martin wanted to put her legal training to good use helping change the plight of African Americans. She made a good start when she became a staff attorney for the U.S. Commission on Civil Rights in 1960. The commission was charged with gathering information on minority groups nationwide. The findings of the commission formed the basis of much of the civil rights legislation in the early 1960s, including the Civil Rights Act of 1964. The landmark act prohibited segregation in public accommodations and discrimination in education and employment—the very things that Martin and her contemporaries had suffered throughout their lives.

In 1965 Martin joined the staff of the Department of Health, Education, and Welfare (HEW). She held a variety of administrative and legal jobs, including assistant to the assistant to the Secretary of the department. Following the passage of the Civil Rights Act of 1964, Congress established the Office of Civil Rights (OCR) within HEW. OCR was charged with ensuring that publicly-funded institutions such as schools and hospitals did not violate Title VI of the act, which expressly forbid discrimination based on race. In 1967 Martin was appointed operations director of the OCR. As she said in a 1968 interview with the *Washington Post*, the government was making a move from "studying to action." Martin was going to be part of the action.

Martin's job was to ensure that Title VI was complied with nationwide. She considered it an honor, and described Title VI to the *Washington Post* as "having the greatest potential for changing the country." Her department would investigate hundreds of institutions nationwide. Their main tool of enforcement would be the withholding of federal funds. Though the landmark 1955 Supreme Court case *Brown v. the Board of Education* had declared segregated schools to be unconstitutional, desegregation was slow in coming. In 1957, nine black students had faced vicious mobs to attend a high school in Little Rock, Arkansas. Federal troops had to be called in. Later, school districts across the country tried to avoid desegregation by redrawing school district lines to follow the racial boundaries of neighborhoods. In other districts, threats from the Ku Klux Klan kept black parents from sending their children to white schools.

Erased Segregation, if Not Racism

Martin and company had their work cut out for them. "Where I work is probably the most controversial area of government," she told *The Washington Post* in 1968. "Every day I come with my armor on wondering what's going to happen." She was often in direct confrontation with local officials and as a result incurred the wrath of several powerful politicians. In February of 1968, a congressman from Georgia demanded Martin's resignation when she found that the school districts in his territory had no plans to develop a desegregation strategy.

Despite the difficulties, most Southern school districts complied with her office's mandates. She told the *Washington Post,* "I've been amazed how Deep South school officials have gritted their teeth, closed their eyes, and gone about the business of conforming with the law." Yet she was not naive enough to think they were happy about it. She acknowledged that the reason for the South's compliance was "not that they are behind us, but that people there are basically law-abiding citizens." In fact, racial tensions were reaching an all-time high in the country. She was one year into her post with the OCR when Reverend Martin Luther King was assassinated.

In her final two years as the operations director of the OCR, Martin turned her attention on Northern schools. She told the *Washington Post* at the time that her office did not foresee busing—transporting children to schools outside their neighborhoods to achieve racial integration—as a method she would employ. Instead she hoped to focus on the quality of education. "The criteria we apply is this: what is the quality of education being dispensed in the schools?" she told the *Washington Post*. "If the schools are equal in opportunity, even if they're all white or all Negro, we'll pack up our bags and move elsewhere."

Martin left the OCR in 1969 after two mostly successful years. She was awarded for her work with a Distinguished Federal Women's Award from President Johnson. At 34, she was the youngest woman ever to receive the honor. During Johnson's awards ceremony speech, reprinted on *The American Presidency Project* Web site, he cited Martin "for her courageous and effective administration of the civil rights compliance program and her exceptional contribution to racial justice in the field of education."

Rose to Political Prominence in Virginia

In 1969 Martin became co-director of the Washington Research Project, a public-interest law firm that provided legal counsel for poor people and minorities. She returned to government work in 1972, joining the legal team of the House Committee on the District of Columbia, the agency that oversaw the affairs of the district. At the time the District of Columbia was slowly moving from federal control to local control. Martin played a key role in the development of the Home Rule Act of 1973, which allowed the district to elect its own mayor and council. She also advised on the establishment of the University of the District of Columbia. In 1978, Martin and her husband, dentist Henry S. Martin, relocated to nearby Richmond, Virginia, where she went into private law practice. She focused mainly on social issues dealing with underserved communities: the poor, minorities, women, and children. She also raised three children of her own.

Martin was called back into public service by her former Howard University classmate, Virginia governor L. Douglas Wilder. He was the first African-American governor in the nation and he wanted Martin on his cabinet. She became his Secretary of Administration in 1990, the first woman and the first African American to hold the post. She was in charge of ten state departments and had responsibility for areas as diverse as employee benefits, property management, and human rights. According to the *Washington Post* she was also "the moving force behind the governor's African trade mission," accompanying Wilder on several trade and cultural visits to Africa. When Wilder's administration ended in 1994, Martin became a consultant to the governor of North Carolina on African trade. She also served as a member of Virginia's State Council on Higher Education and as chairwoman for the Port of Richmond. Along with Wilder, she also founded the National Slavery Museum.

Martin was recognized throughout her career for her contributions to civil and human rights. She received two honorary doctorates, Howard University's Distinguished Alumni Award, and two awards from the NAACP—the Freedom Fund Award and the Public Service Award. "I never thought of what I have done through the years as prize worthy or award winning," Martin said in her 1991 acceptance speech for the Freedom Fund Award. "I just always thought that I was simply doing my job—doing my part—pushing and shoving to help make this Nation, this State, and this Community, a better, more humane, more responsible, and more responsive place for people who can't always help themselves." By the time of her death on May 8, 2003, there was no doubt she had succeeded. A speech given during a Virginia Senate meeting commemorating her death summed up the legacy she left behind. "Those who loved her and had the privilege of knowing and working with her, will treasure the memory of her astounding intellect and her quiet persuasive leadership…[we] hereby mourn the loss of Ruby Grant Martin, a brilliant legal mind, a remarkable Virginian, and gentle lady."

Sources

Books

Notable Black American Women, *Book 2*, Gale Research, 1996.

Periodicals

Essence, July 1972.
Washington Post, February 17, 1968; May 10, 2003.

On-line

"Celebrating the Life of Ruby Grant Martin, Former Secretary of Administration," *Senate Joint Resolution No. 23, State of Virginia*, http://leg1.state.va.us/cgi-bin/legp504.exe?041+ful+SJ23 (October 25, 2004).
"Remarks at the Federal Woman's Award Ceremony," *The American Presidency Project*, www.presidency.ucsb.edu/ws/index.php?pid=28736&st=ruby+grant&st1= (October 25, 2004).

Other

Martin, Ruby Grant, "Reinventing Race Relations" (address given at the Richmond Urban Forum, Richmond, Virginia), December 8, 1992.

Martin, Ruby Grant, "Acceptance Speech, NAACP Freedom Fund Award," (given at the Richmond Center, Richmond, Virginia), October 23, 1991.

—Candace LaBalle

Roland McFarland

1940—

Television executive

Roland McFarland is senior vice president of broadcast standards and practices at Fox Broadcasting, overseeing broadcast standards for Fox's prime time, late night, and children's programming, in addition to comedy and drama development and on-air promotions. In the course of a 30-year career, he has worked on numerous popular television shows on ABC and Fox, monitoring accuracy, appropriateness, and potential positive or negative impact.

Studied Speech and Theater

McFarland was born on August 13, 1940, in Devers, a small town in eastern Texas, the fourth of seven children born to Booker and Ada McFarland. His father was an engineer for Southern Pacific Railroad in Texas and Louisiana; his mother had been a nurse and midwife, "the only nurse to the only doctor in that county for 25 years," McFarland told *Contemporary Black Biography*. The family moved to Baytown, near Houston, when he was a child, following his father's work at the Standard Oil Company.

After completing junior high in segregated Texas, McFarland was sent to California, where his older sister was living, to attend Lincoln High School in San Diego. "I did the same thing with a younger brother once I was married," McFarland told *CBB*. "That was our way of supporting each other and assuring ourselves the best life."

In San Diego, McFarland was a cross-country and track enthusiast but, encouraged by a teacher, Polly Mayne,

he discovered that he excelled at public speaking and drama. He became the captain of the school speech team, competing at interscholastic events. "I remember finishing cross country meets and changing from running togs into tie and shirt and going to City Hall for a debate with rival schools in the area," he recalled to *CBB*. His abilities, he believed, were inherited from his mother, who "was and still is a tremendous public speaker and avid reader."

McFarland graduated from high school in 1958 and attended San Diego State College on scholarship, majoring in speech arts. McFarland studied both acting and directing, and wrote one-act plays. He became close friends with Cleavon Little, a young black actor who went on to appear on film and television. "We flipped a coin," McFarland said to *CBB*, "to see who would compete for a scholarship from the American Academy of Dramatic Arts in New York. He won the coin flip, and I stayed on the west coast to focus on theater and television."

Began Television Career

After graduating from college in 1961, McFarland spent most of the 1960s working as an actor and director, first for the Old Globe Theater in San Diego and then, in Los Angeles, for the repertory company of the Inner City Cultural Theater, a group with high-profile supporters and associates, including Sidney Poitier and Frank Silvera. Someone from ABC Television saw McFarland on stage and invited him to ABC for a meeting. "I thought: oh good, I'm going to get a

At a Glance . . .

Born August 13, 1940, in Devers, Texas; married 1961 (divorced); married Paulette, 1981; children: two. *Education*: San Diego State University, BA in speech arts, 1961.

Career: Repertory actor and director, San Diego and Los Angeles, CA, 1961-70; ABC Television, page, 1970; ABC TV, department of broadcast standards, editor and manager, 1970-93; Fox TV, department of broadcast standards and practices, director, vice president, and senior vice president, 1993–.

Selected Memberships: Broadcast Standards Executives; Academy of Television Arts and Sciences; San Diego Alumni Association; NAACP (Hollywood/ Beverly Hills Chapter); Entertainment Industries Council; Director's Council of Public Representatives of the National Institutes of Health.

Addresses: *Office*—Fox TV, PO Box 900, Beverly Hills, CA 90213.

show," McFarland told *CBB*. "But when I met with the executive, he asked if I wanted to join the network. I didn't know what that meant at the time. I was married, I had a child, I said sure, I'll try this on until I get another role acting or directing. Flash forward for the rest of my life!"

McFarland began work at ABC in 1970. His first job was as a page in guest relations—where he was able to get a broad overview of production—and he soon joined the department of broadcast standards as an editor. In his new position as "the person who in simpler times was known as the censor," according to *U.S. News & World Report*, McFarland was assigned children's shows and a popular situation comedy, *The Ghost and Mrs. Muir.* He went on to work on a number of ABC's classic television shows from the 1970s and 1980s, including *The Brady Bunch, The Partridge Family, Starsky and Hutch,* and *Dynasty.*

Unlike many executives in broadcast standards, McFarland did not train as a lawyer. He believed that his background in theater made him sympathetic to writers and producers as well as responsible to the audience. "I'd done everything from directing to set design to lighting, even sewing!" he told *CBB*. "I really identified with the process." McFarland believed himself to be "part of a creative team" more involved with the early stages of show development rather than in editing and censoring. "We're involved from the time the story is

pitched to signing off on the 'air print' that's going to be broadcast," he told *CBB*. "Censorship is a small part of our day."

Moved to Fox Broadcasting

In 1989, McFarland was approached to join the fledgling Fox Broadcasting network. McFarland believed that moving there would be "folly," he told *CBB*. Fox only offered one night of shows and industry pundits believed it could not compete with the "big three" of ABC, NBC, and CBS. But Fox survived, expanding to three nights of programming by 1990. In 1993 a former colleague, now working at Fox, persuaded McFarland to "walk across the street" to become director of broadcast standards.

McFarland soon adjusted from working for a department of more than 50 people to a team of just three, keeping busy with hits such as *Beverly Hills 90210, Melrose Place, In Living Color,* and its biggest ongoing success, *The Simpsons,* which "still has issues," McFarland told *CBB*, "and still turns me gray." In 2001, a character called Roland McFarland was murdered in an episode of *The X-Files.* "It's part of the price you pay for being an irritant," says McFarland. "The producers have finally found a way to kill me off!"

As Fox expanded its programming to seven days a week, McFarland's workload and travel schedule grew. By 2004, McFarland had a staff of ten, overseeing all aspects of programming except for news and sports. The rise of cable television in the 1980s resulted in increased competition for networks as well as increased public acceptance of stronger language and subject matter, as did the more recent rise of reality television.

The New York Times, calling MTV and Fox "perhaps the most daring" in their programming, recently quoted McFarland talking about acceptability as "an ever expanding and retracting elastic band." A 2004 article in the *International Herald Tribune* suggested that the band is about to retract, because "networks' standards and practices divisions are being strengthened after they were scaled back about a decade ago." McFarland, quoted in that article, projected "a greater degree of separation between networks and cable, with broadcasters settling in as the family medium." In his interview with *CBB*, McFarland described monitoring standards today as "very challenging—gauging America's taste, following and not leading, keeping a finger on the pulse of public acceptance. In programming, if you get 50 percent public acceptance, it's a hit. We have to be on the mark every day." Television shows, he said, are "guests in the home of viewers in this country, and need to exercise decorum."

Supported Community Initiatives

An advocate of diversity in television, McFarland is proud that Fox "developed a lot of shows with strong

African-American characters," he told *CBB*. He personally brokered the deal to bring the NAACP Image Awards to Fox, even though the organization had an antagonistic relationship with the network in the mid-1990s, complaining to the FCC that Fox "has brought the greatest debasement of taste, character, quality, and decency in television history," according to a 1995 story in *U.S. News & World Report*.

McFarland served as chair of the Image Awards for three years in the late 1980s, and has also served on the boards of a number of other organizations, including the San Diego Alumni Association, the Chrysalis Foundation for the Homeless, and the Challengers Boys and Girls Club of America. He currently sits on the board of directors of both the Hollywood/Beverly Hills chapter of the NAACP and the Entertainment Industries Council. He is most proud, he told *CBB*, of his work representing the entertainment industry on the director's council of public representatives of the National Institutes of Health, serving on the board from 1999 until 2002, working to find "a better method of disseminating public health messages."

McFarland has two children from his first marriage, which ended in divorce. In 1981 he married Paulette McFarland, a teacher in early childhood development.

After more than thirty years in broadcast standards, McFarland believes that he's "made a difference in the culture and entertainment industry," as he told *CBB*. "No matter where I am around the world, I see a television show that I had something to do with. It's an amazing realization of the impact of this medium and how diligent we have to be in crafting messages."

Sources

Periodicals

International Herald Tribune, March 16, 2004, p. 13

New York Times, February 5, 2003, p. E1.
U.S. News & World Report, September 11, 1995, p. 68.

Other

Additional information for this profile was obtained through an interview with *Contemporary Black Biography* conducted on November 1, 2004.

—Paula J.K. Morris

Patricia Mell

1953—

University administrator

With twenty years of experience at faculty level in several major law schools, Patricia Mell was appointed Dean of the John Marshall Law School in Chicago in 2003. She became the first black and first female dean of the 104-year-old school and on her appointment was the only black woman to be leading a United States law school where white students form a majority. A graduate of Wellesley College, her career includes appointments at some of the most prestigious law schools in the country, including Michigan State University-Detroit College of Law, where she was Professor of Law before moving to the John Marshall Law School. The daughter of a Cleveland police detective, Mell's list of professional affiliations, academic appointments, and legal positions held is impressive. She served as assistant attorney general for the state of Ohio (1978-82), was made full professor of law at Michigan State University-Detroit College of Law aged just thirty-nine in 1992, and in 2004 was named one of Chicago's 100 most influential women. Her position as dean of the John Marshall Law School makes her one of the most important legal practitioners in the United States.

Born on December 15, 1953, in Cleveland, Ohio, Patricia Mell is the daughter of Julian Cooper Mell, a Cleveland police detective, and Thelma (Webb) Mell, an elementary school principal. She graduated from Collinwood High School in Cleveland in 1971 and went on to Wellesley College, graduating with a bachelor's degree in 1975. Mell progressed to Case Western Reserve University Law School and graduated with a Juris Doctorate (JD) in 1978. She was certified by the Ohio bar and the US District Court, Ohio, in 1979. Mell is married to Dr. Michael Ragland, an obstetrician and gynecologist, and has three stepchildren.

When Mell finished law school she joined the Ohio attorney general's office, where she served as an assistant attorney general specializing in consumer fraud, charitable foundations, and began to develop an interest in corporations and corporate law. She then became corporation counsel for Ohio's secretary of state, where she served from 1982 to 1984. Mell began teaching in 1984 at Capital University Law School, in Columbus, Ohio, where she spent a year as a visiting assistant clinical professor before becoming a visiting professor at the University of Toledo College of Law. She continued to be involved in practical legal work as a mediator with the night prosecutor's program in Columbus and at Toledo found time to serve on the scholarship screening committee of the Black American Law Student Association from 1985 to 1986 and on the governing body of Case Western Reserve University Law School, from 1985 to 1988. She was assistant professor of law at Widener University, Wilmington, Delaware, from 1986 to 1988 before moving to Michigan to join the firm of Lewis, White, and Clay in Detroit in 1991. After a year during which she also worked as an adjunct professor at Wayne State University Law School, Mell was made professor of law at Michigan State University Detroit College of Law in 1992, where she was later promoted to associate Dean for academic affairs in 2000.

Mell's experience in education and in the commercial legal world, as well as her background in administration

At a Glance . . .

Born Patricia Mell on December 15, 1953, in Cleveland, Ohio; married Dr. Michael Steven Ragland; stepchildren: Lauren, Steven, Camille. *Education:* Wellesley College, AB, law, 1975; Case Western Reserve University Law School, JD, 1978.

Career: Assistant Attorney General, State of Ohio, Columbus, 1978-82; Secretary of State Corporation counsel, State of Ohio, Columbus, 1982-84; visiting assistant professor, Capital University Law School, Columbus, Ohio, 1984-85; mediator on the night prosecutor's program, Columbus, 1984-85; visiting assistant professor, University of Toledo Law School, 1985-86; assistant professor of law, Widener University (formerly Delaware Law Sch.), Wilmington, 1986-88; professor of law, Michigan State University, Detroit College of Law, East Lansing, Michigan, 1992-2003; associate dean for academic affairs, Michigan State University Detroit College of Law, 2000-02; dean, John Marshall Law School, Chicago, Illinois, 2003-.

Memberships: Alliance of Black Women, Columbus, Ohio, 1983-85; Black American Law Student Association, University of Toledo Law School, scholarship screening committee, 1985-86; Case Western Reserve University Law School, Cleveland, governing body, 1985-88; American Bar Association; National Bar Association; National Conference of Black Lawyers; American Arbitration Association; National Black MBAs, 1986-91.

Awards: International Associated Corps of Administrators, award, 1983; *Crain's Chicago Business,* Chicago's 100 Most Influential Women, 2004.

Addresses: *Office*— John Marshall Law School, 315 S Plymouth Court, Chicago, IL, 60604.

were given as the reasons why she was chosen for the position of Dean at the John Marshall Law School. But in an interview for the *Chicago Law Bulletin* her predecessor in the post, Dean Robert Gilbert Johnston also pointed to her personality. Mell is known as a friendly and outgoing person who is also ambitious and imaginative. She took over the post at a time when the John Marshall Law School was struggling with falling bar passage rates and other structural problems, and

her appointment can be seen as an attempt to revitalize the school with a fresh approach. Her specialties also fit well with the school's traditional strengths, including its annual hosting of an international moot court competition in information technology and privacy law, both of which are among Mell's interests. She is especially interested in the implications for privacy raised by the growth of e-commerce.

Mell's vision for the school is to widen its reach, connecting with people outside the core legal profession, delivering courses to business people, government workers, and others for whom legal concerns have become increasingly important. She said in her convocation speech that she also intended to open up the law school to students from a wider range of backgrounds than before. The location of the school in Chicago's business and legal district gives its students a close relationship with potential employers and this is something Mell hopes to exploit, refashioning John Marshall as an archetype for urban law schools by strengthening its links with the wider community, businesses, and other organizations. Mell's own career has been defined by her willingness to adapt to new situations and new opportunities and this is an attribute she hopes to bring to the position as Dean, but she has also shown steely determination in order to reach such a position of influence in a profession dominated by white men. She said at her convocation: "We will not let the pursuit of popularity or the inconsistencies of fashion deter us from doing the right thing, from crafting a future for our law school that continues to set us apart from the ordinary and the mundane." Though generally considered a good "second tier" law school, Mell has said that her goal is to lift it into the top ten.

In 2004 Mell was recognized as one of Chicago's 100 most influential women, but she acknowledged that she has not succeeded alone and listed as one of her greatest inspirations the black female Judge Jean Murrell Capers, for whom Mell campaigned as a member of the "Capers for Judge" committee from 1980 to 1986. Capers eventually became the first black woman to serve as assistant county prosecutor in Cuyahoga County, Cleveland. Like Capers, who received many honors for her public service, Mell has also put a great deal of effort into helping others achieve their goals. She was a member of the Alliance of Black Women in Cleveland in the mid-1980s and has been politically active throughout her adult life. She served as chair of the black law student committee of the Young Black Democrats organization from 1982 to 1984 and has consistently represented the interests of black and minority students throughout her career.

Mell's appointment as Dean at John Marshall made her the only black female head of a law school with predominantly white students. This achievement comes after twenty years working in higher education at faculty and administrative level, as well as in private law firms. Since the late 1990s Mell has developed an interest in computers, privacy law, and the law of artistic rights, but her main areas of interest remain commerce, corporations, consumer, and white-collar criminal law. Her recreational interests involve opera and fine art, and she volunteered as a docent at the Detroit Institute of Art.

Sources

Periodicals

Black Issues in Higher Education, December 4, 2003.
Chicago Law Bulletin, March 13, 2003.
Jet, November 10, 2003.
The Plain Dealer (Cleveland, OH), October 30, 2003 p. F2.

On-line

"JMLS News and Events: John Marshall Readies Itself as 21Century Urban law School," *John Marshall Law School,* www.jmls.edu/finditem.cfm?itemid=1920 (December 29, 2004).
"JMLS Faculty—Patricia Mell," *John Marshall Law School*, www.jmls.edu/finditem.cfm?itemid=1916 (December 21, 2004).
"Patricia Mell," *Biography Resource Center*, www.galenet.com/servlet/BioRC (December 21, 2004).

—Chris Routledge

Barbara C. Moore

1949—

University administrator, international sorority administrator

In 2002 Barbara C. Moore became, by unanimous vote, the 22nd international president, or Grand Basileus, of Zeta Phi Beta Sorority, a black Greek letter organization with 750 chapters and 100,000 members located in the United States, Germany, and the Virgin Islands. In addition she is vice president of Institutional Advancement at Benedict College in Columbia, South Carolina, and has been an educator and advancement officer for more than 30 years. Moore received the Living the Legacy Award from the National Council of Negro Women and has been inducted into Zeta Phi Beta's South Carolina and Southeastern Regional Halls of Fame. Moore is a member of many organizations and sits on the board of the YWCA and the Richland County, South Carolina, National March of Dimes Foundation.

Moore was born on December 27, 1949, in Columbia, South Carolina. She was the youngest of three daughters of Wilhelmina and Albert Crockett. Moore grew up in a home filled with love, a sense of family, and a deep awareness of issues facing blacks. As a teenager during the 1960s she experienced the forced integration of public schools, an experience that exposed her to the many disparities that existed between African-American communities. "I had a family who was concerned with what was going on and they talked about it to me," Moore said in an interview with *Contemporary Black Biography* (*CBB*). "They were cognizant of what was happening relative to our civil rights."

Influenced by Church and Family

Moore's father passed away when she was 13 years old, leaving Wilhelmina to raise her youngest child alone. Attributing her own sense of values to her mother, Moore says, "I watched her never giving up. She encouraged me to strive and encouraged my spirituality." In addition Moore credits her church community for providing leadership skills. She recalls the summer revivals, a tradition in southern Baptist churches, as a special homecoming event that served as a sort of family reunion and training ground. "I watched my aunts and the women of the church during a time when women were not in the forefront. Often they were the Sunday school teachers and the fundraisers. At the time we didn't think of them as fundraisers. To us they simply brought the pies and planned the Christmas and Easter programs. It was in the church that young African Americans learned patience, obedience, and respect for authority," Moore told *CBB*. Moore's grandmother, with her soft-spoken, low-key manner, was assistant superintendent of the Sunday school. Although it was an unusual role for a woman at that time, she was an effective leader who inspired Moore. Watching her, Moore said, "I never had to doubt that I too could do things."

Moore feels that the influence of family in a child's life is a key factor in their growth and well-being. "Children today don't understand that having a sense of family strengthens you and gives you a sense of belonging,"

At a Glance . . .

Born Barbara C. Moore on December 27, 1949, in Columbia, SC; married Norman Moore, 1971; children: Walletta. *Education:* Benedict College, BS, biology, 1971; University of Chicago, MS, education, 1986. *Religion:* Baptist.

Career: Benedict College, Columbia, SC, admissions counselor, recruiter, director of alumni affairs, and vice president of institutional advancement, 1975–; Zeta Phi Beta Sorority, Washington, DC, international president, 2002–.

Selected memberships: National Association of Female Executives; Council for the Advancement and Support of Education; National Council of Negro Women; Midlands YWCA, board member; Richland National March of Dimes Foundation, board member.

Selected awards: National Council of Negro Women, Living the Legacy Award, 1983; Zeta Phi Beta Southeastern Region, Hall of Fame, 2000.

Addresses: *Office*—Zeta Phi Beta Sorority, Inc., 1734 New Hampshire Avenue NW, Washington, DC 20009.

Moore told *CBB.* "I never questioned where I belonged and I knew I was loved. In most cases a child can't tell you why they know someone loves them. But when they are going to school they can tell you when they feel unloved."

Moore graduated from high school in 1968 and began undergraduate studies at Benedict College with plans to become a biologist or medical technologist, but her interests changed while working on a local television show called *Job Man Caravan.* Because of limited employment opportunities, the show was of particular value to African Americans: it offered them a means to seek and apply for jobs around the state. At the station Moore came to realize her strengths, particularly her ability to communicate. The experience motivated her to consider other career possibilities. For this reason Moore said that students should place an emphasis on communications, regardless of their major. "You'll find out that your ability to articulate can make a difference," said Moore.

Found Career and Civil Rights Movement

Upon college graduation in 1971 Moore found it difficult to get accepted into the medical technology certification program. After marrying a local businessman, Norman Moore, she focused her efforts on helping her husband with their dry cleaning business. Learning to operate her husband's family business allowed Moore to get to know the community, and she began to get more involved in the civil rights movement. "My in-laws had been in the dry cleaning business for decades," Moore told *CBB.* "They knew the people of our community and were very active in the movement."

Although still supportive of the family business, in 1975 Moore decided to embark on a career of her own and applied for a position as an admissions counselor and recruiter at Benedict College. When they called one year later for a second interview Moore was hired. Her work required extensive travel and there were few female recruiters on the road at the time. Moore accepted the position as a challenge and, she said, "I decided I would survive." In fact, she excelled at the job, and a year later Moore moved into another male-dominated department, the office of development, as director of alumni affairs. Development work involves a great deal of fundraising; during this time Moore conducted a successful citywide campaign for the United Negro College Fund.

As a strategic career move Moore spent a year in New Hampshire at Dartmouth College as an intern learning to become a development officer. Her work was supported by a program called CASE (for Council for the Advancement in Support of Education), funded by the Ford Foundation. "I took a big chance going there," Moore said. "I had a three-year-old child whom I left with my family." Despite the difficulties, taking advantage of this opportunity paid off, for Moore was soon promoted to vice president for institutional advancement at Benedict. This position gives Moore oversight of several departments including the offices of alumni affairs, public relations, church relations, corporate and foundation support, government affairs/grants and contracts, and Title III. As such she is in charge of generating funding for the institution and responsible for media and public relations activities.

Encouraged by Educators and a Vision

Inspired by the community service activities of Zeta Phi Beta and especially impressed with the work of Dr. Annie Hanberry, a Benedict College graduate, retired high school principal, and sorority member, Moore joined the local graduate chapter in 1976. Although Moore had no thoughts of seeking an officer position, she was urged on by others in the organization. "Sometimes leaders are encouraged to assume roles that maybe they did not initially set out to do," she told *CBB.* "I was encouraged by Dr. Hanberry and Dr. Eunice Thomas. Somehow they saw something I did not see in myself." With their support Moore became South Carolina state director for Zeta Phi Beta.

Moore's accomplishments and hard work with the organization led her to its top office in 2002. Moore told *CBB* that the path to the president's office requires an "understanding and desire to improve conditions in the African-American community. It allows you to have a vision of what you would want to see happen." Moore also works to raise the visibility of the sorority's accomplishments. "We have done excellent work throughout the years with little recognition," Moore said.

"In many instances black Greek letter organizations have been front runners in efforts to improve our communities, but have not gotten that story out," Moore told *CBB*. "Black Greek letter organizations were formed by college educated men and women during the early 1900s at a time when it was a privilege to be educated. They should have been the front-runners; they should have led a fight in everything you could think about as it relates to the betterment of our communities. They had an obligation."

Started Sorority Service Initiatives

Moore started Z-HOPE (Zetas Helping Other People Excel) because of her belief that blacks must give back to help others excel. Z-HOPE, which Zeta Phi Beta has expanded into Africa, was developed to "enhance, cultivate and empower" participants in the community to develop healthier lifestyles through a multi-dimensional outreach program. With a holistic approach, it seeks to improve the "spirit, body, and mind of women, youth, seniors, men, and international women of color." In reviewing reports like "The State of Black America," an annual report on the progress and plight of African Americans, and "Healthy People 2010," a national report on health objectives issued by the federal government, the sorority found that there is still plenty of work to be done to eliminate inequities in the black community. "We continue to experience more preventable diseases then anyone else," Moore said. "You can't do anything without good health."

Zeta Phi Beta selected ten health indicators from the reports that would receive their focus: physical activity, substance abuse, obesity, responsible sexual behavior, tobacco use, mental health, immunization, environmental quality, injury and violence, and access to health care. "These are important areas we need to work on," Moore told *CBB*. "We need to develop programs that will create an awareness of these matters. For instance, we can teach our children to eat better. It needs to start in the home. We need to talk to the community about depression. Or if you are allowing someone to beat you then you are probably ruining your life." In response to these issues the sorority has developed a program to deal with domestic violence called Love Should Not Hurt. In support of Z-HOPE, local chapters invite healthcare professionals to speak to groups about the issues. Sorors are assessed and awarded for their efforts.

The Zetas Organizational Leadership Program (ZOL) was implemented by Moore as a means to develop and train strong leaders in the organization. "It has a certification component for national officers and its goal is to empowers women of color to help themselves and their communities," Moore told *CBB*. "Zeta plans to take this program abroad."

In addition, Moore encourages local chapters to continue to form coalitions with other organizations to attain common goals. Zeta Phi Beta teams with the March of Dimes to promote better prenatal care for mothers through the Stork's Nest program and through various fundraising activities. Local chapters work with social service agencies to supply mothers and their newborns with layettes and much needed items. The sorority also partners with the American Red Cross, the National Cancer Society, and many other sororities and black churches to expand its outreach. Moore is also seeing the organization through a $2 million renovation of its national headquarters in Washington, DC. Next she would like to see the sorority build a women's health and prenatal care clinic in Africa.

Moore is passionate about her work to improve the health and living standards of blacks and told *CBB*: "I have a real desire to make a difference. That is why I built an evaluation piece into the program. I don't want to be someone who says that my chapters have done something. I want to be able to prove that they've done it."

To enlighten young black women today about the true purpose of black sororities, Moore said, "They should understand that joining a black sorority means making a life-long commitment to serving one's community. It is not about anything other than that. It's about strengthening our commitment and keeping the right perspective. Stay focused on what you desire to be in life and be good at it."

Sources

Periodicals

For Your Information (Washington, DC), November 15, 2004, p.1.
The Louisville Scene (Louisville, KY), November 15, 2004, p. 1.

On-line

"Benedict College Vice-President Elected as Zeta's New Leader," *Black Greek Network,* www.black-greeknetwork.com/site/newsletter/zetanews_aug02.htm (November 13, 2004).
"Division of Institutional Advancement," *Benedict College,* www.benedict.edu/divisions/insadv/title3/bc-title3.html (November 20, 2004).

"National Social Action Committee," *Zeta Phi Beta Sorority, Inc.,* www.zphib1920.org/socialaction/index.shtml (November 18, 2004).

Other

Additional information for this profile was obtained through an interview with Barbara C. Moore on November 24, 2004.

—Sharon Melson Fletcher

Marilyn Murrell

1947—

Mayor

For Marilyn Murrell, the tiny Oklahoma town of Arcadia has always been a big enough world to live in. Born and raised in Arcadia, Murrell has never lived away from her hometown for more than a few years. However, within her tightly woven community of family and friends, she has created a groundbreaking career of public service. When it appeared that Arcadia might be absorbed into the boundaries of a neighboring city, Murrell led the fight to preserve the town's identity. As the first mayor of the reestablished town of Arcadia, she has continued to work to keep Arcadia a vibrant, energetic, and safe place to live. Though her business and organizing skills could easily qualify her for a job in any big city, Murrell has chosen to remain in the town she loves and to focus on preserving a culture and a way of life that has become increasingly rare in the modern world.

Raised in Large Family

Born in the fall of 1947 at her parents' Arcadia home with the aid of a midwife, Sylvia Marilyn Parks was the eighth of nine children. Her father Ebbie Parks was an entrepreneur; throughout his career her owned and operated nightclubs, restaurants, and dry cleaning shops, as well as serving on the school board and participating in the community life of Arcadia. Her mother Inez Parks kept busy running the household and caring for her large family. She was also very involved in the school activities of their children, serving as PTA president, home room mother and chaperone for athletic teams and school events.

Young Parks was an introverted child who loved staying at home with her mother learning to garden and cook, reading books, or riding horses in the country lanes. Her playmates were her sisters and brothers or nearby neighbor children. Weekends often found the Parks family piled in the car for an educational day trip to a nearby state park or a visit to members of their large extended family.

When it was time to go to school, Parks was reluctant to leave her mother's side to enter the unfamiliar world of teachers and classes. With so many siblings going through school before her, she felt a great deal of pressure to do well, and she did, graduating from high school when she was only sixteen.

Parents Encouraged Learning

Ebbie Parks encouraged learning among his children. Besides the family trips to interesting sites, he led mealtime discussions of current events and expected his children to read the newspapers and keep themselves informed. He also expected them to excel in school and go on to college. When Ebbie and Inez Parks were in school, Arcadia's black school offered classes only through the eleventh grade. Therefore, the Parks, like many other African-American Arcadians, never completed their last year of high school. Perhaps because of this, both worked hard to provide higher education for of their nine children.

Marilyn Parks attended Central State College, now called the University of Central Oklahoma. The college

At a Glance . . .

Born Sylvia Marilyn Parks on September 7, 1947, in Arcadia, Oklahoma; married Alfred Murrell, October 12, 1965 (divorced); children: Monica, Alfred "Buzz," Cypreanna. *Religion:* African Methodist Episcopal Church.

Career: Oklahoma City Minority Business Development Center, project manager, assistant director, and executive director, 1975-94; Oklahoma Department of Transportation, special project director, 1988; Oklahoma Minority Supplier Development Council, program administrator, 1988-90; M and M Business Consultants , Inc., president & chief executive officer, 1988–; Town of Arcadia, Oklahoma, mayor, 1988–; Oklahoma City Northeast, Inc., independent consultant, 1991-93; Oklahoma Consortium for Minority Business Development, Inc., chairman, 1991–.

Selected memberships: National Association for the Advancement of Colored People; National Conference of Black Mayors Inc., president, 2002-3; National Small Town Alliance; Oklahoma Conference of Black Mayors, Inc., secretary, 1988-2003; Women's Foundation of Oklahoma.

Addresses: *Office*—P.O. Box 268, Arcadia, OK 73007.

was close enough that she could live at home, and she planned to major in English. However, in 1965, during the fall of her sophomore year, she married fellow student and basketball star Alfred Murrell. Alfred completed his senior year in 1969 and was offered a job playing basketball in the minor league Continental Basketball Association. The Murrells moved to Wilkes-Barre, Pennsylvania, where Alfred's team was located. Alfred's career with the CBA later took them to Scranton, Pennsylvania.

However, after less than three years, they returned to live in Arcadia, where Murrell was happy to raise her family in her own hometown. She began to develop her business skills by working in some of her father's businesses and as an office manager of a construction company. In 1975 she went to work in nearby Oklahoma City at the Minority Business Development Center, working to help independent businesspeople run successful businesses.

Marilyn Murrell did not have great ambitions. She was happy with her small-town life, her family, and her

work in the business community of central Oklahoma. However, during the mid-1980s something happened that changed the course of her career. The nearby city of Edmond was growing larger and decided as part of its growth to annex Arcadia into its borders.

Understood Oklahoma's Rich History

When this annexation was suggested, the town of Arcadia had a population of about 300 people. Many had lived in Arcadia for several generations, stretching back well over a hundred years in the town's history. Arcadia was a largely black town, with African Americans making up approximately 75 percent of the population. Around ten percent of the town's residents were Native American, and about fifteen percent were the descendents of European settlers.

This African-American majority was not unusual in the state of Oklahoma, where many black settlers made their home during the 1800s. Some came as slaves of the Cherokee people who were forced to leave their homes in the southeastern United States in 1938. In 1939, after a march so difficult it was dubbed the "Trail of Tears," they arrived in Oklahoma, where the Cherokee and the blacks made their homes alongside white European settlers.

Other black settlers came to Oklahoma as soldiers, many of whom had joined the army to help the Union defeat the Confederate States during the Civil War. These soldiers often remained in the army, serving on the western frontier of the United States from 1873 until 1903. Native Americans nicknamed these black servicemen "buffalo soldiers," a term used perhaps because the soldiers' dark skin and wooly hair resembled the coat of the great bison of the plains.

By 1907 so many African-American soldiers, farmers, and cowhands had settled in Oklahoma that they outnumbered both the Native Americans and the settlers of European origin. There were more all-black towns in the state of Oklahoma than in the other states combined. Though many of these early black towns no longer exist, several well-known towns still remain, including Langston, Boley, Taft, Meridian, and Arcadia.

The racially mixed population of Arcadia had lived in relative harmony for many years, even during the severe racial segregation of the 1950s. Though blacks and whites attended different schools then, when integration became the law the schools simply merged without hostility or resistance. Many of the families themselves have merged, and Arcadia became home to many interracial families.

Fought to Preserve Town's Identity

When Murrell heard about the city of Edmond's plans to annex her hometown, she was prompted to take action. Rather than see her town lose its identity, she organized a campaign to gather signatures for a petition against the annexation. A citizens' group called Arcadians Against Annexation elected her as spokesperson. Though some thought of seeking help from national groups like the NAACP, Murrell felt it was important that the work to save the town be done by the townspeople themselves. The Arcadians collected 2,000 signatures, twice as many as they needed to stop the annexation. They had taken their case into the city of Edmond, gathering signatures from citizens there who admired the town's energy and enthusiasm.

Once annexation was defeated, Murrell and other Arcadians spent the next four years in legal battles to reestablish the town's official identity. With the help of several lawyers who donated their labor, they set about to prove that Arcadia had been considered a town for at least twenty-five years. They gathered documents, from birth certificates and military papers to state road maps, which named the town of Arcadia. Finally, they proved their case to Governor Henry Bellmon, and in 1988 he signed an order making Arcadia the first Oklahoma town to exist by executive order.

Even then, the work of reestablishing the town of Arcadia had just begun. Towns need administrative officers, fire and police departments, and civic centers. One of the first official acts of the new town of Arcadia was to elect Marilyn Murrell mayor, an office she has held since 1988. Mayor Murrell set to work immediately to organize the town's support systems. Within a few years, Arcadia had a full-time paid police department with 15 reserve officers, a volunteer fire department, and a city hall, sold to the town for $500 by the local chapter of an international service and social group called the Oddfellows. In order to accomplish all this, Murrell set goals, sought grants to raise money, and promoted citizen responsibility, such as a volunteer maintenance department and beautification committee.

Though Murrell has continued to work as a consultant to small businesses, she took her duties as mayor very seriously, often working up to 80 hours a week. In an effort to learn more about local governance, she completed The Program for Senior Executives in State and Local Government at Harvard University in July 2001. She has also taken a national role as part of the National Conference of Black Mayors, where she became the second woman president in 2002. In 1999 she made international connections as part of a U.S. Conference of Mayors delegation to West Africa. Welcomed like a returning sister by mayors and other citizens of African cities and towns in Senegal, Ivory Coast, and Ghana, Murrell learned more about just how far the borders of a small town can reach.

Sources

On-line

"Heritage Step-on Guide: Marilyn Murrell," *Oklahoma Native America*, http://66.102.7.104/search?q=cache:H4O5fAGxAcQJ:www.travelok.com/travelProf/step_on_guides.asp++mayor+Arcadia+oklahoma&hl=en (November 1, 2004).

"Marilyn Murrell Shows Saavy Style At National Mayors' Conference," *African American News and Issues*, www.aframnews.com/html/2003-05-07/lead3.htm (November 1, 2004).

"Oklahoma's History," *A Look at Oklahoma*, www.otrd.state.ok.us/StudentGuide/history.html (November 1, 2004).

Other

Information for this profile was obtained through an interview with Marilyn Murrell on November 9, 2004.

—Tina Gianoulis

Barack Obama

1961—

Politician, attorney

Obama, Barack, photograph. AP/Wide World Photos. Reproduced by permission.

Elected to represent Illinois in the United States Senate in November of 2004, Barack Obama had already become the subject of speculation as to his future on the national political stage. The speculation had grown exponentially in August of that year, when Obama delivered an electrifying keynote address at the Democratic National Convention in Boston. In that speech, Obama used the language of patriotism to frame an appeal to Americans to transcend their divisions. "There's not a black America and white America and Latino America and Asian America; there's the United States of America."

Indeed, Barack Obama's story resonated with the durable narrative of the American melting pot. "Barack is the American dream," Democratic National Committee chairman Terry McAuliffe told *Ebony*. Obama himself in his convention speech said that "in no other country on earth is my story even possible." Obama was born on August 4, 1961, in Honolulu, Hawaii. He was named after his father Barack, a Kenyan exchange student; the name is an African one and means "blessing" in his father's native Swahili. Obama's mother Ann was a white American born in Kansas who had moved to Honolulu with her parents.

Obama's family unit dissolved when he was two, as his father won a scholarship to Harvard that wasn't large enough to support the whole family and went to Massachusetts alone. After finishing his degree, the elder Obama went home to Kenya and took a job as an economic planner for the country's government. He continued to write letters to his son, and visited him once when he was ten, but his marriage to Obama's mother ended. She married an Indonesian oil company executive, and Obama lived in Indonesia between the ages of six and ten. His half-sister Maya Soetoro-Ng was born in Indonesia and later moved to Honolulu.

Conflicted Identities in Honolulu

Sent back to Hawaii to live with his mother's parents in a small Honolulu apartment, Obama had a tough adolescence. Considered black by the world of which he was learning to be a part, he was nevertheless shaped most directly by the values of his small-town, white, Midwestern-grown immediate family. Later, when he was running for the Senate in the farm belt of

At a Glance . . .

Born on August 4, 1961, in Honolulu, HI; son of Barack Obama, a Kenyan government economist; raised by mother, a Kansas native; lived with mother in Indonesia as child; raised as teenager in Honolulu by maternal grandparents; married Michelle; children: Malia Ann and Natasha. *Education:* Columbia University, 1983; Harvard Law School, law degree, *magna cum laude*, 1991. *Religion:* United Church of Christ.

Career: Community organizer, Chicago, 1983-86; civil rights attorney, Chicago, 1991-96; University of Chicago, lecturer, early 1990s-2004; Illinois State Senator, 1996-2005; U.S. Senator, 2005–.

Selected awards: Presidency of *Harvard Law Review*, 1990.

Addresses: *Office*—U.S. Senate Office Buildings, Washington, DC 20515.

downstate Illinois, he found that this Midwestern background worked to his advantage. "I know these people," he told the *New Yorker*, referring to downstate voters. "The food they serve is the food my grandparents served when I was growing up. Their manners, their sensibility, their sense of right and wrong—it's all totally familiar to me."

As a teenager, though, Obama was a young man with a confused identity. He experimented with marijuana and cocaine, and though he had inherited a quick-study intelligence from his father and won admission to the top-flight Punahou School, his grades were inconsistent and his commitment to bodysurfing and basketball was bigger than his interest in school. One of seven or eight black students at Punahou, he found that whites had low expectations when they met him. "People were satisfied so long as you were courteous and smiled and made no sudden moves," he wrote in his 1995 memoir, *Dreams of My Father.* "Such a pleasant surprise to find a well-mannered young black man who didn't seem angry."

Inside, Obama was worried about fitting in and was on the way to developing a classic example of W.E.B. DuBois's double consciousness. "I learned to slip back and forth between my black and white worlds," he wrote, "convinced that with a bit of translation on my part the two worlds would eventually cohere." Despite these feelings, Obama's innate charisma began to show itself as he left the Punahou campus to flirt with

college-aged women at the nearby University of Hawaii.

That coherence was still hard to find at New York's Columbia University, where Obama transferred as a third-year student. Obama enjoyed New York but found that racial tension infected even "the stalls of Columbia's bathrooms ...," he wrote, "where, no matter how many times the administration tried to paint them over, the walls remained scratched with blunt correspondence between niggers and kikes. It was as if all middle ground had collapsed."

Wrote Letters to Community Organizations

After earning his degree in 1983, however, Obama responded with activist commitment instead of hedonistic escapism. He wrote to community service organizations all over the United States asking what he could do to help, and he signed on with the one group that replied, a church-based Chicago group doing neighborhood work on the city's economically reeling South Side. For three years, Obama was a community organizer—a tough job, but one in which he notched accomplishments ranging from job-training programs to a successful attempt to improve city services at the Altgeld Gardens housing project. The biracial outsider gathered with black Chicagoans at a South Side barbershop that he continued to patronize even after he became famous.

Obama applied to Harvard Law School—"to learn power's currency," he wrote in his autobiography. His academic brilliance flowered fully and propelled him to the presidency of the prestigious *Harvard Law Review* in 1990, making him the first African American to hold the post, and to a *magna cum laude* graduation in 1991. One of his teachers was famed litigator Laurence Tribe, who told *Time* that "I've known Senators, Presidents. I've never known anyone with what seems to me more raw political talent." Back in Chicago for a summer internship, he met his wife Michelle, an attorney and South Side native who was assigned to supervise him. The couple has two daughters, Malia Ann and Natasha (Sasha).

Obama passed up job offers from Chicago's top law firms to practice civil rights law with a small public-interest law office and to lecture at the University of Chicago, holding the latter position until he ran for the U.S. Senate in 2004. He jumped into politics by chairing a voter-registration drive that helped carry Illinois for Democratic presidential candidate Bill Clinton in 1992, and his political ambitions became clearer when he turned down a chance to apply for a tenure-rack University of Chicago professorship. When an Illinois state senate seat in his home South Side district came open in 1996, he ran and was elected. In the Illinois senate Obama was noted for legislation to curb racial profiling and for a bill that mandated the video-taping of police interrogations carried out in death-penalty cases.

Despite his varied background, Obama identified himself as black. "When I'm catching a cab in Manhattan they don't say, there's a mixed-race guy, I'll go pick him up," he pointed out to *Ebony* writer Joy Bennett Kinnon. "Or if I was an armed robber and they flashed my face on television, they'd have no problem labeling me as a black man. So if that's my identity when something bad happens, then that's my identity when something good happens as well." But when Obama ran for the U.S. House of Representatives in the 2000 Democratic primary against entrenched South-Side congressman Bobby Rush, a former Black Panther, he suffered from a perception that he was an exotic, elite outsider and was trounced by a two-to-one margin.

Triumphed in Crowded Primary

South Side residents (including Rush) rallied around Obama during his next try for higher office, however. Obama jumped into a primary race that pitted him against two formidable opponents (and several others): longtime Chicago politician Dan Hynes, who was favored by the city's vaunted Democratic Party "machine" political organization, and businessman Blair Hull, who spent a $29 million personal war chest on the campaign. Obama put together an unusual coalition of blacks, "lakefront liberal" white Chicago voters, and downstate supporters to win the primary with a convincing outright majority of 53 percent. His victory was partly attributable to a fervent corps of volunteers who worked on his campaign, many inspired by Obama's early and unequivocal opposition to the Iraq war and by other unrepentant liberal positions. "People call it drinking the juice," Obama political director Dan Sherman explained to the *New Yorker.* "People start drinking the Obama juice. You can't find enough for them to do."

Then came Obama's Democratic National Convention speech, which *Time* called "one of the best in convention history." The speech really put Obama on the national political radar, and the phone in his South Side home rang nonstop with interview requests in the days after the convention. "I didn't realize that the speech would strike the chord that it did," Obama told *Ebony.* "I think part of it is that people are hungry for a sense of authenticity. All I was really trying to do was describe what I was hearing on the campaign trail, the stories of the hopes, fears, and struggles of what ordinary people are going through every day."

On the campaign trail Obama shone as he showed an ability to connect with voters across class, racial, and geographic lines. "I just never heard anybody speak like him before," a downstate Democrat told the *New Yorker.* "It's like he's talking to you, and not to a crowd." One reason Illinois voters reacted to Obama this way was that the candidate, in meeting individual voters one on one, drew effectively on the various dialects of English he had absorbed as a result of his diverse background. Working-class black Chicagoans, highly educated professionals and academics, and small-town business owners all felt that they had encountered one of their own when Obama gave a speech in their neighborhoods.

The Illinois Republican party floundered as its anointed candidate, Jack Ryan, struggled with allegations that he had forced his ex-wife, television actress Jeri Ryan, to visit sex clubs with him against her will. Ryan eventually dropped out of the race and was replace by Alan Keyes, an ultraconservative black radio commentator from Maryland who had previously criticized New York Senator Hillary Clinton for moving to that state solely for the purpose of running for the Senate. Obama won in a landslide, garnering seventy percent of the vote and spending much of his time in the final phases of the campaign stumping for Democratic candidates in neighboring states.

Beginning with the Democratic convention speech, talk began to swirl around Obama suggesting that those who had heard him speak at this early stage in his career had been looking at the man who would become the first African-American president of the U.S. Obama contributed nothing to such speculation, and many of his early statements regarding his intentions for his Senate term focused on the problem of Illinois's declining job base. Yet few could doubt that the state that had produced Abraham Lincoln was now home to another figure able to exert a powerful healing force to the nation's still-gaping racial wounds.

Sources

Books

Obama, Barack, *Dreams of My Father: A Story of Race and Inheritance* (1995), reprinted Three Rivers Press, 2004.

Periodicals

Black Enterprise, October 2004, p. 88.
Ebony, November 2004, p. 196.
New Yorker, May 31, 2004, p. 32.
Time, November 15, 2004, p. 74.
U.S. News & World Report, August 2, 2004, p. 25.

—James M. Manheim

Vivian Pinn

1941—

Medical doctor, administrator, pathologist

From a very young age, Vivian Pinn felt herself to be a person with a mission. Having seen pain and illness in the family members she loved, she developed a drive to ease suffering and to cure disease. At the age of four, she announced her intention to become a doctor, an almost unheard-of ambition for a black girl in the United States of the 1940s. By the time she reached college, her mission had broadened. Pinn not only wanted to treat the ill, but to make sure that all patients were taken seriously and treated with respect by those entrusted with their health care. Throughout her career, whether as a doctor, a teacher, or the director of an office of a major government agency, she has remained true to the goals she set in her youth and added another: to help and encourage other young African Americans and women to pursue careers in medicine.

Pinn was born in Halifax County, Virginia, close to the North Carolina border. Her mother, Francena Evans, was a high school home economics teacher, and her father, Carl Francis Pinn, taught physical education. They had met and fallen in love while teaching at the same Halifax County school. However, school rules did not allow married couples to teach at the same school, so Carl Pinn took a job in his hometown, Lynchburg, about 50 miles away. Young Vivian's childhood was divided between her parents' home in Lynchburg and her grandparents' farm in rural Halifax County.

Growing up in this warm extended family, she developed close relationships with her parents and grandparents. Her grandfather had cancer, and her grandmother had diabetes, and these diseases became a part

of young Vivian's childhood experience. Her father showed her how to help care for her grandparents, even teaching her to give injections of medication and insulin. From these early experiences with disease and the death of her grandfather, Pinn developed an interest in science and the desire to help the sick. Her family's support and belief in education gave her the assurance that she could achieve her goals.

Education had become a tradition in the Pinn family. Unlike many African Americans of the time, both of Vivian Pinn's parents had graduated from college, and even one of her grandfathers had completed his studies at Hampton Institute in 1901. Her family also included another side of the black American experience: her other grandfather had quit school in seventh grade to support his brothers and sisters by working as a carpenter. Pinn learned to value both of her grandfathers' achievements as the products of hard work and dedication. Her chosen career would require both manual skill and academic excellence.

When Pinn announced to her family at the age of four that she wanted to become a pediatrician, or children's doctor, her parents did not point out that there were very few black women doctors. They merely told her that she would have to work hard in school to become a doctor.

Pinn did work hard in school. After graduating from Lynchburg's Dunbar High School in 1958 as valedictorian of her class, she attended Wellesley College in Massachusetts, one of the most distinguished women's colleges in the United States. One of only four black

At a Glance . . .

Born Vivian Winona Pinn on April 21, 1941, in Halifax County, Virginia; married Henry Wiggins, 198? (divorced). *Education:* Wellesley College, BA, zoology, 1963; University of Virginia School of Medicine, MD, 1967.

Career: Massachusetts General Hospital, research assistant, 1962-63; Tufts University School of Medicine, Boston, instructor in pathology, 1970-71; Tufts-New England Medical Center Hospital, assistant in pathology, 1970-71; Tufts University School of Medicine, assistant professor of pathology, 1971-82; Chelsea Soldier's Home, consultant in pathology, 1972-77; National Cooperative Study of Adult Nephrotic Syndrome and of Adult Glomerular Diseases, Central Pathology Laboratory, director, 1972-84; Tufts University School of Medicine, associate coordinator for Minority Student Affairs, 1972-82; Tufts University School of Medicine, assistant dean for Student Affairs, 1974-82; Boston Veteran's Administration Hospital, consultant in nephrology, 1976-77and 1978-79; Tufts-New England Medical Center Hospital, Pathologist, 1977-82; Howard University College of Medicine, Washington, DC, Department of Pathology, professor and chairman, 1982-91; Hadley Memorial Hospital, Washington, DC, chief of pathology, 1991; National Institutes of Health, Bethesda, Maryland, Office of Research on Women's Health, director, 1991–.

Selected memberships: National Medical Association, president, 1989-90; International Academy of Pathology, councilor, 1990-93; American Medical Association; American Medical Women's Association; Delta Sigma Theta Sorority.

Selected awards: Howard University College of Medicine, Women in Medicine, Woman of the Year Award, 1989; University of Virginia, Distinguished Alumna Award, 1992; Wellesley College, Alumni Achievement Award, 1993; Black Woman Hall of Fame Foundation, Chicago, Bethune Tubman Truth Award, 1990.

Addresses: *Office*—Office of Research on Women's Health, National Institutes of Health, Building 1, Room 201, Bethesda, MD 20892.

women in her class at Wellesley, Pinn had left the segregated South to come North, where she had to negotiate a less familiar series of racial lines and barriers. With so few African American students in her class, she grew to depend on the black Greek system for support. College fraternities and sororities are named for letters of the Greek alphabet, and so are sometimes called "Greek." The black Greek system is a national network of nine black fraternities and sororities, which provide friendship and support for African American students. Pinn joined Delta Sigma Theta and attended many social events with other African American college and university students in the region.

In 1960, Francena Pinn became seriously ill. Pinn took time away from her studies at Wellesley to care for her mother, who died that year from bone cancer. Pinn felt that her mother's doctor had been cold and unresponsive to her mother's complaints, diagnosing her pains as a problem with posture that could be corrected by wearing more supportive shoes. Pinn was convinced that the doctor had missed her mother's bone tumor because he had not paid close enough attention to the complaints of a black female patient. This painful experience only increased her determination to become the kind of doctor who would attend to all of her patients with thoroughness and kindness. Thirty-one years later, Pinn herself would survive the same kind of cancer that killed her mother, because a more careful doctor would discover her tumor much sooner.

Back at school in Massachusetts, Pinn took a summer job that would change the course of her career. Working as a research assistant with Dr. Benjamin Barnes at Boston's Massachusetts General Hospital, she began to learn about the field of immunopathology. Pathologists are doctors who study tissue, cells, and fluids from various parts of the body in order to find the cause of disease. Immunopathologists are particularly concerned with organ transplants, and what factors in the body make them successful or unsuccessful.

After her graduation from Wellesley in 1963, Pinn went south again to attend the University of Virginia School of Medicine. She was the only person of color and the only woman in her class and often felt isolated. During the summer, she returned to Massachusetts to continue her research training in immunopathology. After her graduation from medical school in 1967, she went to work and study with Dr. Martin Flax at Massachusetts General Hospital, learning about kidney disease and transplants.

When Flax got a job offer from nearby Tufts University in 1970, he asked Pinn to go with him to teach pathology. She agreed and began a new career as a teacher. Pinn welcomed the chance to encourage young students, especially minorities and women, to go into medical fields, "I don't think you're truly a good doctor or a good researcher if you don't reach back to help others coming along," she said. Whether as a doctor, a teacher, or a mentor, her career goals had always revolved around helping others.

Pinn taught pathology at Tufts until 1982 when she was offered a job at Howard University in Washington, D.C., one of the nation's most respected traditionally black colleges. Howard hired Pinn as professor and chair of the pathology department, where she continued to encourage and support young African Americans to seek careers in medicine.

In 1991, the director of the National Institutes of Health (NIH) contacted Pinn about an exciting new project. The NIH, part of the U.S. Department of Health and Human Services, is the nation's major center of medical research. Pinn was invited to be the first director of a new office of the NIH, the Office of Research on Women's Health. The new office was the first of its kind, established to ensure that women would be included in research studies about new medical techniques and therapies. Traditionally, issues of women's health had focused only on the reproductive organs and breast cancer. However, Pinn's new office began to research how a wide variety of health issues affect women in special ways. This included studies of what particular diseases women get and the ways treatment and diagnosis may differ between women and men. This work to uncover the specific ways disease and the medical system affect women was directly related to the promise Pinn had made to herself when her mother died. She would work to make sure that all people had responsive and thorough health care.

Pinn has also continued her work as a mentor. In her role as director of the Office of Research on Women's Health, she has focused on drawing girls and women to careers in scientific fields. In her personal life, she maintained close connections with many of her thousands of former students, who she considered part of her extended family.

Selected writings

"Heart Disease and Blacks," *Ebony* Magazine, February, 1990, p.176.
"Putting Women First," *The Journal of Minority Medical Students*, Fall 1994.
"The Status of Women's Health Research: Where are African American Women?" *The Journal of the National Black Nurses Association*, 1996, pp. 8-19.
"Women's Health Research for the Twenty-first Century," *Journal of Dental Education*, March 1999.
"Sex and Gender Factors in Medical Studies: Implications for Health and Clinical Practice," *Journal of the American Medical Association*, 2003, pp. 397-400.

Sources

Periodicals

Ebony, December 1989, pp. 126-27; April 1990, pp. 84-85.
Gender Medicine, 2004.
Richmond Times-Dispatch, February 2, 2004.

On-line

"High Standards Are a Plus," *Women Working 2000*, www.womenworking2000.com/feature/index.php?id=58 (November 15, 2004).

Other

Information for this profile was obtained through an interview with Vivian Pinn on December 8, 2004.

—Tina Gianoulis

Helen Gordon Quigless

1944-2004

Poet, librarian, community leader

Known as an energetic, imaginative individual, Helen Quigless's passion for writing poetry was equalled by her dedication to community projects, including the Partners in Art program, which provides guidance in the arts for disadvantaged children. She was a respected community leader in her home town of Tarboro, North Carolina, where her involvement in the Phoenix Historical Society of Edgecombe County helped develop the town as a major historical site. In her professional life as a librarian Quigless was no less driven. Despite struggling with rheumatoid arthritis and progressive blindness she was responsible for developing the library holdings at the University of the District of Columbia from its inception in 1974. Quigless is most widely known as a poet; her work appeared in several prestigious anthologies, including *Black Southern Voices* (1968) and *Today's Negro Voices* (1970).

Helen Gordon Quigless was born in Washington, D.C., on July 16, 1944, the daughter of Milton D. Quigless and Helen McAlpine Gordon Quigless. Quigless grew up with her brother Milton and her sister Carol in Tarboro, North Carolina. Her father was a noted physician and general surgeon; he was one of the first black doctors in Edgecombe County. In 1946 he opened a clinic on Main Street, in Tarboro, to provide medical care for blacks who were prevented from seeking treatment at "white" health centers and hospitals; he died in 1997. Her father's position in the community may well have inspired Quigless in her own community work. She attended Putney School in Putney, Vermont, before earning a bachelor's degree in English at Fisk University (1966); in 1969 she was awarded a master's degree in library and information science at Atlanta University. From the age of 19, she suffered with rheumatoid arthritis, a painful illness that left her blind and bedridden in the final months of her life.

Quigless began working at Federal City College, later to become part of the District of Columbia University, in 1968 and remained there until illness forced her retirement. She began as a media specialist, but was eventually responsible for developing the library and information holdings at the university. Despite her time-consuming and demanding job, Quigless also found time to write poetry. She was linked with the Black Arts Movement, a group of black writers, musicians, poets, and artists whose work provided cultural and intellectual weight to the civil rights movement. In 1967 her poetry appeared in *For Malcolm*, an anthology to commemorate civil rights leader Malcolm X, and for the next few years she could be listed alongside Marvin X, Etheridge Knight, and Gwendolyn Brooks, as one of those who provided a poetic voice for the black community. She published poems in two other anthologies, *The New Black Poetry* (1968), and *Today's Negro Voices* (1970), as well as the 1970 edition of *New Negro Poets*.

Quigless was well known as a poet for a relatively short period, but the direct approach she took in her poetry also made her a dedicated community leader in her home town of Tarboro. Struggling with illness, Quigless nevertheless worked hard on community projects, using her connections in the literary and art worlds in

At a Glance . . .

Born Helen Gordon Quigless on July 16, 1944, in Washington, DC; died on January 17, 2004. *Education:* Fisk University, BA, English, 1966; Atlanta University, MS, library and information science, 1969. *Religion:* Episcopalian.

Career: Poet, 1967-2004; Federal City College (now University of the District of Columbia), Washington, DC, media specialist and librarian, 1968-(?).

Memberships: Edgecombe County Cultural Arts Council; Edgecombe County NAACP; American Association of University Women; president of Phoenix Historical Society of Edgecombe County.

fundraising and publicity. She founded Partners in Art, an award for middle and high school students in Edgecombe County. The annual award, funded by a coalition of local businesses, is presented each spring. It provides access to art materials, and professional tuition, as well as allowing students to display their work for the public. Meade Horne, former executive director of Edgecombe ARTS, who worked with Quigless on the Partners in Art program, told *The Daily Southerner* that "She had a great spirit and great determination. I never met someone more determined in my life." Besides her involvement with Edgecombe County Cultural Arts Council, Quigless was also a leading light in Edgecombe County NAACP, and the American Association of University Women. She served as president of the Phoenix Historical Society of Edgecombe County, using her position to promote genealogical research in and around Tarboro, one of the United States' oldest towns. She was also influential in the development of Tarboro's historic district, which is one of the largest in the South-Eastern United States.

Quigless's life was overshadowed by the illness that finally took her life at the age of 59. Yet her dynamic personality, determination, and creativity brought her influence that went far beyond the small town where she was raised; as a poet she was part of a literary movement that helped define American literature in the late twentieth century. Yet it was for the culture, history, and the people of Tarboro that Quigless reserved her greatest dedication and effort. Sister Mary Ann Czaja told *The Daily Southerner* "Her creativity was the gift she gave to society."

Selected works

Poetry

Helen Gordon Quigless' poetry has been published in anthologies, including *For Malcolm: Poems on the Life and Death of Malcolm X*, Broadside Press, 1967; *The New Black Poetry*, International Publishers, 1968; *Today's Negro Voices: An Anthology by Young Negro Poets*, Messner, 1970; *New Negro Poets* (1970).

Sources

Periodicals

Jet, February 23, 2004.

On-line

"County at a Loss for Words," *The Daily Southerner*, http://dailysoutherner.com/articles/2004/01/20/news/news3.txt (November 22, 2004).

"Helen Gordon Quigless," *Biography Resource Center*, www.galenet.com/servlet/BioRC (November 18, 2004).

—Chris Routledge

Gregory Reeves

1952—

Non-profit executive, advocate

Gregory Reeves is the national president of Blacks in Government (BIG), a non-profit advocacy group dedicated to preserving and enhancing government employment for blacks. The organization was founded in 1975 by black federal employees of the Department of Health, Education, and Welfare in Rockville, Maryland, in order to respond to concerns regarding their employment, health, housing, and education. BIG now has 225 chapters in 11 regions throughout the United States. The organization advocates on behalf of 3 million blacks working for federal, state, county, and municipal agencies. Working with the combined strength of its members to confront issues, BIG has testified before the U.S. House of Representatives and met with White House officials on matters regarding employment opportunity, employee rights, and affirmative action. BIG operates by its founding principles: to promote equity in all aspects of American life, excellence in public service, and opportunity for all Americans.

Reeves has established himself as an important supporter for BIG's initiatives in education and training. In addition to developing leadership and training programs, Reeves has been instrumental in efforts to increase the number of local chapters and provide direction and support in technology and policy development.

Remembered Racism and Unsung Heroes

Reeves was born on November 21, 1952, in Marianna, Florida, to William and Eloise Reeves. Because William Reeves was in the air force, Reeves and his four siblings lived in many cities around the world. When Reeves was young his father was sent to Panama; he remembers well their ringside seat during the U.S.-led invasion of Cuba in 1961, the Bay of Pigs invasion. The Reeves family watched as Central America and the world reacted to events of the Cold War and, in 1963, to the assassination of U.S. President John F. Kennedy. "The events were very traumatic; they gave me a sense of my own history," Reeves told *Contemporary Black Biography* (*CBB*).

Reeves believes that life in the military gave his family access to opportunities and a perspective on the world that most African Americans never see. "Although discrimination and racism were alive and well in the military, the beauty of it was if you could stay focused on the fact that through everything, on the other side, with an education, you could win," he told *CBB*.

Reeves enjoyed life in Panama, but eventually the family left for Albuquerque, New Mexico, and in 1966 relocated to Marianna, Florida, where they stayed while his father completed a tour of service in Alaska. After living outside the country and in the American southwest, the level of racial intolerance Reeves experienced in the deep south surprised him.

By the time Reeves reached his teen years he had developed a comfort level meeting people from various backgrounds. Many young people raised in the military learn to negotiate the unknown world with ease and diplomacy. "It makes you more open-minded," said

At a Glance . . .

Born on November 21, 1952, in Marianna, Florida; married Roye Jacobs, 1974; children: Barry Brown. *Education:* Hampton Institute, BS, industrial education, 1974. *Military Service:* United States Army, 1971-73. *Religion:* Baptist.

Career: Brown & Root, Austin, TX, draftsman, 1974; Alcoa Aluminum, Austin, TX, intern/engineer, 1974-75; General Services Administration, Austin, TX, facilities engineer, 1975-78; Internal Revenue Service, Austin, TX, computer specialist, 1978-80; Department of Veterans Affairs, Austin, TX, chief of information systems, 1980–; Blacks in Government (BIG), Austin, TX, chapter president, regional council officer and vice president, national board of directors, 1990-94; BIG, national executive committee third vice president, 1994-98; BIG, national executive vice president, 2000-02; BIG, national president, 2002–.

Selected Memberships: 100 Black Men; NAACP; National Guard Association.

Address: *Office*—Blacks In Government, 3005 Georgia Avenue, NW, Washington, DC 20001-3807.

Reeves. Certain personality traits smoothed the transition: Reeves inherited an easygoing, affable nature from his parents. "When friends came to our home they were always welcome and my parents had an open-door policy. They taught us to be fair, to treat others as we wanted to be treated, and they taught us to believe in God. They are wonderful people," he told *CBB*. "My father is my hero."

Reeves observed other heroes at work in the Marianna area as tensions continued to rise during the years of forced integration of public schools. "The untold story" of this time, he told *CBB*, "is what happened to all the teachers and administrators who helped to prepare African-American children for integration as schools were closing. These are the people who lost their jobs after many years of making a difference, particularly for those who needed that extra help. These were the people who developed the best and brightest."

There were white heroes as well, as Reeves found when his family relocated to Edwards Air Force Base, California. "I remember a tap dance instructor at a recreation center near my home," Reeves recalled. "All her students were white. I used to watch as she taught

her class, and one day she invited me to join. I did for a while. She reached out to make a difference."

Discovered Technology and Career Path

In 1971 Reeves graduated from high school, joined the army, and entered Hampton Institute in Hampton, VA. Reeves graduated from college in 1974 and moved to Fort Hood, near Austin, Texas, to begin doing layout work for Brown & Root, a large construction company. His plan was to become an architect, but realizing a lackluster economy and little creative experience would inhibit his career, Reeves left there and started work for Alcoa Aluminum installing a voice activated monitoring system in 1974. There his career focus began to settle on information technology. Reeves left there in 1975 to work for the General Services Administration of the federal government, moving from there to the Internal Revenue Service in 1978, and the Veterans Administration in 1980, where he currently holds the position of chief of information systems at the Austin Automation Center.

Reeves has been employed in technological fields with the federal government for over 30 years, and says his career has benefited greatly due to ever-changing applications and the opportunity to learn and stay on the cutting edge of the industry.

Joined BIG

Reeves joined Blacks in Government (BIG) in 1982 and although he doesn't remember what his first elected position was, he is sure about one thing: he had found the right organization to voice his concerns. Since 1982 Reeves has held many elected positions within BIG, from the chapter level in Austin, to regional positions, to two terms as national executive vice president, and—after 2002—to national president.

"Our focus at BIG comes from our founders, who in 1975 determined they would form an organization with the vision of working in behalf of African Americans working for the federal government," Reeves related to *CBB*. "We speak for those who cannot speak for themselves, or assist in some way. What we do best is we advocate, often through our chapters."

BIG advocates for issues that face African Americans employees, such as the kind of legislation that will determine health benefits and measures that affects how agencies report on their hiring practices. BIG monitors various areas of achievement by federal agencies and addresses issues that relate to affirmative action goals as part of their compliance and review program. "I meet with agency and department heads to talk about their mission and goals and to find out what they are trying to achieve in terms of equal opportunity within the workplace and career development. We discuss where the government is going and what the agency is doing in terms of structure from a legislative perspective," Reeves told *CBB*.

"BIG helps eliminate the isolation an African American outside of Washington, D.C., can feel while pursuing senior management positions with the federal government," Reeves explained, citing his chance meeting of a senior executive at a federal agency. "I met him in 1989. He mentored me for the next ten years and would check on me from time to time. You need to develop those kinds of relationships to be successful."

Reeves described the variety of programs offered by BIG. "We do professional development and offer educational programs." Through the years Reeves has established partnerships with organizations like the NAACP, the Congressional Black Caucus, and the Urban League to achieve mutual goals on behalf of blacks. The Training in Communication Program (TIC), a component of BIG's youth program, partners with corporate sponsors to train young people for oratorical and technology competitions. The goal is to enhance communications skills and increase interest in information technology.

BIG is a major player in "Operation Big Vote," a national effort to inform citizens about the electoral process and their rights as voters, while stressing the importance of registering. To assist its members BIG offers *Winning Ways*, an employee development kit created to help members protect themselves against discrimination on the job. The kit offers audio tapes and fact sheets focused on increasing knowledge of rules affecting the workplace and stressing the value of individual achievement. BIG offers an Attorney Assistance program that makes referrals and gives grants to members seeking legal counsel on matters relating to their employment. BIG keeps its membership informed with three publications: *BIG Bulletin*, *BIG Reporter*, and *Daily Updates*. Reeves' office often responds to current issues of the day by press release.

Reeves sees major challenges on the horizon for BIG as it works on behalf of displaced workers. "With jobs being contracted out to private firms and the overall reform taking place in the government, the merging of departments now under Homeland Security and the reforming of the personnel system within the Department of Defense will affect a lot of people, pushing more authority to the supervisors in promotions and hiring practice," Reeves told CBB. "It's a huge issue."

Reeves' skill, diplomacy, and hard work are essential ingredients in his advocating for African-American workers' rights. Sharing insights he feels will aid the young people who will be the workers of tomorrow, Reeves told *CBB*, "Know who you are as a person and know your family roots. I see a lot of young people who are confused about these things. It's not related to race. Ask what contribution you can make on this earth, stay focused spiritually, define early what you want to do, and set goals." The formula has certainly worked for Reeves.

Sources

On-line

"Mr. Gregory Reeves," *Blacks in Government,* www.bignet.org/national/Gregg2003.htm (October 11, 2004).
Blacks in Government, www.bignet.org (October 15, 2004).

Other

Additional information for this profile was obtained through an interview with Gregory Reeves on October 6, 2004.

—Sharon Melson Fletcher

Hilda Richards

1936—

Educator, health care activist

Dr. Hilda Richards is immediate past president of the National Black Nurses Association (NBNA), an organization representing 150,000 nursing professionals across the United States. She is Chancellor Emeritus and Professor Emeritus of Indiana University Northwest in Gary, Indiana, and was the first dean of the College of Health and Human Services at Ohio University. In addition she is the first black academic dean and the first female academic dean in the school's history. Richards is a sought after advisor and lecturer, and is know for her generosity and persistence. This tireless educator has been a board member and advisor to many education and health organizations throughout her career and was the editor for the *Journal of the National Black Nurses Association,* a research publication for members of the NBNA. Richards retired in 2001 but remained active with organizations such as the Gary Education Development Foundation and the AIDS Foundation of Chicago, and worked with hospice care.

Hilda Richards was born in St. Joseph, Missouri, on February 7, 1936, to Rose Avalynne (Lynne) and Togar Ballard. Richards' parents separated when she was very young and because of family issues she spent her early years living between her father's home and the home of relatives in Hutchins, Kansas. As a child Richards had been told that her mother was deceased, but in 1942 Lynne purchased a new car and left her home in San Francisco en route to Chicago where young Hilda and Togar lived. On her way she stopped to purchase a motel near a small mining town in Wyoming. In Chicago, Richards was reunited with her mother. One day Lynne told the six year old she would take her shopping; instead they drove to Wyoming.

Needed Better Climate and Catholic Education

After some time in Wyoming managing the motel, doctors warned Lynne that the weather in Wyoming was unsuitable for the young child's health, so the two moved to San Francisco. There Lynne completed a degree in mortuary science, and later mother and daughter relocated again, this time to Hawaii were Lynne met and married Willis Young in 1949. The family eventually returned to the mainland and settled in tiny Sunflower, Kansas.

Lynne had strong opinions about the type of schooling her daughter should receive. "Mother believed in a good Catholic education, and she did not believe in a segregated education," Richards said in an interview with *Contemporary Black Biography* (*CBB*). But there was a problem; there were no Catholic schools in the area. In order to complete her education Richards was allowed to live in St. Louis in the home of an elderly white lady, where she earned seven dollars per week for being the woman's companion and serving at dinner parties.

Richards graduated from high school in 1953 and hoped to attend college. "My mother reared me to go to college," Richards said. "Paying for it was my problem. We had no money and there was no financial aid at that time." Richards did receive a partial scholarship to Webster College but it was not enough and

At a Glance . . .

Born Hilda Ballard on February 7, 1936, in St. Joseph, MO; married Alfredo Richards, 1961 (divorced). *Education:* St. John's School of Nursing, diploma, 1956; Hunter College, BS, nursing education, 1961;Columbia University, MED, psychiatric/mental health nursing, 1965; New York University, MPA, health administration, 1971; Columbia University, EDD, teaching in educational institutions, 1976; Harvard University, Certificate, education management, 1981. *Religion:* Catholic.

Career: Payne Whitney Clinic, New York, NY, staff nurse, 1956-58; City Hospital at Elmhurst, Elmhurst, NY, head nurse, 1958-63; Harlem Rehabilitation Center, New York, NY, deputy chief and coordinator of clinical services, 1965-71; Ohio University, Athens, OH, dean, 1979-86; Indiana University Northwest, Gary, IN, president and chancellor, 1993-2003; National Black Nurses Association, Silver Spring, MD, president, 1999-2003.

Selected memberships: National Black Nurses Association, lifetime member; National Black Nurses Foundation, secretary and member; National Coalition of Ethnic Minority Nurse Association, board member and advisory committee member; Chicago State University, College of Health Sciences Community Advisory Board, member.

Selected awards: *Ebony* Magazine, 100+ Most Influential Black Americans, 1999-2003; Teachers College Nursing Education Alumni Association, Nursing Hall of Fame, 2000; Association of Black Nursing Faculty, Lifetime Achievement Award, 1996; Black Opinion Magazine, Achiever Award, 1989.

the school did not offer a degree in medicine. "I wanted to be a doctor," Richards said. When Lynne weighed in on the matter, her advice was, "Don't just be a doctor, be a neurosurgeon." Richards wondered how she would be able to afford it, and there were other obstacles. The Midwest was very segregated.

Stung by Racism in the Midwest

During a high school assembly Richards met a representative from St. John's School of Nursing who

invited her to apply to their nursing program. Richards attended an open house at the school and upon meeting the Mother Superior she asked about the possibility of attending the school. Mother Superior agreed, not realizing that, as Richards said, "I was sixth in my class and I could pass any old test they gave me." Richards took the tests but didn't hear from the school. She contacted the Mother Superior who told her that she tested well but that they had never had any Negro students, there were no private rooms, and white parents wouldn't be very happy if their daughters roomed with her. She suggested that if Richards pretended to be Mexican she would allow her to attend. Richards responded, "I have been Negro for seventeen years. If my parents find out that now I am something else they would be very upset." Richards told *CBB*, "Mother Superior was not amused; nor was I."

Richards' mother urged her to "push forward." Richards spoke with a priest who promised to discuss it with the local bishop, but going over Mother Superior's head only provoked anger. "If the archbishop tries to get a colored child into the school, she'll never get in," she told Richards. She could have stopped Richards; instead she suggested Hilda attend their sister school in Springfield, Missouri. She applied and was accepted.

By her second year in one of the most racist parts of the country, Richards was ready to leave. She was at the top of her class, but she felt the sting of prejudice personally because, as she told *CBB*, "I wasn't subservient." Fortunately she had a friend in one of the nuns who was appalled that racism was forcing Richards to leave. Nuns from the Springfield campus contacted the Mother Superior at the St. Louis campus, Richards' original choice. Richards was allowed to complete her coursework there, and in 1956 she became the first black nurse to graduate from the school. It had been a tough year; when it was over, Richards left for New York City where she had friends.

Found Psychiatry, Education, and NBNA

Planning to become a psychiatrist, Richards worked as a psychiatric nurse at Payne Whitney Hospital in New York and was among the first black nurses on the staff. After 11 months Richards left to join City Hospital of New York's new psychiatric facility and eventually became head nurse of the adolescent psychiatric unit.

Richards then aimed higher. She returned to school and secured a bachelor's degree in nursing education and married Alfredo Richards in 1961. In 1965 she completed a master's degree in education, and another in public administration in 1971. In 1976 Richards earned a doctorate degree in education.

The 1960s had been a time of great social change and activism. Richards did her part by joining the New York chapter of NBNA at its start in 1969 and was instrumental in organizing the national association, becoming a member in 1973. She became a national board member in 1974 and became first vice president in 1984. Richards later became parliamentarian in 1998 and took the president's seat in 1999, a post she held until 2003.

Raised Visibility of NBNA

Richards set out to raise the visibility of the NBNA. In 1985 she created the *Journal of the National Black Nurses Association,* a research publication targeting the nursing and academic communities. She testified on behalf of the NBNA on Capitol Hill on matters relating to the shortage of nurses and funding for nursing education. "The goal of the organization is to look at the health of the black community and to try to move forward the number of African-American nurses and their education levels," Richards told *CBB.* "Too many of our people go into the associate degree programs and never get to the baccalaureate level, the true professional degree," Richards added. "More of us need to move up to positions where we can make decisions."

Richards' accomplishments with NBNA are many. "We have increased the number of scholarships we offer and our linkages with other organizations, like the American Nurses Association," Richards said. "We are part of the National Coalition of Ethnic Minority Nurse Associations (NCEMNA) and recently received a $2.6 million grant from the National Institute of Health to increase the number of nurse researchers among the five ethnic groups we represent: Blacks, Hispanics, Asian Americans, Filipinos, and Native Americans." With these funds the organization sets up research-oriented conferences and mentors students. NBNA also partners with women's health organizations and pharmaceutical companies who provide funds for research projects. NBNA presents issues to both major political parties through the Black Congress of Health, Law and Education (BCHLE), a group formed to make an impact on political issues important to the minority nursing community.

Richards does not forget the obstacles she had to overcome, and along the way her dedication and concern has helped many others achieve their own goals. Her "play daughter," Sefi Yadeta, a young Ethiopian student attending college in the United States, is just one example. Helping the young student during her college years in the United States, Richards came to view her as a permanent member of the family. Of helping others, Richards says, "I had a mother there for me every step of the way and I've had a lot of supporters. Young people should know that they need a support system. Also, understand that your history is behind you. Set your goals and be persistent. I integrated schools and I am still alive!"

Sources

On-line

National Black Nurses Association, Inc., www.nbna. org/index1.htm (November 15, 2004).

Other

Additional information for this profile was obtained through an interview with Dr. Hilda Richards on November 3, 2004, and through material obtained from Dr. Richards.

—Sharon Melson Fletcher

Smokey Robinson

1940—

Singer, songwriter, record producer

Robinson, Smokey, photograph. © Fred Prouser/Reuters/Corbis.

Smokey Robinson, the "poet laureate of soul music," has been composing and singing rhythm and blues hits for more than four decades. As the lead singer of the Miracles, Robinson, who moved to SBK Records later in his career, helped to put Detroit and its Motown Records on the music map; his solo performances have netted Grammy Awards and praise from pundits who usually shun the pop genre. *People* contributor Gail Buchalter labeled Robinson "one of the smoothest tenors in soul music," a romantic idol whose 60 million-plus in record sales "helped turn Motown into the largest black-owned corporation in the world."

According to Jay Cocks in *Time*, Robinson has written, produced, and performed "some of the most enduring rhythm and blues [songs] ever made. The church kept easy company with the street corner in his rich melodies, and his lyrics had a shimmering, reflective grace that, at his pleasure, could challenge or seduce. With the Miracles, Smokey helped make a kind of soul music that balanced ghetto pride and middle-class ambition. Some of the group's best tunes…stayed true to the R&B roots even as they beckoned, and found, a larger pop audience." In *Rolling Stone*, Steve Pond concluded that Robinson has written "some 4000 songs and recorded hundreds that have made him a true poet of the soul and a voice of the soul, too."

William "Smokey Joe" Robinson, Jr., not only rose from obscurity, he brought along a number of other now-famous black recording stars when he began to find success. He was born and raised in Detroit, in the rough Brewster ghetto, where, as he recalled in *People*, "you were either in a [music] group or a gang or both." Young Smokey grew up listening to his mother's record collection, which included the works of B. B. King, Muddy Waters, John Lee Hooker, Sarah Vaughan, and Billy Eckstine. These black artists, he commented in *Rolling Stone*, were "the first inspirational thing I had." When Robinson was ten, his mother died, and his sister Geraldine took him in, raising him along with her ten children. The family was poor but close-knit, and Robinson spent his youth writing songs and singing in local bands.

Robinson would not consider a professional career until he graduated from high school, and even then he tried barber school and courses in dentistry before giving his full attention to music. In 1954 he formed a rhythm

At a Glance . . .

Born William Robinson, Jr., February 19, 1940, in Detroit, MI; married Claudette Rogers (a singer), November 7, 1959 (divorced); Frances (an interior designer), 2002; children: Berry William, Tamla Claudette.

Career: Singer and songwriter, 1954–. Founder of group the Matadors, 1954; group's name changed to the Miracles, 1957; performed with the Miracles, 1957-72; solo performer, backed by group Quiet Storm, 1972–; cofounder, with Berry Gordy, Jr., of Tamla record label, 1959; vice-president of Motown Records, 1972-91.

Awards: Grammy Award nomination for best rhythm and blues song, 1979, for "Cruisin'"; inducted into Rock and Roll Hall of Fame and Songwriters Hall of Fame, both 1986; Grammy Award for best male rhythm and blues vocal performance, 1987, for "Just to See Her"; Grammy Legend Award, 1990; lifetime achievement award, Motor City Music Awards, 1992; BET Walk of Fame Award, 2004.

Addresses: *Home*—Los Angeles, CA; *Agent*—Michael Roshkind, 6255 Sunset Blvd., 18th Floor, Los Angeles, CA 90028; *Label*—SBK Records, 1290 Avenue of the Americas, New York, NY 10104; *Web*—www.smokey-robinsonfoods.com.

and blues group called the Matadors; the name was changed to the Miracles three years later to accommodate a female singer, Claudette Rogers, who married Robinson in 1959. At first the members of the Miracles—who were each paid five dollars per week by their agent, Berry Gordy—found the music business difficult. "For a while," Claudette Robinson related in *Essence*, "we lived basically in one bedroom. But we didn't stay in that house very long. Fortunately, the music started to happen."

Robinson was lucky to have encountered Berry Gordy during an audition for another agent; Gordy, then a fledgling music producer on a shoestring budget, was equally fortunate to have found Robinson. Gordy began to produce the Miracles's singles in 1958, collaborating with Robinson on lyrics and tunes. Their first release, "Got a Job"—an answer to The Silhouettes's number one hit "Get a Job"—hit Number 93 on the nationwide Billboard Top 100 chart. The debut was encouraging, but nothing prepared Gordy and Robinson for the

limelight they would attain in 1960. Late in that year they released an upbeat single, "Shop Around," that became a chart-topping million-seller. The Miracles subsequently became a national phenomenon, and Gordy was able to launch Motown Records, a landmark production company that introduced such talents as Diana Ross and the Supremes, Stevie Wonder, Marvin Gaye, and the Temptations.

Robinson and the Miracles were Gordy's first star-quality group, and they continued their association with Motown as the company gained prestige. Indeed, Robinson wrote hit songs not only for his group but for other Motown headliners as well. He explained the Motown philosophy in *Rolling Stone*: "We set out to...make music for people of all races and nationalities. Not to make black music—we just wanted to make good music that would be acceptable in all circles.... All we were doing, man, was just putting good songs on good tracks, songs that anybody could relate to.... We had good, solid songs that would fit your particular life situation if you were white or Oriental or Chicano or whatever you happened to be. And that made a world of difference."

Throughout the 1960s, especially in the latter half of the decade, the Motown sound competed with the music of the British invasion for popularity among the young. Robinson and the Miracles were favorites among the Motown personnel, earning more than six gold records containing such hits as "The Tracks of My Tears," "You've Really Got a Hold on Me," "I Second That Emotion," and "Ooo Baby Baby." Still, Robinson was on the verge of quitting the group in 1968 when his son Berry was born. He reconsidered almost immediately, however, when a Miracles single, "The Tears of a Clown," became a Number One hit, first in England and then in the United States. Robinson noted in *Rolling Stone* that "The Tears of a Clown" became "the biggest record we ever had. It catapulted us into another financial echelon as far as what we made on dates, and I felt that the band was entitled to reap the benefits."

The Miracles, a model group in terms of road behavior, endured until 1972, when Robinson quit. For a time after leaving the Miracles, Robinson concentrated on his business duties as vice-president of Motown Records. He soon returned to recording, however, this time as a solo artist. His solo albums are, on the whole, more reflective and mellow than his work with the Miracles. All of them highlight the singer's particular talent—the creation and performance of meaningful love songs at a time when many erstwhile romantics have become jaded cynics. Stephen Holden summed up the reason for the immense popularity of Robinson's music in *Rolling Stone*: "Smokey Robinson is that rare pop singer whose rhapsodic lyricism hasn't diminished with approaching middle age. Indeed, time has added a metaphysical depth to his art.... Smokey Robinson's faith in the redemptive power of erotic love continues unabated."

In Robinson's musical world, "sexual happiness isn't the product of spiritual equilibrium but its source.... Don't think, however, that Robinson's songs aren't filled with sex. They are. But in this man's art, sex isn't a fast roll in the hay, it's sweet manna shared during a leisurely stroll into paradise. Smokey Robinson creates that paradise every time he opens his mouth to sing," according to *Rolling Stone*. Robinson's records of the late 1980s, when he was well into his third decade in the music business, continued to garner popularity and the approval of critics. A *People* reviewer found that on *Smoke Signals* of 1986, for example, the singer "remains a uniquely resilient performer," and 1987's *One Heartbeat* was termed "another winning package of sharp, sophisticated soul" in *Rolling Stone*. Robinson hits like "Cruisin'," "Just to See Her"—a Grammy Award winner—and "Being With You" became both rhythm-and-blues and pop hits and were rendered in a voice *Essence* contributor Jack Slater hailed as "a hypnotic, airy aphrodisiac that puts tens of thousands in the mood for love." Coupled with his success with the Miracles and as a prolific Motown songwriter, Robinson's solo achievements in the music industry led to his 1986 induction into the Rock and Roll Hall of Fame, and in 1989 he was named a Grammy Living Legend. Coping with such enormous fame has not always been easy for Robinson. He chronicles his personal struggles in his 1989 collaboration with David Ritz, *Smokey: Inside My Life*. *Musician* contributor Jon Young remarked that the autobiography "documents everything from [Robinson's] family history and the early days of the Miracles to his extramarital affairs and, most striking, a graphic account of two years in thrall to cocaine in the mid-'80s." When asked why he chose to provide such candid details about his drug addiction, Robinson responded to Young, "I wrote it because it was God's will.... I was saved from drugs in 1986 when my pastor prayed for me. I never went to rehab or to a doctor. It was a miracle healing from God, so that I could carry the message about the perils of drugs. At the time I was saved, I was already dead. You are now speaking to Lazarus."

With the onset of the 1990s, Robinson's contract with Motown Records expired, and after a long and productive career with the record company, he moved to SBK Records. According to Gary Graff of the *Detroit Free Press*, the singer said simply, "My contract with Motown was up, and I was just out of there." He also pointed to the sale of Motown Records to MCA and Boston Ventures in 1988 as one of the reasons for his departure. "After we sold the company," he continued to Graff, "it was never really quite the same for me." With SBK Records, Robinson released a well-received LP he co-produced and recorded in less than six weeks, 1991's *Double Good Everything*. "It feels like a new day or something, man," he divulged to Graff. "This is the first thing I've ever done outside of Motown; that's a big deal to me.... I feel like a new artist, almost."

Also in 1991, Robinson ventured into previously uncharted areas of the music world, considering an album

of country-western tunes and penning the score for a Broadway musical titled *Hoops*, which presents the history of the Harlem Globetrotters basketball team. "I've written 22 pieces so far," Robinson told Young in February of 1992. "I want this to be like [the Broadway musical] *South Pacific* and produce several hits. The title track is a funk thing that I can envision being a halftime song for the NBA [National Basketball Association]."

Robinson had declared to Young in 1992 that "If the world lasts until the twenty-second century, I hope they're still playing my music." And, yes, in the 2000s, Robinson's music vibrated over the airwaves. Creator of more than 4,000 songs, Robinson's soul and his spiritual music, which he began producing in 2004, were cherished by fans. BET's tenth anniversary *Walk of Fame* program honored Robinson's career in 2004, and attracted 2.6 million viewers, according to *PR Newswire*. He continued to speak out about the perils of drug addiction and went "anywhere I'm called to go," including churches, prisons, and rehab centers, he told *Ebony*. And he launched a frozen food venture, selling "Smokey Robinson's: The Soul is in the Bowl" gumbo, red beans and rice, and jambalaya at Chicago-area groceries in 2004. But at age 64, when he performed with 17-year-old, up-and-coming white soul singer Joss Stone at Motown's 45th anniversary concert, Robinson made a point of proving his long-standing belief, as he told *People*, that "Everybody has a soul. I don't think there's an age range or color attached to it." With no sign of retiring, Robinson seemed primed to pursue his career to a ripe old age. He told *America's Intelligence Wire* that "I've been blessed enough to have a job that I love and it's by God's grace that I'm doing what I'm doing.... I'm living beyond my wildest imagination."

Selected discography

Albums (with the Miracles)

Hi, We're the Miracles, Motown, 1961.
Shop Around, Motown, 1962.
Doin' Mickey's Monkey, Motown, 1963, reissue, 1989.
The Fabulous Miracles, Motown, 1964.
The Miracles on Stage, Motown, 1964.
Going to a Go Go, Motown, 1964, reissue, 1989.
The Miracles From the Beginning, Motown, 1965.
Away We a Go Go, Motown, 1965, reissue, 1989.
Make It Happen, Motown, 1968.
Greatest Hits, Vol. 2, Motown, 1968, reissue, 1987.
The Miracles Live, Motown, 1969.
Special Occasion, Motown, 1969.
Time Out for Smokey Robinson and the Miracles, Motown, 1970, reissue, 1989.
Four in Blue, Motown, 1970.
What Love Has Joined Together, Motown, 1970, reissue, 1990.
Smokey and the Miracles, Motown, 1971.

1957-1972, Motown, 1973.
Anthology, Motown, 1974.
The Miracles, CBS, 1977.
Compact Command Performance, Vol. 2, Motown, 1986.
Going to a Go Go/The Tears of a Clown, Tamla, 1986.
Christmas With the Miracles, Motown, 1987.

Solo albums

Renaissance, Motown, 1973.
Smokey, Motown, 1973.
Pure Smokey, Motown, 1974, reissue, 1982.
Do It, Baby, Motown, 1974.
A Quiet Storm, Motown, 1974, reissue, 1989.
City of Angels, Motown, 1974.
Love Machine, Motown, 1975.
Smokey's Family Robinson, Motown, 1975.
Power of the Music, Motown, 1977.
Deep in My Soul, Motown, 1977.
Love Crazy, CBS, 1977.
Smokey's World, Motown, 1978.
Love Breeze, Motown, 1978.
Smokin', Motown, 1978.
Where There's Smoke, Motown, 1979, reissue, 1989.
Warm Thoughts, Motown, 1980.
Being With You, Motown, 1981.
Yes It's You, Lady, Motown, 1981.
Touch the Sky, Motown, 1983.
Great Songs and Performances, Motown, 1983.
Essar, Motown, 1984.
Smoke Signals, Tamla, 1986.
One Heartbeat, Motown, 1987.
Blame It on Love and All the Great Hits, Motown, 1990.
Love, Smokey, Motown, 1990.
Double Good Everything, SBK, 1991.
Intimate, SBK, 1999.
Food for the Spirit, Liquid 8, 2004.

Books

(With David Ritz) *Smokey: Inside My Life* (autobiography), McGraw-Hill, 1989.

Sources

Books

Given, Dave, *The Dave Given Rock 'n' Roll Stars Handbook,* Exposition Press, 1980.
Robinson, Smokey, and David Ritz, *Smokey: Inside My Life*, McGraw-Hill, 1989.
The Rolling Stone Record Guide, Random House, 1979.

Periodicals

America's Intelligence Wire, July 23, 2004.
Detroit News, October 20, 1991.
Down Beat, June 1983.
Ebony, October 1971; October 1982; March 1989; May 1989; June 2004.
Essence, February 1982.
High Fidelity, June 1980; May 1981; May 1982; July 1982; April 1986.
Jet, January 31, 1980; July 9, 1981; August 3, 1987; March 13, 1989; November 13, 1989; December 18, 1989; April 8, 1991; November 11, 1991.
Musician, February 1992.
New Republic, July 15, 1991.
Newsweek, January 27, 1986.
People, March 10, 1980; April 28, 1980; April 12, 1982; May 16, 1983; August 13, 1984; May 20, 1985; December 16, 1985; March 10, 1986; May 18, 1987; March 13, 1989; April 3, 1989; November 8, 2004.
Playboy, July 1985; June 1986.
PR Newswire, October 28, 2004.
Publishers Weekly, January 27, 1989.
Rolling Stone, April 16, 1981; September 17, 1981; February 12, 1987; April 23, 1987; December 17, 1987; February 9, 1989.
Stereo Review, July 1980; May 1982; January 1984; November 1986.
Variety, May 22, 1985; October 15, 1986; December 23, 1987; March 1, 1989.

—Anne Janette Johnson and Sara Pendergast

Al Roker

1954—

Television weathercaster

Roker, Al, photograph. AP/Wide World Photos. Reproduced by permission.

Al Roker may describe himself as "goofy-looking" and "nothing special," but his combination of accurate forecasting and warm, relaxed delivery have won him possibly the most visible weather anchor position on television. Roker is the weekday weathercaster for the National Broadcasting Company's *Today Show*, a morning news-and-information program watched by millions and millions of Americans. Roker inherited his position on *Today* from the equally affable Willard Scott in 1995, adding a new laurel to a two-decade career in the television weather forecasting business. He is also host of his own cable channel weekend talk show, *The Al Roker Show*. Success has done little to alter Roker's working methods—or his opinion of himself. "We know weather is one of the main reasons people tune in to the news," he said in the *New York Times*. "So I try to do my best to be accurate. Then I hope for the best."

Roker comes from a blue-collar background where his hard-working parents stressed education and achievement. His father, Albert Lincoln Roker, was a bus driver who also served as a labor-relations negotiator for New York City's Transit Authority. His mother was a homemaker who raised the six Roker children in a home in the St. Albans section of Queens, New York. Al Jr., the oldest in the family, graduated from Manhattan's Xavier High School, where he spent four years developing his comic skills and indulging his interests in graphic art.

The cost of tuition at a private college was out of reach for the Roker family, so Al attended the State University of New York at Oswego. There he majored in graphic communications, but he took classes in meteorology to satisfy the university's science requirements. Roker found he had a talent for meteorology, and his interest in the science grew as his studies progressed. While still a sophomore in college, he landed a part-time job as weekend weather forecaster at nearby WTVH-TV in Syracuse. By the time he earned his bachelor's degree in 1976, he had been promoted to weekday weathercaster at the station. Roker did not earn a degree in meteorology, but few television weather forecasters do. In fact, his back ground contains more science than that of many of his colleagues, and he became known

At a Glance . . .

Born Albert Lincoln Roker, Jr., on August 20, 1954, in New York, NY; son of Albert Lincoln (a bus driver and union negotiator); married third wife, Deborah Roberts (a television journalist), September 16, 1995; children: two daughters and one son. *Education:* State University of New York at Oswego, BA, communications, 1976.

Career: WTVH-TV, Syracuse, NY, weekend weather anchor, 1974-75, weekly weather anchor, 1975-76; WTTG-TV, Washington, DC, weather anchor, 1976-78; WKYC-TV, Cleveland, OH, weather anchor, 1978-83; WNBC-TV, New York City, 1983–, began as weekend weather anchor, worked as local weekly weathercaster, currently weather anchor for *Today Show*; CNBC-TV, New York City, host of weekend talk show *The Al Roker Show*, 1995–.

Awards: Recipient of two Emmy Awards for weather forecasting; twice named Best Weatherman by *New York* magazine; holder of American Meteorological Society's Seal of Approval.

Addresses: *Office*—NBC-TV, 30 Rockefeller Plaza, New York, NY 10112; *Web*—www.roker.com.

for writing his own forecasts and using NBC's radar—rather than the National Weather Service—to keep him up-to-date on local and national weather.

Soon after graduating from college, Roker took a job as weathercaster for WTTG-TV in Washington, DC. WTTG is a local independent station, and while there the young Roker had ample opportunity to study other weather anchors' techniques. One local hero Roker studied was the chubby and avuncular Willard Scott, who was then forecasting weather at the NBC affiliate in the nation's capital. Today Roker credits Scott with teaching him the secret to a long career on the air. "I used to be crazy, do all kinds of gimmicky things," Roker admitted in the *New York Times*. "Willard took me aside one day and said, 'Just be yourself. It'll last a lot longer.'"

From WTTG Roker moved on to WKYC-TV in Cleveland, Ohio. The job in the Midwest was Roker's first with an NBC affiliate, and—as an avid weather-watcher—he admits that he misses the assignment in Cleveland. After five years at WKYC, Roker moved on in 1983 to WNBC-TV in New York City. His parents, who were still living in Queens, were thrilled to welcome him home.

Roker's first position with WNBC was weekend weather anchor. By 1985 he had worked his way up to weekly weather forecaster, earning *New York* magazine's "Best Weatherman" award. Roker had the same easygoing, ordinary-guy delivery that characterizes his weather spots now, but he also exhibited a keen understanding of meteorology on both a local and national level. He seemed at ease urging New Yorkers to play hooky from work on sunny spring days, and deeply committed and serious when tracking Atlantic hurricanes and other dangerous weather. With an 80 percent accuracy rate, he quickly earned the American Meteorological Society's prestigious Seal of Approval.

Asked in a 1987 *New York* magazine profile if he would like to replace Willard Scott on the *Today Show* at some point, Roker disclaimed any ambitions. "Willard is my idol. The idea of stepping into his shoes terrifies me," he said. Over the next decade, Roker had ample opportunity to shed his fears and prepare to be Scott's replacement. In addition to his duties with the weekly local NBC newscast, he became weathercaster for the weekend edition of *Today* and a substitute for Scott on weekdays. By the time Scott retired in 1995, Roker had firmly established himself as the heir apparent and continued to hold the position a decade later.

A yo-yo dieter with thick glasses who stands about five-feet-eight, Roker thinks a great deal of his appeal lies in his "ordinary Joe" persona. "It's part of my stock in trade," he explained in the *New York Times*. "People look at me and feel superior." Whatever the secret of his success, Roker has achieved what many would consider the pinnacle of television weather forecasting success as the national weather correspondent for the highly rated *Today Show*. Unlike his predecessor, however, Roker has not just settled into the staff of *Today* with no further ambitions. Late in 1995 he inaugurated The *Al Roker Show*, a weekend talk show run on the cable channel CNBC. He also served as narrator for a Public Broadcasting System documentary on weather entitled *Savage Skies*.

Roker's fans are many and diverse. *Entertainment Weekly* once dubbed him a "Cool Ordinary Guy." MTV did a feature on him called "What It's Like To Be Al." And everyone from New York's mayor Rudolph Giuliani to reporter Barbara Walters turned up at his 1995 wedding to television journalist Deborah Roberts. Roker, who lives in New York, seemed truly content with his celebrity status and his high-profile job at NBC. "Our problem is that sometimes we have too much fun," he said of himself and his *Today* co-hosts in the *New York Times*. "We forget we're on television."

While Roker continued to hold his spot on the *Today Show*, he continually branched out in diverse directions. He set up Al Roker Productions, Inc. in 1994 to do "all things Al," according to Roker's Web site. He has published a parenting book and two cookbooks. He appeared on *Dateline* in 2004 to report on his health status two and a half years after undergoing gastric bypass surgery to reduce his weight. He hosted a special on NBC called "All Roker Investigates: Katie. com," which offered viewers information about Internet predators. And he hosted a Court TV show called "Faulty Forensics" that revealed the devastating consequences in the criminal justice system due to poor procedures in a Houston crime lab. His travel series called *Going Places* won high ratings on PBS. Whatever his interest, Roker seemed able to craft it into a package for audiences, making *TV Guide* contributor J. Max Robins wonder: "Is Al Roker laying the groundwork to be the next Oprah?" It seems the answer is yes.

Selected writings

Don't Make Me Stop This Car: Adventures in Fatherhood, Scribner, 2000.
Al Roker's Big Bad Book of Barbecue, Scribner, 2002.
Al Roker's Hassle-Free Holiday Cookbook: More Than 125 Recipes for Family Celebrations All Year Long, Scribner, 2003.

Sources

Periodicals

Chicago Tribune, June 27, 2004.
Entertainment Weekly, February 11, 1994, p. 42.
Grand Rapids Press, August 25, 2004.
Houston Chronicle, November 5, 2004.
New York, August 17, 1987, p. 20.
New York Times, September 2, 1992, pp. C1, C10.
People, January 23, 1995, p. 73; October 2, 1995, p. 72.
TV Guide, September 2002.

On-line

Al Roker, www.roker.com (January 31, 2005).

Other

Additional information supplied by NBC News, Inc.

—Anne Janette Johnson and Sara Pendergast

Millicent Scarlett

1971—

Singer

Her voice has been called sublime, radiant, commanding, and quite simply, beautiful. In operas, jazz concerts, and show-stopping recitals, Millicent Scarlett has sung her way into a resounding career. "I love singing very dearly," she told *The Diamondback,* the student paper of the University of Maryland. "I hope the love of what I'm doing shows through in my performances." Apparently it does, with everyone from her second-grade music teacher to opera legend Luciano Pavarotti having fallen sway under her vocal charms.

Surprised by Her Singing Skill

The youngest of seven, Veronica Millicent Scarlett was born on April 25, 1971, in the Canadian city of Winnipeg, Manitoba. Her parents Neville and Veronica Scarlett, both born in Jamaica, provided a solid middle-class upbringing for Scarlett and her siblings. "My mom was an LPN nurse at Deerlodge Hospital and my dad was a welder and worked for Old Dutch Potato Chips," Scarlett told *Contemporary Black Biography (CBB).* Nonetheless, the Scarletts found it difficult to afford to raise their large family and provide the youngest Scarlett with voice lessons at the same time. "I really appreciate the sacrifices [my parents] made for me, for my training," Scarlett told *The Winnipeg Free Press.* "There were lessons, and many trips to Europe. It was not easy."

Those sacrifices began when Scarlett was in second grade. "One day after music class the teacher took me aside and said she wanted to speak to my mother and that she would take me home after school," Scarlett

recalled to *CBB.* "[She told my mom], 'I think that Millie should take voice lessons.' My mom was surprised as I never sang at home. I was surprised too. I had only been doing what the teacher told me to do." The teacher was insistent, and Scarlett soon found herself in singing lessons.

Scarlett was a natural. "Singing was never a difficult thing," she told *The Winnipeg Free Press.* "Learning the theory, and what makes it all come together was more difficult for me." By the age of ten, Scarlett began participating in local and regional singing competitions including the Winnipeg Music Festival. She also began studying for the Canadian Royal Conservatory of Music exams. She sang for her school choir and participated in three school musicals. She also sang in the choir at Holy Trinity Anglican church. While still a high school student, she was hired to sing for productions of Rainbow Stage, a professional theater company in Winnipeg. Despite her busy performance schedule, she was 16 before she realized she was good. "[I began] winning competitions and scholarships and actually getting money from singing," she told *CBB.* "By that point I hadn't decided if I'd be a singer or not, but I realized I was good at it."

Earned Singing Scholarships

In 1989, after graduating from high school, Scarlett headed to Brandon University on a performance scholarship that included a full tuition waiver. There Scarlett was introduced to opera by her vocal coach. "She helped me...develop an appreciation of opera, to make

At a Glance . . .

Born on April 25, 1971, in Winnipeg, Manitoba, Canada. *Education:* Brandon University, Canada, BA, applied voice performance, 1993; University of Maryland College Park, MA, opera, 1997. *Religion:* Anglican.

Career: University United Methodist Church, Washington, DC, soprano soloist, 1998–; George Washington University, Department Of Music, Washington, DC, adjunct professor in voice, 1998–; professional singer, 2000–.

Selected awards: University of Maryland, Homer Ulrich Graduate Voice Competition, winner, 1995; Luciano Pavarotti International Competition, winner, 1996; Metropolitan Opera Auditions, Mid-Atlantic region winner, 1999; Metropolitan Opera Auditions, national semi-finalist, 1999.

Addresses: *Office*—George Washington University, Music Department, Phillips B-144, Washington, DC 20052. *Web*—www.millicentscarlett.com.

contacts, to be prepared for anything," Scarlett told *The Winnipeg Free Press*. Until that time she had sung mostly jazz, chorals, and Broadway-style musicals. While at Brandon, Scarlett also realized that music was more than just something she was good at. "In my first year in college, I went to a summer camp in Tampa, Florida, sponsored by the International Institute of Vocal Arts," Scarlett told *CBB*. "While I was there I realized for the first time that a career in music was very possible for me to do." During her senior year, Scarlett received Brandon's coveted Silver Medal for the highest GPA in applied performance and in 1993 she graduated with a Bachelor of Music in applied voice performance.

Scarlett left Canada for Washington, D.C., in 1994 and enrolled as an opera graduate student at the University of Maryland College Park. She knew only the director of the school's opera program. "He is Canadian as well, and he was the reason I moved to Maryland," Scarlett told *CBB*. She earned several scholarships to cover the costs of her tuition and settled into the program. She traveled to Salzburg, Austria, to study at the Mozarteum music school. She also traveled several times to the International Institute of Vocal Arts in Chiari, Italy, though she told *CBB* that she was "just a tag-along" on those trips. "At the time I was living with another singer who I thought was just fantastic. Her

manager had taken her to Italy through the International Institute, and I went along too." And when Scarlett's roommate enrolled in the Luciano Pavarotti International Voice Competition, Scarlett did too. "But I assumed she would be the one to be called back, not me," Scarlett told *CBB*. She was wrong.

Performed with Pavarotti

Of the over 2,000 singers from around the world who entered the 1996 Pavarotti competition, only 145 advanced to the semifinals. Scarlett was among them. She performed the aria from *The Marriage of Figaro* for Pavarotti. "When I finished he said in Italian, 'Thank you very much, that's enough.' He had listened to everyone else sing two arias. But he stopped me at one," she told *CBB*. "On the way upstairs to get my things I just assumed I had sung badly. By the time I got back downstairs, one of Pavarotti's assistants was waiting for me. He told me, 'Maestro Pavarotti said to tell you that he only needed to hear you sing once. It was enough for him.'" Scarlett had made it to the finals.

When Pavarotti called her name as one of the winners, Scarlett was so shocked that the other contestants had to push her forward to shake his hand. "All I could think was here I was, this girl from Winnipeg who came to Maryland for school, not knowing anyone, not knowing about the Pavarotti competition," she told *CBB*. "And I became one of the winners. I knew then that my parents' money hadn't gone down the drain. All the encouragement I had received over the years, all the hard work from my teachers, all of it wasn't wasted. That was the best for me."

As a winner, Scarlett performed onstage with Pavarotti in the Luciano Pavarotti Opera Extravaganza in Philadelphia. "[That] was another high," Scarlett told *CBB*. "Meeting him, performing with him, he was very nice and very encouraging," she told *The Winnipeg Free Press*. However, Scarlett's real joy in performing with Pavarotti came from knowing her parents were watching her. "He was the only opera singer my mom knew," Scarlett told *CBB*. "Until the day I die, I'll never forget the look on my mom's face when she and my dad walked into the auditorium the day of the winners' performance and saw him on stage rehearsing. My mom nudged me and asked me, 'Is that him?' I said 'Yes.'"

Began Building Professional Career

Almost immediately on the heels of her Pavarotti win, Scarlett had her operatic debut in Washington in *Dido and Aeneus*. "I got a fantastic review from *The Washington Post*," she told *CBB*. Over the next year she participated in nearly a dozen productions both with the University of Maryland Opera Studio and professionally. Notable among them were roles in the North American premier of *La Fiamminga* and in the world premiere of *Fatal Song*. After graduating with a masters of music in opera in 1997, Scarlett began a heavy schedule of singing, teaching, and touring. In 1998 she became a national finalist at the prestigious Metropolitan Opera auditions in New York. She performed a solo with the National Symphony at the National Cathedral in Washington, D.C. She also made her debut in Italy as soloist with the Internationale Orchestra di Italia. Meanwhile Scarlet joined the faculty of George Washington University as an adjunct professor of voice and also began giving private classes and lectures including master classes in voice at the University of Manitoba.

In 2000 Scarlett made her professional opera debut with the Illinois Opera playing the role of Clara in *Porgy and Bess*. *The Winnipeg Free Press* quoted reviews of her performance calling Scarlett "radiant and enchanting" and "a standout in the cast." Since then Scarlett has graced dozens of stages. She has sung soprano solos in famed operas such as Mozart's *Requiem*, Verdi's *Requiem*, Haydn's *Creation*, Handel's *Israel in Egypt*, and Lord Nelson's *Mass*. She has also performed with Opera International at the Lisner Auditorium in Washington, D.C. However Scarlett doesn't classify herself as an opera singer. "I love all genres of music," she told *CBB*. "I love opera and love performing it, but I also love doing recitals too, and singing with orchestras. I love doing concerts and smaller cabaret-style shows." This diversity is reflected in her roles. She has sung show tunes in *Celebration of Music by Bernstein and Gershwin* with the Washington Theatre Orchestra and gospels in *Let My People Go* with the Master Chorale of Washington. She has also performed at churches, fundraisers, political dinners, and in 2000 she was a featured soloist on ESPN's live broadcast of the Outback Bowl's half-time show.

Poised to Keep Performing

Of all her performances, Scarlett told *CBB* about one that was very dear to her. "Performing with Pavarotti was amazing, and doing *Porgy and Bess* was unbelievable, but a more personal thing for me was going back to Winnipeg [in 2004] and doing my first solo recital as a bona fide professional." Scarlett was invited to do the recital as a guest of the Women's Musical Club of Winnipeg. The group supports young Canadian musicians with scholarships and had awarded a $500 scholarship to Scarlett in 1990. At the recital Scarlett performed songs ranging from Mozart's "Exultate Ju-

bilate" to Gershwin's "Summertime." "[It was] probably the best recital I've ever done," Scarlett told *CBB*. "My family was there, my friends, teachers, other singers I had competed against while growing up. It was so great to come back and sing in front of them…. I was not little Millie anymore. Now, I am Millicent Scarlett. The reaction I got I will never forget. They treated me as if I were a rock star."

A singing career is never easy to pursue, and Scarlett encountered the usual disappointments along the way—rejections, bad auditions, insecurities. However she also had to deal early on in her career with a subtle racism. "Sometimes it is hard being a black soprano," she told *CBB*. "We have to be very, very good to get noticed. I am not blonde, nor skinny, and I think that has had an effect on the way I've been treated, but I have never let it bother me." Reflecting on her current career, she added, "I don't notice if it is happening now. I can't afford to allow that to occupy my mind. I am going out to sing, if they don't like me, well, I move onto the next person."

As Scarlett considered her future, she looked forward to simply singing. "I don't know where that will lead me," she told *CBB*. "I don't know if that means opera or recitals. I just want to be singing." With a calendar bulging with performances, classes, and a CD in the works, she seemed poised to do just that.

Sources

Periodicals

The Winnipeg Free Press, April 21, 2004, April 22, 2004.

On-line

"Student to Sing with Pavarotti," *The Diamondback,* www.inform.umd.edu/News/Diamondback/1996-editions/02-February-editions/960213-Tuesday/NEWS-student_to_sing_w_Pavarott (October 20, 2004).

Other

Additional information for this profile was obtained through an interview with Millicent Scarlett on November 7, 2004.

—Candace LaBalle

Thomas B. Shropshire

1925-2003

Business executive

Thomas B. Shropshire was one of the first African Americans to break the color barrier in corporate America when he became a top executive at the Miller Brewing Company in the 1970s. His position was of note because he was not promoted merely to meet diversity quotas at the corporation. *The Business Journal* of Milwaukee wrote that Shropshire did not have "the title of VP for urban affairs, minority affairs, or numerous other corporate labels that were specifically crafted to employ minorities in high-profile positions. Shropshire had bottom-line responsibility throughout his corporate career." Even as he forged his place in the executive suite, Shropshire worked to help other African Americans join him. "He believed in reaching back and helping others along the way," his wife Jacqulyn told Milwaukee's *Journal Sentinel*. "He didn't believe that once you arrived, you forgot where you came from."

Went from Arkansas to Africa

Thomas B. Shropshire was born to William and Irene Shropshire on October 15, 1925 in Little Rock, Arkansas. After graduating from Little Rock's Dunbar High School, Shropshire did a two year stint in the U.S. Navy during World War II. When he got out, he headed north to Missouri's Lincoln University, where he earned a bachelor's degree in 1950. Next he traveled to New York University and enrolled in the School of Business, graduating a year later with an Master's in Business Administration (MBA) degree.

Following graduate school, Shropshire took a job as a sales representative with Philip Morris. His initial territory was Brooklyn, New York; later the company moved him to Chicago. Eventually he became a college supervisor for the company, creating marketing aimed at college-aged consumers.

In 1961 Philip Morris entrusted Shropshire with distribution and sales of its products in West and Central Africa. Two years later he was promoted to sales manager for tropical Africa. Another promotion came in 1967, when he became marketing and sales coordinator for all of Africa. In 1968 Shropshire made a huge leap when he was appointed managing director and CEO of Philip Morris Nigeria, becoming "the first African American to crack the CEO ranks in corporate America," wrote *The Business Journal*.

Shropshire moved to Nigeria to oversee Philip Morris's manufacturing and marketing operations in the country. Over the next four years, he trained nearly 1,000 Nigerian employees. He also established a 1,200-acre experimental farm to teach farmers the most efficient methods of growing and curing tobacco. This innovative method helped Philip Morris Nigeria do business with more than 12,000 farmers throughout the country. Shropshire was also committed to community service in Africa. He volunteered on several boards, including the All-African Games Committee, the Nigerian National Swimming Association, the Nigerian-American Chamber of Commerce, and the University of Lagos Medical School.

At a Glance . . .

Born on October 15, 1925, in Little Rock, AR; died on August 14, 2003; married Jacqulyn Calloway; children: Terilyn, Thomas Jr. *Education:* Lincoln University, BS, 1950; New York University, MBA, business, 1951. *Military Service:* U.S. Navy. 1944-46.

Career: Philip Morris, Brooklyn, NY, sales representative, 1952; Philip Morris, college supervisor, 1953-1960; Philip Morris, African sales representative, 1961-63; Philip Morris, sales manager, Tropical Africa, 1963-66; Philip Morris, sales coordinator, Africa, 1967-68; Phillip Morris-Nigeria, chairman and managing director, 1968-72; Miller Brewing Company, vice president for market planning, 1972-78; senior vice president and treasurer, 1978-85.

Selected memberships: Milwaukee Urban League, treasurer; Howard University, trustee; Joint Center for Political and Economic Studies, board of governors; National Urban League, trustee; Sigma Pi Phi Fraternity, Grand Sire Archon.

Selected awards: NAACP, Freedom Award for Business; B'nai B'rith, Human Rights Award; Alpha Phi Alpha, Distinguished Service Award; Miles College, honorary doctorate, 1984; Talladega College, honorary doctorate, 1987.

Took Miller to Number Two Spot

In 1970 Philip Morris bought the Milwaukee-based Miller Brewing Company and tapped Shropshire to be part of a four-man team to oversee the transition. As head of marketing and sales, Shropshire was in charge of completely reorganizing Miller's sales department and distribution networks. He also oversaw the introduction of new products including the famous "tastes great, less filling" beer, "Miller Lite." It was one of his most brilliant and successful career moves. The *Milwaukee Courier* wrote, "[Miller Lite] revolutionized the brewing industry and made Miller the second-largest brewer in the world." It also solidified Shropshire's place as one of Philip Morris's most valuable executives.

During the first two years of Philip Morris's ownership of Miller, Shropshire held down both his role as CEO of Philip Morris Nigeria as well as the new title of vice president for market planning at Miller. He had also ascended to the board of directors of Philip Morris. In

1972 he left the company's Nigerian operations and focused completely on Miller. In 1978 he was promoted to senior vice president and treasurer of Miller. That same year he was also made a vice president at Philip Morris. In the late 1970s and early 1980s, Shropshire's marketing skills were integral to the phenomenal success of Miller. He conceived and implemented marketing strategies and programs aimed at ethnic and college-aged consumers. The result, according to *The Business Journal*, was that "Miller held the overwhelming share of the beer market among minority consumers, and a quarter of the market for all beer consumers." Shropshire also managed sports sponsorships for Miller, including deals with the National Baseball Association, the National Basketball Association, and NASCAR.

Shropshire's appointment to senior vice president at the Miller Brewing Company was significant because he was one of the first African Americans to rise so high in corporate America, solely as a result of work performance. *The Business Journal* noted, "When Philip Morris sent Shropshire to Milwaukee as part of Miller's new management team, he was not a token minority." Miller was one of the first corporations in the nation to actively promote diversity as a business strategy. Upper management at Miller believed that the best way to promote their products to all consumers, regardless of race, creed, or class, was by building a corporate structure that reflected that same diversity. It was an environment that allowed Shropshire to flourish, both personally and as a manager of Miller. "[His] skill in developing goodwill and networks within and across communities positioned Miller to make a run for the No. 1 position in the beer industry," wrote *The Business Journal*.

Built Business Opportunities for Minorities

Because of his prominent role at the company, Shropshire was in a position to influence Miller's hiring practices. He ensured that the diversity that Miller displayed at the top was reflected at all levels of the corporation, from the administrative offices to the shop floor. *The Business Journal* wrote in 2003, "Even today, hundreds of minority production workers in Miller's plants speak fondly of Shropshire's role in their acquisition of blue-collar, middle-income wage jobs."

Shropshire's commitment to the African-American community did not stop with marketing campaigns nor employment policies. Along with his wife, Jacqulyn Calloway Shropshire—one-time director of Milwaukee's Urban League—Shropshire gave both time and money to promoting economic opportunities for minorities. The couple was so dedicated to this cause that the Opportunities Industrialization Center (OIC), a Milwaukee-based organization that promotes minority-owned businesses, created an award in their name.

"Thomas was a pillar in this community," the president of OIC told the *Journal Sentinel*. "He was a leading national and local businessperson who worked to promote black businesses here." General Electric vice president Fred H. Black—also a top African-American executive—reiterated that praise, telling the *Journal Sentinel*, "Tom was a man who used his enormous talents to help our people."

Shropshire was also very active in community and corporate programs, serving on dozens of boards. They included Howard and Talladega universities; civic and charitable groups such as the Joint Center for Political and Economic Studies, the National Urban League, and Big Brothers/Big Sisters; and corporate boards ranging from Key Banks of Puget Sound to the Seven-Up Company. He was also heavily involved with Sigma Pi Phi, a national fraternity of African-American men dedicated to leadership in civic, social service, educational, and charitable pursuits. Shropshire served on several local and national committees for the group and from 2000 to 2002 held a top leadership position as Grand Sire Archon. He also served as vice-chairman of the Boule Foundation, the charitable wing of the fraternity which provides scholarships for minority students.

Forged Path to Success for Others to Follow

Shropshire received many awards for both his corporate and community service. They included five honorary doctorate degrees from universities around the country, the prestigious NAACP Freedom Award for Business, induction into the Mid-Eastern Athletic Conference's Hall of Fame, the Philip Morris Gold Ring Award, and the B'nai B'rith Human Rights Award. However, recognition was never the goal of Shropshire's hard work. "Tom never needed any titles or accolades," his wife told the *Journal Sentinel*. Instead Shropshire took satisfaction in knowing that he was helping others find their own way to success.

In November of 1985 Shropshire retired from Miller, though his 33-year-long career with Philip Morris did not come to an end. Though he and his wife relocated to Las Vegas, Shropshire continued to work for Philip Morris as a consultant for marketing and community affairs. The consultancy work, along with numerous charitable pursuits, kept Shropshire busy long after he had exited his corporate suite. When he died peacefully in his home on August 14, 2003, he left a sudden and sad vacancy. He also left a legacy that has continued to inspire minority executives who are following in the path he forged back when affirmative action was in its infancy and racism was rampant.

Sources

Periodicals

The Business Journal (Milwaukee), September 5, 2003.
Jet, Sept 8, 2003 *Journal Sentinel* (Milwaukee), August 16, 2003.
Milwaukee Courier, August 22, 2003.
The Prince George's Post (Marlboro, MD), August 28/September 3, 2003.
The Sun Reporter, February 16, 1994.

—Candace LaBalle

Charlie Sifford

1922—

Golfer

Sifford, Charlie, photograph. AP/Wide World Photos. Reproduced by permission.

Charlie Sifford has been called the "Jackie Robinson of golf." The first black man to break the color barrier in one of the nation's most elitist sports, Sifford endured humiliation, threats to his life and limb, and even mistreatment from some of his fellow pros. Nothing stopped him. He challenged a "Caucasian only" clause in the Professional Golfers' Association of America (PGA) by-laws and won, he teed off at clubs that would not allow him to use the restaurants and on fairways filled with heckling fans, and he kept his cool, knowing that his best years were behind him well before he was allowed to join the PGA. "There's not a man on this tour who could have gone through what I went through to be a golfer," Sifford admitted in the *Chicago Tribune.* In the *Atlanta Constitution* he concluded: "I still can't believe I went so long without breaking down or quitting the game."

A popular character on the Super Seniors Tour who always sports a cigar—even while playing—Sifford bristles when he is compared to Robinson, the first black baseball player in the major leagues. "If I was the Jackie Robinson of golf, I sure didn't do a very good job of it," he said in the *Chicago Tribune.* "Jackie was followed by a hundred great black ballplayers. I was followed by no one. There are now two blacks (Calvin Peete and Jim Thorpe) playing on the regular PGA Tour. There are six of us...on the Senior Tour.... There is no place for a black man in professional golf." Sifford cited cases of prejudice that lingered more than 30 years after he was allowed to join the PGA. He also noted that black youngsters are not encouraged to play golf—and if they like the sport, are often barred from private clubs. "There are still closed doors," Sifford told the *Lexington Herald-Leader.* "There aren't equal opportunities. Things are far from being equal.... It's been a long, tough battle, but the job is not done. We still have a lot to overcome. We have a lot of things that need to be changed."

Charles Luther Sifford was born in Charlotte, North Carolina, in 1922. He grew up in a racially mixed area that was surprisingly free of prejudice, but the insulation did not last long. At the age of ten he began to earn pocket money as a golf caddie at the Carolina Country Club. In those days before motorized golf carts, young men could earn wages for carrying the heavy bags of clubs from hole to hole for golfers.

At a Glance . . .

Born Charles Luther Sifford on June 2, 1922, in Charlotte, NC; married Rose; children: Charles, Craig. *Education:* High school graduate.

Career: Professional golfer, 1948–. Won Negro National Open six times; joined Professional Golfers' Association as first black card-holding member, 1960. Remained among top 60 money winners on PGA Tour, 1960-69; has won more than $1.2 million with PGA Tour and Senior PGA Tour. Victories include 1957 Long Beach Open, 1963 Puerto Rico Open, 1967 Greater Hartford Open, and 1969 Los Angeles Open. Senior PGA Tour Victory, 1980 Suntree Classic. Member of Super Senior Tour, 1991–.

Awards: World Golf Hall of Fame, Inductee, 2004.

Addresses: *Home*—Kingwood, TX. *Publisher*—Simon & Schuster Inc., 1230 Avenue of the Americas, New York, NY 10020.

The country club was closed on Mondays, so the caddies were allowed to use the golf course that day. Sifford took advantage of the situation. He found that he loved the game, and better, that he had a gift for it. Sometimes he and a few friends would sneak inside the grounds before the club opened and practice some more. By the age of thirteen, he occasionally broke par on the course. Because he had to play undetected so often, he developed a powerful and accurate drive as well as the tendency to hurry on the green—the most likely spot that he would be seen by club security. "I was always moving fast to keep from being thrown off the course," he told the Memphis *Commercial Appeal.* "I never learned how to take my time on the greens and develop a decent stroke."

The Carolina Club owner, Sutton Alexander, and future PGA pro Clayton Heafner, saw Sifford play and helped to teach him the game. In 1939, Alexander took the 17-year-old Sifford aside and told him it might be best if he left the caddie service and stayed away from the club. Sifford was hurt, but the worst blow came when he found out the reason for his exile. "I had gotten too good, and the members didn't like it," he told the *Atlanta Constitution.* "Mr. Alexander was concerned about my physical well-being."

This news, combined with a minor scrape with the law, convinced Sifford to move elsewhere. He ventured north to Philadelphia, where he had some family, and there he found the public golf courses he needed to

perfect his game. "I always did want to be a pro," he said in the *Lexington Herald-Leader.* "But the pro tour wasn't open to us [African-Americans] then." Instead, Sifford entered segregated golf tournaments and made friends among the black golfers of his day. The early 1940s found him on the United Golf Association tour, and between 1948 and 1960 he won the Negro National Open six times.

Like many other black athletes, Sifford could only dream about competing for the big money prizes alongside white athletes in the PGA. His life did offer some opportunities, however. His association with Teddy Rhodes—an African-American golfer and personal golf coach to Joe Louis—led to a job. Sifford became golf teacher and valet to Billy Eckstine, an immensely popular jazz singer. Eckstine was in great demand as an entertainer during the 1950s, and Sifford had the chance to meet some of the nation's top contemporary musicians, including Miles Davis, Charlie Parker, and Sarah Vaughan. Eckstine himself challenged Sifford to buck the racist restrictions of the PGA. From the singer Sifford also acquired his nickname, "Little Horse," a memory he preserves today by wearing a golden horse charm on a chain around his neck.

Sifford first met Jackie Robinson at the Negro National Open in 1947. Robinson too encouraged Sifford to challenge the PGA, but the baseball star knew just how tough a fight Sifford would face. Robinson advised patience, and Sifford agreed. "I think it had to be done right," Sifford told the *Sacramento Bee.* "Jackie Robinson told me not to do it until I was ready." As early as 1953 Sifford began to try to enter PGA events. On one occasion, in Phoenix, Arizona, he and three other black players trying to qualify reached the green on the first hole and found the cup filled with human waste. Fellow golf pro Charles Owens told the *Sacramento Bee* that Sifford "went through tar in hell. What he went through was like being tied down in a room with a spigot going 'drip, drip, drip.' It'll drive you crazy. But Charlie's too tough to go crazy."

Sifford remembered those days too. "In 1955, I qualified for a tournament," he told the *Lexington Herald-Leader.* "At the time, black players were only able to play in Canada, Chicago, or Los Angeles. I shot a 68 and got in the tournament, but I couldn't get in the locker room. I knew the risks, but I went ahead." Sifford won the Long Beach Open in 1957, and thereafter he simply could not be ignored. Even so, the stodgy PGA tried to thwart him when he sued for membership, moving tournaments from one state to another while clinging tightly to the "Caucasian only" clause.

A California lawsuit caused the PGA to strike the clause in 1960, and Sifford got an official PGA Approved Players card for a one-year trial. Renewal depended upon his ability to win among the ranks of whites. He was almost 40 at the time and was thus a good bit older than the average PGA golfer. Nevertheless, he managed to remain among the top 60 money winners for a whole decade, from 1960 until 1969.

"The first official tournament I played in with my card was in Greensboro, North Carolina, and that was hell," Sifford remembered in the *Houston Post*. "The first day of the tournament I led it with a 68. And that night I got people calling me up in the hotel, threatening my life, saying what they were going to do to me if I showed up for the next round. I just told them whatever they were planning to do, be prepared to do it because I still planned to tee off at 9:30." He won second place in that tournament and pocketed $700. On other occasions he was heckled ruthlessly by fans, who called him "nigger" and "boy" and suggested he return to caddying. Several times he was turned away from the gates of private clubs despite his official PGA status. Often he had to change clothes in his car or eat lunch in the locker room because the dining facilities were segregated. Sifford admitted in the *Sacramento Bee*: "It's hell, naturally, when a black man breaks into a white man's world."

Sifford endured, and he was rewarded with victories in the 1967 Greater Hartford Open and the 1969 Los Angeles Open. He earned $341,345 as a PGA pro and repeatedly applied for the prestigious Masters Tournament. His application was always denied, even during the years of his tour victories. One year he led the Canadian Open after the first round. Traditionally, the winner of that tournament received an automatic invitation to the Masters. That year, however, the PGA cabled the Canadian Open that it would not necessarily invite the winner to the Masters Tournament—right in the middle of the Canadian Open. Stung yet again by the blatant racism, Sifford did not win the tournament. Another time, a promise of a $100,000 bonus and a new car for anyone who hit a hole-in-one was mysteriously rescinded when Sifford managed to do just that. He sued and won his cash and car.

No black athlete played in the Masters Tournament until 1975, the year Tiger Woods was born. By that time Sifford had retired from the PGA tour and was working as a teaching pro at a country club near Cleveland, Ohio. Sifford never cared much for teaching, however. He liked the challenge of the tournament. Therefore he happily joined the PGA Seniors Tour when it began in 1980. He toured with the Seniors for more than a decade and later moved to the Super Seniors Tour for those over 60 years old. Even as a member of the Seniors Tour Sifford often teed off against men much younger than himself, but he managed to stay among the top 50 earners from 1981 until 1989. His record with the Seniors helped to boost his career earnings to better than $1.2 million. In 1991 Sifford told the *Arizona Republic:* "Only the strong can survive out here. They counted me out 25 years ago, but I'm still here."

Sifford's 1992 autobiography, *Just Let Me Play*, recounts in vivid detail his years of trial in the battle against racism. Although one of the better-known pros, especially among the Seniors Tour, he had few product endorsement offers; his first came from the Toyota company. "For 35 years this cigar has been my trademark, but I've never had a cigar sponsor," he noted in the *San Francisco Chronicle*. Sifford also laments the lack of young black talent rising in golf's ranks. "Blacks who go to school these days are taught football, basketball and baseball, but not golf." He predicted that fewer, not more, blacks would become PGA golfers within the next decade. Indeed, in 2004 Tiger Woods was the only American black of African descent on the PGA tour. Woods related to *Golf International* that "If it wasn't for Charlie and players like Teddy Rhodes, Bill Spiller and others, we wouldn't be here. I certainly wouldn't probably have been introduced to the game of golf because my dad wouldn't have played. Without Charlie's diligence and dedication…we owe everything to him and to others like him."

His cigar ever clamped in his mouth, Sifford claimed that he is not bitter, even though much work remains to be done for the proper integration of golf. Married for more than fifty years, he resides in Kingwood, Texas, a suburb of Houston. The "Jackie Robinson of golf" continued to play the Super Seniors Tour into his seventies. If not bitter, he did sound just a bit wistful in the *Lexington Herald-Leader* when he said: "Sometimes, I think what it would have been like if I could have played the tour when I was at my best. Really, I think it's unbelievable. I know I could have done well. I know I would have been up there with the best. Don't get me wrong. Golf has been good to me. It just could have been a whole lot better." He added: "But, you can't dwell on that. It's gone. It's not important, I guess, that I didn't make it real big. It's important that I made it. At least it did open the door for a few more blacks." Indeed Sifford has opened doors and inspired others to follow him. Tiger Woods' father Earl told *Golf International* that Sifford "took the punishment, the ridicule and he still persevered. For that, he should always be remembered. Because nobody else did it but him. He was the first one."

Sifford's accomplishments were honored in 2004 when he was inducted into the World Golf Hall of Fame. As the first black golfer to be so rewarded, Sifford remarked upon accepting his induction: "It's a wonderful thing that a little black man from Charlotte, N.C., a caddie, can go through all the obstacles he went through and wind up being inducted into the Hall of Fame," according to the *Tampa Bay Online*. "This makes me believe they accepted me as one of the professional golfers."

Selected works

Just Let Me Play (autobiography), Simon & Schuster, 1992.

Sources

Books

Sifford, Charlie, *Just Let Me Play,* Simon & Schuster, 1992.

Periodicals

Arizona Republic, November 10, 1991.
Atlanta Constitution, June 8, 1992.
Chicago Tribune, July 19, 1992.
Commercial Appeal (Memphis, Tennessee), June 2, 1992.
Houston Post, January 6, 1991.

Lexington Herald-Leader, August 28, 1986.
Los Angeles Times, August 12, 1990.
Sacramento Bee, July 1, 1988.
San Francisco Chronicle, August 14, 1987.
Upscale, February 1993.

On-line

"Charlie Sifford Breaks Hall of Fame Barrier," *Golf International,* http://www.golfinternationalmag.co.uk/News/121104_4.htm (January 14, 2005).
"Charlie Sifford Is Right Where He Belongs," *Tampa Bay Online,* http://golf.tbo.com/golf/MGBAVWW7D3E.html (January 13, 2005).

—Mark Kram and Sara Pendergast

Dr. Lonnie Smith

1942—

Jazz organist and pianist

A turban-wearing jazz institution, and one of the few jazz players to specialize in the difficult Hammond B-3 electric organ, Dr. Lonnie Smith has had a long musical career that may be divided into three distinct sections. In the first, shortly after his discovery, Smith played as a sideman in jazz bands led by others, most notably guitarist George Benson. In the second, Smith led his own band in the late 1960s and early 1970s, at the height of the movement known as soul-jazz. Finally, after a long hiatus from recording, Smith returned in the 1990s with fresh, experimental takes on his earlier styles.

Lonnie Smith—not to be confused with keyboardist Lonnie Liston Smith—was born in Buffalo, New York, on July 3, 1942. His mother sang around the house and introduced him to a potent mix of gospel, jazz, and classical music. Members of his extended family came by to play gospel music as well. "That was all in my bones," Smith told the *University of Idaho Argonaut*. "It was in my heart and soul in the beginning." By the time he was old enough to get on stage, Smith was singing in a group called the Teen Kings for a salary of six dollars a night. The group, which for a time included Buffalo sax player Grover Washington Jr., later changed its name to the Supremes—no relation to Diana Ross's group in Detroit.

Smith didn't really play an instrument at the time, but he dreamed of a career in music. He started spending time at a music store owned by Art Kubera, who finally asked him what he was doing there. "If I had an instrument, I could play," Smith said (as he recalled in a *Palm Beach Post* interview). "If I could play, I could make a living." The store owner took Smith into a back room and showed him a new Hammond B-3 organ, an instrument worth several thousand dollars. "If you can get it out of here, you can have it," the merchant said. "He did it for me," Smith told the *Post*. "I really owe everything to him."

About 20 at the time, he learned to play the organ quickly by ear. His biggest influence was organist Jimmy Smith, whom he met a few months after he started playing. "I liked everything that I heard when he played," he told *Down Beat*. "Jimmy has a flare, he has fire, and he has warmth. And he generates a beautiful sense of humor. He definitely has great technique, and he knows just what to play." Before long, Smith had enough keyboard skills to accompany traveling Motown-label vocalists when they came to town needing a pickup band.

About a year after he started playing, Smith rented his organ for a week to Brother Jack McDuff, another of the reigning organ players of the time, for a $25 fee. While McDuff was performing with alto saxophonist Lou Donaldson (probably at Buffalo's Pine Grill club), friends of Smith's in the audience called out to McDuff, encouraging him to let Smith play. The organist complied, and Smith had a ready-made audience of influential jazz people that included guitarist George Benson, a major pop star a decade later.

Smith made the most of the opportunity. Jazz promoter Jimmy Boyd arranged for Smith to join a recording session with guitarist Grant Green, but the young organist, feeling he wasn't ready, didn't show for

At a Glance . . .

Born on July 3, 1942, in Buffalo, NY; six children.

Career: Musician, mid-1960s–.

Address: *Office*—Palmetto Records, 9 Desbrosses Street, Suite 101, New York, NY 10013.

the session. It didn't matter—those who had heard Smith had become well aware of his talent. Benson at the time was forming a band of his own and offered Smith a place in it. After a quick rehearsal at Benson's mother's house, Smith became a touring jazz musician. Times were hard for the little-known group, and Smith recalled at one point having to grab waitresses' tips from restaurant tables in order to get by.

But things improved fast. Working with Benson for several years, Smith began his recording career on Benson's albums on the Columbia label. He sometimes played piano as well as organ, but the organ was his central focus. "Well, it's a passion for me," he told *All About Jazz.* "Right from the beginning I was able to play and I didn't even know how. I learned how to work the stops and that was it; everything else came naturally. It's a difficult instrument because you have two keyboards and the bass pedal, so you are the orchestra." Once the instrument was in place for a gig it couldn't be moved easily, so Smith often showed up early at the club to practice in an empty room.

Smith moved to New York and worked with Lou Donaldson later in the 1960s, contributing organ grooves to Donaldson's modestly successful commercial hit "Alligator Boogaloo." Around the same time, Smith formed a band of his own and recorded his *Finger Lickin' Good* album for Columbia. In the late 1960s, one branch of jazz moved away from modernist experimentation and toward a closer relationship with the rhythms and harmonies of commercial soul music. The resulting "soul-jazz" was just the ticket for Smith, whose Hammond organ had a long background in the African-American church music from which soul was originally derived.

Moving to the Blue Note label, Smith recorded the best-known music of his career. Such albums as *Think!* (1968) and *Lonnie Smith Drives* (1970) fit the basic soul-jazz pattern but showed Smith's tremendous talents as a sheer improviser with massive ten- or fifteen-minute jams built on a composition of Smith's own, another jazz piece of the time, or even on "Three Blind Mice" (as heard on *Think!*). Joining Smith in his band and on records were several noted jazz players of the1970s, including trumpeter Lee Morgan and saxo-

phonist David "Fathead" Newman. In 1969, Smith was named top organist of the year by *Down Beat* magazine.

Smith recorded for a variety of smaller labels throughout the 1970s, slowing down somewhat as soul-jazz lost its appeal but never falling out of favor with his fellow musicians. During the period of his Blue Note albums he was still simply Lonnie Smith, but later he became Dr. Lonnie Smith—a title bestowed not by any academic institution but by musicians who called on Smith to "doctor" pieces they were struggling with. Smith also began wearing a turban. It didn't have any religious connotation, but it added to the already rather mystical feel of his music.

During the 1980s, Smith was mostly absent from the recording scene. He continued to perform, occasionally making appearances with rhythm-and-blues singers like Etta James as well as with jazz groups. He developed a reputation in Europe, having recorded his *Lenox and Seventh Avenue* album in Paris in 1985, and he continued to perform there, planning a continent-wide tour in late 2004 and 2005. He appeared as a sideman on albums by other artists, and in 1990 he reunited with Lou Donaldson for the latter's *Play the Right Thing* album.

By the 1990s Smith, who had six children, had moved to Fort Lauderdale, Florida. He recorded several more albums with Donaldson, and the new exposure for his playing led Blue Note to reissue some of his classic albums of the late 1960s and early 1970s. Younger organists had always named Smith as a strong influence, and now they were joined by musicians who were resurrecting all kinds of classic soul and rock sounds. Musicians in the acid jazz movement, which merged jazz with electronic sounds, took an interest in Smith's music.

What they found when they attended one of Smith's concerts, which took place on a regular basis at O'Hara's Pub in Fort Lauderdale and the Jazz Showcase in West Palm Beach, was a unique atmospheric conception that fit well with the sonic experimentation of acid jazz. Smith's style was still rooted in soul-jazz and its underlying blues harmonies, but he stretched the style out to cosmic lengths, offering 20-minute-long improvisations that might begin with almost formless quiet sounds and gradually build to a high pitch of intensity. Often Smith performed as part of a trio: organ, guitar, and drums.

Smith kept things fresh with innovative new album releases, including a Jimi Hendrix tribute album and another, 2003's *Boogaloo to Beck,* devoted to the eclectic and unclassifiable alternative musician Beck Hansen. Smith hadn't heard of Beck before agreeing to record the album, which was suggested by a guitarist friend, but he made Beck's diverse music his own. "It's sampling without the sampler. Beck will be thoroughly amused," noted *San Francisco Chronicle* critic James

Sullivan, and other publications also registered positive reviews. The *All Music Guide* called his next album, the soul-jazz *Too Damn Hot,* "Smith's best record of the decade so far," and the organist showed no signs of pulling back the throttle on his free-spirited jazz life. Asked by the *Miami New Times* whether he planned to incorporate Beck's music into his live shows, Smith answered, "I feel that I'm going to do something a little different. That's what I have plans to do. Something quite different. Yeah."

Selected discography

Finger Lickin' Good, Columbia, 1966.
Think!, Blue Note, 1968.
Turning Point, Blue Note, 1969.
Move Your Hand (live), Blue Note, 1969.
Lonnie Smith Drives, Blue Note, 1970.
Live at Club Mozambique, Blue Note, 1970.
Mama Wailer, Blue Note, 1971.
When the Night Is Right!, Chiaroscuro, 1975.
Lenox and Seventh Avenue, 1985.
Afro Blue, Music Masters, 1993.
Purple Haze: A Tribute to Jimi Hendrix, Music Masters, 1995.
The Turbanator, 32 Jazz, 2000.
Boogaloo to Beck: A Tribute, Scufflin', 2003.
Too Damn Hot, Palmetto, 2004.

Sources

Books

Feather, Leonard, and Ira Gitler, *The Biographical Encyclopedia of Jazz,* Oxford, 1999.

Periodicals

Down Beat, July 2004, p. 70.
Financial Times (London, England), April 29, 2004, p. 15.
Miami New Times, September 18, 2003.
Palm Beach Post, April 13, 1997, p. J4.
San Francisco Chronicle, May 25, 2003, p. 28.
St. Louis Post-Dispatch, March 7, 2003, p. C8.
University of Idaho Argonaut, September 3, 2004.

On-line

Dr. Lonnie Smith, www.drlonniesmith.net (December 1, 2004).
"Dr. Lonnie Smith," *All Music Guide,* www.allmusic.com (December 1, 2004).
"Dr. Lonnie Smith: The Doctor Is In...," *All About Jazz,* www.allaboutjazz.com/php/article.php?id=908 (December 1, 2004).

—James M. Manheim

Lonnie Liston Smith

1940—

Jazz keyboardist

The "fusion" jazz of the 1970s, which merged jazz with more commercially oriented influences from rock, rhythm-and-blues, and funk, fell out of fashion as its leading practitioners either moved into popular music or went on to newer jazz experiments. But keyboardist Lonnie Liston Smith has been fusion's survivor. Resurrecting his career several times after he seemed to have been written off by the jazz world, Smith seemed to have an uncanny ability to connect with younger musicians and yet maintain the core of his blissful, rather meditative style. He remained active long enough to find himself hailed as an elder statesman by acid jazz musicians of the 1990s and early 2000s.

The spiritual feel of Smith's music was shaped early in his life. Lonnie Liston Smith (not to be confused with organist Dr. Lonnie Smith) was born in Richmond, Virginia on December 28, 1940. His father worked in a tobacco factory at the time, but soon joined a gospel quartet called the Harmonizing Four. Virginia was a hotbed of gospel singing, and the elder Lonnie Liston Smith was able to turn music into a full-time job by 1946. Such stars of the gospel genre as the Swan Silvertones and Sam Cooke often stopped by the Smith household. The three male Smith children all became musicians; flutist and vocalist Donald Smith often performed with his Lonnie Liston Smith, and the Rev. Ray Smith served as music minister at the Richmond Christian Center church.

Emulated Saxophonists

Smith learned to play the piano at home but began taking lessons after it became clear that he had some

talent. As a high school student he became interested in modern jazz, but it was saxophonists Charlie Parker and John Coltrane, as well as the cool, unorthodox trumpeter Miles Davis that caught his ear. He intentionally tried to follow their styles and not to emulate the work of jazz pianists like McCoy Tyner and Horace Silver. While still in his teens, Smith was appearing with jazz groups in the Baltimore area and backing such vocal stars as Betty Carter when they came through town.

After earning a degree in music education from Baltimore's Morgan State University in 1961, Smith got a tip from a college bandmate that there was an open keyboard spot in the highly experimental Jazz Messengers band led by drummer Art Blakey. Smith moved to New York City in 1962 to take the job, making his recording debut with Blakey. He also filled a keyboard slot in the band of another very progressive percussionist, Max Roach. In 1965 he joined the band of saxophonist Roland Kirk (later Rahsaan Roland Kirk), appearing on six tracks of Kirk's *Rip, Rip and Panic* album that year.

In 1968 Smith joined the band of saxophonist Pharaoh Sanders, one of the top touring modern jazz ensembles of the time. It was with Sanders that Kirk started experimenting with the electric keyboards he would often use later in his career, creating a wash of sound as an underpinning for Sanders' frenzied soloing. In the early 1970s Smith began performing and recording intermittently with trumpeter Miles Davis, the key creator of fusion jazz and one of the all-time giants of the genre. Davis tabbed Smith to play on his 1974 *Big*

ing texture. Lyrics, when there were any, often referred to spiritual concerns and the expansion of consciousness.

Despite energetic touring, Smith's reputation faded a bit by the mid-1980s. "Smith has tended to regurgitate his better ideas in increasingly vapid cycles," complained the *Washington Post* in 1983. He found himself without a recording contract for a time. "I had a lot of idealistic concepts about music, and about the spiritual message I was trying to get across," Smith told the *St. Louis Post-Dispatch.* "But most record companies only care about demographics and bottom line sales." Still, he retained strong audience loyalty in Europe and Japan, appearing at festivals in both countries.

Venerated by Hip-Hop Artists

Smith made several recordings for the Doctor Jazz label and for the small, Maryland-based Startrak Records. In the late 1980s the hip-hop movement, with its strong basis in funk, began to propel his career upward once again. His debut album for Startrak, *Love Goddess,* featured guest appearances by vocalist Phyllis Hyman and saxophonist Stanley Turrentine, but soon Smith was working with rapper Guru, who was one of the first to attempt to mix the jazz and hip-hop genres. Smith found himself an elder statesman. "Guru and the other rappers would tell me how their uncles used to make them listen to me and Miles and Donald Byrd and how they got the message," Smith told Australia's *Daily Telegraph Mirror* newspaper.

Smith appeared on the *Guru Jazzmatazz Volume One* album but then took another hiatus from recording. He reemerged in 1998 with his *Transformation* CD, which returned to a sound reminiscent of the Cosmic Echoes years. (The Cosmic Echoes, after a series of personnel changes, disbanded in the mid-1980s.) Once again Smith showed his ability to connect with contemporary listeners; quiet storm radio had been reborn as "smooth jazz," and Smith, approaching the age of 60, was once again a frequent radio presence.

Smith established his own label, Loveland, which was distributed by the large Sony conglomerate. Several of his early albums were reissued, and his music of the late 1970s and early 1980s was collected on a two-CD set called *Explorations: The Columbia Years.* Touring the United Kingdom in 2003 and 2004, fusion's cosmic-minded survivor showed no signs of calling it quits. He continued to live and make music according to a philosophy he had expressed nearly 30 years before to the *Tri-State Defender:* "Music is one of the ruling forces in the Cosmos and I constantly stretch for the ultimate. Music should bring a message and I am but a messenger."

Fun album, keeping Smith on his toes by demanding that he learn to play the organ. "It was intimidating," Smith recalled in an essay reproduced on his Web site, *Lonnie Liston Smith Online.* "Then Miles gave me two nights to learn how to make music on the thing. Miles liked to introduce new sounds in a surprising way—that's how he produced such innovative, fresh music."

Made Solo Debut

After a stint with Argentine saxophonist Gato Barbieri, during which he added a persisting Latin accent to his music, Smith was signed to a contract by producer Bob Thiele on his Flying Dutchman label. Smith put together a band of his own, the Cosmic Echoes, and recorded his first album, *Astral Traveling.* Mostly but not exclusively instrumental, the music Smith and the Cosmic Echoes made was fusion jazz that combined a spacious, spiritual feel with a layer of funk and rhythm-and-blues (R&B). As Smith gained popularity with the *Expansions* LP (1975), Flying Dutchman was picked up for distribution by the larger RCA label.

Smith moved to the Columbia label with his 1978 album *Loveland* and kept up a rapid pace of recording through the rest of the 1970s. When he added vocals to the mix, as with 1979's "Space Princess," Smith created a sound close to the commercial R&B of the day and gained a good deal of radio airplay. His fortunes were boosted by the emergence around 1980 of the "quiet storm" radio format, which blended jazz with sophisticated black pop styles; such Smith numbers as "Never Too Late" became staples of the format. His instrumental numbers often established a basic beat and then surrounded it with subtle shifts of a shimmer-

Selected discography

Astral Traveling, Flying Dutchman, 1973.
Cosmic Funk, Flying Dutchman, 1974.
Expansions, Flying Dutchman, 1975.
Visions of a New World, Flying Dutchman, 1975.
Reflections of a Golden Dream, RCA, 1976.
Live!, RCA, 1977.
Renaissance, RCA, 1977.
Loveland, Columbia, 1978.
A Song for the Children, Columbia, 1979.
Dreams of Tomorrow, Doctor Jazz, 1979.
Love Is the Answer, Columbia, 1980.
Love Goddess, Startrak, 1983.
Silhouettes, Doctor Jazz, 1984.
Rejuvenation, Doctor Jazz, 1985.
Make Someone Happy, Doctor Jazz, 1989.
Ankhspansion, Novus, 1991.
Magic Lady, Startrak, 1991.
Transformation, Loveland, 1998.
Exotic Mysteries/Loveland, Sony International, 1998.
Explorations: The Columbia Years, Legacy, 2002.

Sources

Books

Feather, Leonard, and Ira Gitler, *The Biographical Encyclopedia of Jazz,* Oxford, 1999.

Periodicals

Daily Telegraph Mirror (Sydney, Australia), July 21, 1995.
Philadelphia Tribune, December 6, 1996, p. E5.
Richmond Times-Dispatch, August 2, 1995, p. B1.
St. Louis Post-Dispatch, March 22, 1990, p. G8.
Tri-State Defender (Memphis, TN), April 3, 1976, p. 7.
Washington Post, June 24, 1983, p. 35.

On-line

"Lonnie Liston Smith," *All Music Guide,* www.allmusic.com (December 1, 2004).
Lonnie Liston Smith Online, www.lovelandrecords.com (December 1, 2004).

—James M. Manheim

Nate Smith

1929—

Labor activist

From lying in order to enter the navy at the age of 12 to boxing his way into the union at 16, Nate Smith proved that he knew how to get what he wanted. What he wanted in the mid-1960s was to break the color barriers in the construction industry in Pittsburgh. To do so, he laid down in front of bulldozers to stop work at construction sites. He also formed an innovative training program that was emulated nationwide. For his efforts he received death threats and beatings. But he got what he wanted. Not only in Pittsburgh, but across the country, construction unions opened up to blacks. Smith told *Contemporary Black Biography* (CBB) that he estimated that he helped some 2,000 people get union cards over the years. The *New Pittsburgh Courier* placed that number closer to 17,000. No matter the final figure, Smith's legacy lives on daily in the black workers who now have steady work at solid union wages. "He is why I'm here," a 21-year old African-American union worker told the *New Pittsburgh Courier* in 2004. "I'm not here because of what I did. I'm here because of what Nate did."

Fought His Way into the Union

Nate Smith was born on February 23, 1929, and raised in the predominantly black Hill District of Pittsburgh, Pennsylvania. After seventh grade, Smith ran away to the navy. "I always liked the song, "Anchors Away" and I was downtown one day and I heard the song playing. I was near the recruiting office, so I went in," Smith told CBB. The next day he was off to boot camp and soon on a ship to Europe. "I was 12 years old, but I looked much older," he told CBB. It took the navy two years to figure out Smith's real age. By that time he had learned the skill that would change his life—heavy equipment operation.

At 14 Smith was back in Pittsburgh. Instead of returning to school, he decided to become a boxer. "I was boxing on the ship when I was overseas in the navy and I liked it," he told CBB. He began training at a local gym as a middleweight fighter. He was good and personable and soon developed a fan base in the city, including a prominent Pittsburgh millionaire. "One day I was walking downtown … and I ran into this man," Smith told CBB. "He said, 'You're Nate Smith.' I said, 'Yeah, who are you?' It turned out he was Edgar Kaufmann. He owned Kaufmann department stores and he had seen me box." Kaufmann offered to sponsor Smith. "He paid for my training and accompanied me on out of town fights." Eventually the two became like family. "[Kaufmann] used to introduce me to people as his adopted son," Smith told CBB.

Two years and over 100 professional fights into his boxing career, Smith had to quit. "I was doing pretty good, but I left because my body just couldn't take the blows," Smith told CBB. "I was only 16 and the doctor said my body hadn't settled enough." Smith decided to take advantage of his navy training and get a union job as a heavy equipment operator. However he was too young, too inexperienced, and too black for the 1940s union. The civil rights movement was still a few years off, and affirmative action not yet imagined. Only the lowest-paying, most menial of construction jobs were

At a Glance . . .

Born on February 23, 1929, in Pittsburgh, PA; married Minnie Smith; children: Nate Jr., Renee, and Sabrina. *Military service:* U.S. Navy, 1940-42.

Career: Local 66 of the Operating Engineers' Union, Pittsburgh, PA, heavy equipment operator, 1944-196?; Operation Dig, Pittsburgh, PA, founder, 1968–; Nate Smith Enterprises, Pittsburgh, PA, founder, 1969–.

Selected memberships: Operation PUSH/Rainbow Coalition, executive board member; Pittsburgh Cancer Institute, volunteer; Western Hospital, consultant.

Selected awards: Health Education Center, Action Board Member of the Year; Pittsburgh Junior Chamber of Commerce, Man of the Year in Labor; Pittsburgh African-American Legacy Committee, Pittsburgh Freedom Fighter Award, 2004; Pittsburgh Public Schools, honorary diploma, 2004; Allegheny County Council, county proclamation, 2004.

Addresses: *Office*—Operation Dig, 130 Larimer Avenue, Pittsburgh, PA, 15206.

open to African Americans. That fact did not stop Smith.

Bulldozed Path for Blacks in Construction

"The union guys used to go to the fights all the time, so I knew who they were," Smith told *CBB*. "I went to the union office and gave the guys four tickets [to a championship match] in exchange for my union card." Smith became a heavy equipment operator for Local 66 of the Operating Engineers' Union. "I loved operating bulldozers, cranes, all kinds of equipment," he told *CBB*. He was also good at his job, surprising his bosses. "Those two union officials, they thought I wouldn't keep it up, but I proved them wrong," Smith told the *New Pittsburgh Courier*.

In the late 1950s and early 1960s, Smith became involved in the civil rights movement. "I went with Jesse Jackson, and we marched all over Atlanta, and then we came to Pittsburgh and marched some more," Smith recalled to *CBB*. As Smith got involved in the national campaign for civil rights, he realized that closer to home there was serious work to be done. Though Smith had gotten past the color barrier in the Pitts-

burgh unions, he had not broken it. "I couldn't see any black people in the craft unions," Smith told *CBB*. "And I checked it out and found out the unions weren't hiring blacks. The excuse was that there weren't any trained minorities." Not a man to accept excuses, Smith dreamed up Operation Dig.

Operation Dig provided African Americans the skills needed for construction union jobs. "I started training blacks on the weekends. I taught them how to operate bulldozers, cranes, all of it," Smith told *CBB*. Smith financed the program with help from Kaufmann and fellow Pittsburgh philanthropist Elsie Hillman of the Hillman Foundation. Smith also took out loans on his home to help pay for backhoes and scrapers for the program. Operation Dig launched in 1969 and within two years 90 African Americans were card-holding union members working on various job sites throughout Western Pennsylvania. "It just mushroomed from there," Smith told the *New Pittsburgh Courier*. The program was copied in states across the country and Smith became a civil rights star. He was profiled in the *Wall Street Journal* and named one of the 100 most influential blacks in America by *Ebony*.

Laid Life on the Line to Integrate Unions

Despite its initial success, Operation Dig could not overcome the deeply rooted racism within the unions. "There was a problem going on," Smith explained to *CBB*. "The contractors wanted good workers, but the white union workers didn't want to lose their jobs to black workers." He continued, "Operation Dig made sure there were trained black workers but they still weren't getting hired. So we formed the Black Construction Coalition." In conjunction with the NAACP and other community and civil rights groups, Operation Dig formed the coalition to directly confront unfair hiring practices.

The Civil Rights Act of 1964 had prohibited discrimination in employment. Thus Smith and company had the law on their side. They also had a militancy inspired by the Black Power movement that had risen up in anger against the slow march of civil rights. The coalition was ready to fight. It sponsored 800-people strong marches that often slipped into violent confrontations with the police. Marchers were beaten with billy clubs, sprayed with mace, and hauled off to jail. Not intimidated, Smith boldly employed other confrontational tactics. After a job supervisor reneged on an agreement to hire 10 black workers, Smith insisted on a meeting on the tenth floor of the building. "What happened was I held this man out the window," Smith told the *New Pittsburgh Courier*. "I grabbed him and held him out over the edge and told him, 'Look at all those people down there. They want jobs. You're going to hire them or I'm going to drop you.' He said, 'They're hired.' That's all it took." He continued, "He could have pulled me down with him. It wasn't like I was going to take his life. I was going to take our lives." Meanwhile "accidents" began to occur at job sites where African Americans were not employed. Though these actions secured some jobs for blacks, real success came when the coalition confronted the problem at its source—the construction sites.

"I laid down in front of bulldozers and stopped job sites. I said hire me or run me over," Smith told *CBB.* "At the time it seemed kind of crazy, but I really believed that God was on my side." In all, the Black Construction Coalition stopped work on ten building projects, including a highly publicized shutdown of Pittsburgh's Three Rivers baseball stadium site. "Contractors don't like that. When a site shuts down, they lose a lot of money," Smith told *CBB.* "So they listened to me, and they hired blacks." Smith's actions made him a hometown hero. "I'm the most popular man in Pittsburgh," he told the *New Pittsburgh Courier.* They also made him quite a few enemies. He received a bullet wound in his leg during a drive-by shooting attempt. During a ball game at Three Rivers, Smith's son was doused with gasoline and set on fire, suffering third-degree burns. No one was arrested in either incident.

Became Role Model and Mentor

The Black Construction Coalition led to the creation of the Pittsburgh Plan, a joint venture of local government, unions, and community groups designed to oversee the smooth integration of African Americans into the building trades. Though Smith was active with the plan, he began to focus his energies on his own business. "In 1969 I formed Nate Smith Enterprises, my own construction company. I started bidding on jobs and getting contracts." His firm worked on stadiums and schools, roads and highways—always with crews that included both blacks and whites.

In the decades since Operation Dig was founded, Smith has become a role model to children in Pittsburgh. "Our kids need someone to look up to. Someone who is not an athlete or an entertainer, but an everyday person. That's who I represent," he told the *New Pittsburgh Courier.* He visited dozens of public schools to talk about his role in the Civil Rights movement and to tell the kids about the career possibilities in the craft unions. He told *Jet,* "I want to see young minorities take advantage of the opportunities today that I created in the early '70s in the building trades." His work earned him a high school degree. Over 60 years after dropping out of school, Pittsburgh's Westinghouse High School awarded Smith an honorary diploma.

In the mid-1990s he teamed up with Pittsburgh contractor Gill Berry to develop Berry Enterprises in Partnership with Organized Labor, a training program to help inner-city teens acquire the skills needed for a union apprenticeship. In 2000 he helped launch Renaissance III, a recruitment and training program for minorities and women sponsored by 23 local trade unions. As late as 2004, well into his 75th year, Smith was still involved in the ongoing struggle to keep minorities on union jobs. "I still get a lot of calls from black workers. They call me up when they are having a problem on a job. Or if there aren't any blacks or women on a job," Smith told *CBB.* "And if word gets out that Nate Smith is looking into a job site, the contractors shape up. They don't want me coming out to a site."

Smith has received many honors for his activism including a plaque at Pittsburgh's historic Freedom Corner. Located on a former stop on the Underground Railroad, Freedom Corner honors Pittsburgh citizens who fought for civil rights. "It's beyond my wildest dreams that this would happen. I'm glad my name will be up there," he told the *New Pittsburgh Courier.* "This cost us a lot, in terms of getting beaten on the head with police truncheons, going to jail. But really, it's a small price to pay." Another honor that delighted Smith was when he was approached to make a movie about his life. He hoped the title would be *Bacon and Eggs on Sunday Morning.* "That's my philosophy," Smith told *CBB.* "If you live in America, you should be able to have bacon and eggs on Sunday morning. It means you can work. That you got a job." Minority union workers around the country should tip their Sunday morning coffee cup to Smith in salute.

Sources

Periodicals

Jet, March 29, 2004,
New Pittsburgh Courier, November 23, 1994; February 11, 1995; February 6, 1999; March 31, 2001; June 6, 2001; June 16, 2004.

On-line

"Community Leader, Nate Smith, to Receive 'Freedom Fighter' Award," *Pittsburgh Public Schools,* http://cms.pps.k12.pa.us/natesmith.asp?ezprint=6/23/200494741AM (October 28, 2004).
"Regular Meeting," *Allegheny County Council,* www.county.allegheny.pa.us/council/minutes/2004/meet240615.pdf (October 28, 2004).

Other

Additional information for this profile was obtained through an interview with Nate Smith on December 7, 2004.

—Candace LaBalle

Joseph Spence

1910-1984

Guitarist and vocalist

Bahamian guitarist Joseph Spence was a truly original stylist on his instrument. Never famous outside the Bahamas, or even inside that country with the exception of his home island, Spence nevertheless fascinated and influenced a number of prominent American and British guitarists, including slide virtuoso Ry Cooder and the eclectic bluesman Taj Mahal. The explanation for his influence was simple: Spence was a highly virtuosic player who didn't sound remotely like any other guitarist. He developed his style on his own and for most of his long life played for friends and other interested listeners, not worrying much about approval and not at all about commercial success. Fans and folklorists made several recordings of Spence, but he didn't own copies of any of them.

Spence was born in August of 1910 on Andros Island in the Bahamas. When he was nine, he was given a guitar by an uncle who lived in the United States, and the first steps in the formation of his distinctive style were taken as he taught himself to play it. Spence learned more about music at the feet of another uncle, this one in the Bahamas, who was a popular and highly regarded flute player. Along with two percussionists, uncle and nephew would play for dances on Andros Island. He recalled playing a variety of dance rhythms that included quadrilles, waltzes, polkas, and calypso pieces.

Played Music on Sponge Fishing Trips

From the age of 16 until he was 28, Spence made a living as a sponge fisherman. Sponge fishing, like other kinds of work among African-descended peoples, had music associated with it, and Spence would bring his guitar along on trips, wrapping it in a cloth and keeping it below deck when he wasn't using it to avoid having the strings rust in the salt air. It was partly among sponge fishermen that the Bahamian tradition of "rhyming" developed. An early ancestor of rap music, rhyming consisted of extemporized verses often based on hymns or Bible stories. Spence would later be heard on recordings performing in his own heavily guitar-influenced version of the style.

In 1938, a blight struck the sponges in the Bahamas' waters, and Spence was thrown out of work. Far from being discouraged, Spence interpreted the blight as a sign of divine intervention. "God destroy all the sponge," he explained to authors John Stropes and Justin Segel in their on-line article. "You see, when the spongers used to bring the boat to the merchant, sinking down loaded with sponge, when they sell the sponge they still left in debt. They don't hardly get nothing. So I figure the father say, 'Well, I see they're doing too much with this poor people having to kill these sponge. I better put them on something else.'"

Spence moved on to the Bahamian capital of Nassau, and during World War II he and his wife worked as migrant farmers in the southeastern United States, filling a need left by the departure of young Americans for the European and Pacific fronts. The two years Spence spent in the United States were crucial to his development as a guitarist, for he came into contact with a variety of American string traditions and incorporated bits and pieces of them into his own style.

At a Glance . . .

Born in August, 1910, on Andros Island, Bahamas; died on March 18, 1994, in Nassau, Bahamas; married Louise.

Career: Musician. Sponge fisherman, Bahamas, 1926-38; recorded by folklorist Alan Lomax, late 1930s; migrant farm worker, southeastern United States, 1944-46; stonemason, 1946-1970s; night watchman, mid-1970s.

Performing often in places as musically diverse as Mountain City, Tennessee, and Belle Glade, Florida, Spence heard both blues and country music.

Learned American Pieces

"St. Louis Blues" became a staple of his repertory, but for the most part he absorbed American folk and popular music piecemeal, learning individual compositions and adapting them for himself rather than plunging headlong into American styles. Spence also deepened his knowledge of Christian hymns during this period, however, and they shaped his style more fundamentally. He learned to play a variety of music as if he were singlehandedly reproducing the sounds a church organ or choir might make. While most fingerstyle guitarists aim for picking out a bass line with the thumb and adding an elaborated melody line with the fingers, Spence inserted internal harmonies so that several lines of music would be heard at once, even as he kept up a full melody line.

It was no wonder that visiting musicians and folklorists, when they first heard Spence, were sometimes convinced that he had another musician hidden nearby to provide an accompaniment. He sounded like he was playing several guitars at once. Returning to Nassau in 1946, Spence worked as a stonemason by day and performed at hotels and on yachts at night. Gradually he gave that up. "The town gets so wicked, you know," he explained to Stropes and Segel, "and when I coming back home, them fellows know I have been to those boats, and they figure I make money, they try to knock me down."

By then, however, the outside world was beginning to discover Spence. Folklorist Alan Lomax met and recorded Spence in the 1930s, and blues historian Samuel Charters recorded three hours of Spence's playing in the late 1950s. These recordings were released on the Smithsonian Folkways label under the title *Bahamian Folk Guitar* in 1960. Rock and blues guitarists visited the Bahamas to seek Spence out, and many of them left with their own styles deeply enriched

by the experience. Spence toured California in the late 1960s, staying at the home of his admirer Taj Mahal, and in 1972 he appeared along the eastern seaboard. He met Ry Cooder on that trip. In 1975 he turned down an offer to appear at New York's famed Carnegie Hall, saying that he didn't feel like traveling.

Took Night Watchman Job

In the mid-1970s Spence suffered a heart attack and took a less demanding job as an elementary school night watchman. At this advanced age he learned to play the piano at the school, creating a sound similar to his guitar style. He made several more recordings for the roots-oriented Arhoolie label, one of which, *Good Morning Mr. Walker,* contained a version of the 1960s pop hit "Sloop John B." Mostly Spence recorded religious music, sometimes joined by his wife Louise. His guttural voice served mostly as an accompanying percussion instrument, throwing in a word or taking a snatch of melody here and there; it was his guitar that carried the tune.

Spence's guitar—he always played in the key of D at this late date—sounded out-of-tune by conventional standards, but the sounds that came from it were consistent "There is no sloppiness in this," noted Jack Viertal in the liner notes to *Good Morning Mr. Walker.* "He tunes very precisely by playing the same figures over and over again until he is satisfied, and the guitar is always tuned to the same pitches." His playing was complicated and very difficult to imitate.

Spence died in Nassau on March 18, 1984, leaving many admirers and players he had influenced, but no real successors. In the words of Ry Cooder (quoted by Stropes and Segel), Spence was an example of "someone who breaks through whatever the dominant style or conventional approach might be, and makes a new statement." Joseph Spence was truly one of a kind.

Selected discography

Bahamian Folk Guitar (Music of the Bahamas, Vol. 1), Smithsonian Folkways, 1960.
Happy All the Time, Elektra, 1964 (reissued 2003).
Living on the Hallelujah Side, Rounder, 1987.
Good Morning Mr. Walker, Arhoolie, 1990.
Glory, Rounder, 1991.
Joseph Spence: The Complete Folkways Recordings, Smithsonian Folkways, 1992.

Sources

Periodicals

Guitar Player, September 2003, p. 87.
New York Times, June 12, 1960, p. 129.

On-line

"Joseph Spence," *Musicians and Entertainers of the Bahamas,* http://mail.vandercook.edu/~cjustilien/Artist/JosephSpence/spence_bio.html (November 30, 2004).

"Joseph Spence," *All Music Guide,* www.allmusic.com (November 30, 2004).

"Joshua Gone Barbados: A Joseph Spence Appreciation," *Chris Smith Reference Materials,* www.indiana.edu/~smithcj/cjsbvoi2.html (November 30, 2004).

Stropes, John, and Justin Segel, *Joseph Spence / Fingerstyle Phenomenon,* www.stropes.com/refdocs/spence.pdf (November 30, 2004).

Other

Liner notes to *Good Morning Mr. Walker,* Arhoolie 1061, 1990.

—James M. Manheim

Olivia Lee Dilworth Stanford

1914-2004

Businesswoman, pianist, and community leader

Olivia Stanford packed many full and successful lives within the almost ninety years she lived. First known nationally as the co-owner of the largest black beauty salon in the United States, she was also an accomplished musician and producer of musical performances. In addition to raising her three children and creating elegant homes in New York, St. Thomas, Portugal, Washington, D.C., and Florida, Stanford continued to be active in business, political work, and charity fundraising throughout her life. Growing up as the only child in a house full of doting adults, Stanford learned confidence and social skills that would allow her to rise above the racism and sexism of the society around her and feel at home anywhere in the world.

Stanford was born in the small town of Suffolk, Virginia, on December 10, 1914. Her grandparents were Lemuel and Lizzie Bynum, whose parents had once been slaves in North Carolina. Lemuel Bynum worked as a horse driver. He met Lizzie Roberts, a baby nurse, when she offered him water as she drove his wagon past the home where she worked. When they married, they moved into a house Lemuel had built in Suffolk on a piece of land he had bought for $75. The Bynums had three daughters, Lessie Mae, Maude, and Grace. Rather than moving out when they got married, each of the Bynum girls brought her husband to live in the family home. Into this large family of sisters and brothers-in-law, only one child was born, a baby girl named Olivia Lee, daughter of Grace Bynum and her husband George Dilworth.

During the first half of the twentieth century, limited employment opportunities existed for African-Ameri-

can women. One kind of work that was available was that of service in the homes of wealthy white families. As her mother had been, Grace Dilworth was a skilled baby nurse, and she traveled up and down the East Coast working as a nurse for white families with new babies. This meant frequently leaving her own daughter behind in the care of her sisters and their husbands. Since Grace was estranged from George Dilworth, who died in 1944, her loving extended family was extremely important in young Olivia's life.

First in Family to Graduate from College

Though she was the pampered darling of her aunts and uncles, Stanford was also a hard worker. Both of her uncles had their own businesses, one a tailor and dry cleaner and the other a funeral director. By age thirteen, young Olivia had learned to drive the business vehicles, and by fourteen she was helping her uncle prepare bodies for burial in his funeral home. Perhaps this early work inspired her future interest in business. Stanford was also a good student and especially liked her biology classes. Her family had great confidence in her abilities, and they both encouraged and helped Stanford to attend a local college, Virginia Normal Institute, later renamed Virginia State University.

While studying physical education in college during the mid-1930s she met and married her first husband, Edward Glass Trigg, DVM, a professor of veterinary medicine and bacteriology at Virginia Normal Institute.

At a Glance . . .

Born Olivia Lee Dilworth on December 10, 1914, in Suffolk, Virginia; died on February 9, 2004, in St. Augustine, Florida; married Edward Trigg, 193(?), (divorced); married Charles Clarke, 1941 (divorced); married Donald Stanford, August 19, 1949; children: Madalin (first marriage), Donald and Bruce (third marriage). *Education:* Virginia State University, BA, physical education.

Career: Rose-Meta House of Beauty and Olivia's House of Beauty, co-owner, 1943-55; L'Escale Inc., co-owner with her husband, 1955-65; United States Equal Employment Opportunity Commission, Public Awareness department, 1967-70.

Memberships: Inner Wheel of St. Thomas, founder, 1975; Partners for Health, founder, 1977.

Selected awards: Partners for Health, "My Fair Lady of St. Thomas" Award, 1990; Rotary International, Paul Harris Fellow. 1990.

The couple had one child, named Madalin, but the marriage ended a few years later. After her divorce, Stanford, always independent and adventurous, decided to make a big change in her life. Remembering stories her mother had told of her travels to New York City, she decided to move north, leaving Madalin with her family in Suffolk.

World War II had begun, and Stanford contributed to the war effort by working for the United Service Organization (USO). Founded in 1941, the USO is a national organization that allows non-military citizens to provide moral support and recreation for soldiers. Stanford had learned to play the piano when she was a child and had continued to love the instrument, teaching herself new songs and styles as she grew up. While in New York during the early years of the war, she frequently entertained soldiers, playing in USO shows. She was married again to a serviceman named Larry Clarke, but the marriage did not last long.

Built Own Business in New York

During the mid-1940s, Stanford met Rose Morgan, a beautician and businesswoman, who had moved to New York from Chicago. Both Stanford and Morgan had grown up in families of entrepreneurs, and both possessed a strong confidence that they too could succeed in business. Together they opened a beauty salon, relying on Morgan's skill as a beautician and Stanford's knowledge of business. Within a few years, the Rose-Meta House of Beauty in Harlem had become the largest black beauty salon in the United States. Stanford and Morgan not only created their own line of beauty products, especially designed for African-American women, but they expanded the business into several shops around the city, including one called Olivia's House of Beauty.

One of the revolutionary ideas behind Rose-Meta's success was Morgan and Stanford's belief that African features, such as kinky hair and dark skin, were not defects to be covered up or changed. They celebrated the beauty of these features and sold products to enhance them. Along with hairstyling and cosmetics, their salons offered massage and health advice, and there was a waiting list of black women who wanted their services.

In 1949 Stanford, then called Olivia Clarke, met a New York real estate developer named Donald Stanford. Both successful business people with imagination and an adventurous spirit, they found they had much in common. In August of the same year, they married. By 1954 they had two small sons, Donald Lemuel and Bruce, and had built their own house in Croton-on-Hudson, a Westchester county suburb of New York City.

Though they both had flourishing businesses and full lives in New York, the Stanfords began to think of moving. They were angered and frustrated by the racism and segregation they saw everywhere in the United States during the 1950s, and they were concerned about raising their children in this atmosphere. Donald had heard about investment opportunities in the Caribbean. His own parents had come from Jamaica, so he was familiar with Caribbean culture. Though many European cultures have colonized the nations of the Caribbean, most have large black populations. The Stanfords began to think that raising their children in a place where black people were in the majority would be a good idea.

Relocated to the Virgin Islands

In 1954 the family took an exploratory trip to Haiti, an island nation in the Caribbean. The unstable political situation in Haiti convinced them to leave and head for St. Thomas in the U.S. Virgin Islands. The Stanfords fell in love with St. Thomas, so they went back to New York, sold all their businesses and properties, and moved to the Caribbean. Olivia's first daughter Madalin chose to remain on the mainland, however, and follow in her mother's footsteps at Virginia State University.

In the budding economy of St. Thomas, Donald Stanford found ample opportunities for real estate development. Working side by side, Donald and Olivia Stanford leased quantities of unused U.S. government property and started many businesses, including the first gift shop, bar, and restaurant in the St. Thomas airport. Olivia threw herself into volunteer community work as well and began to produce musical shows to raise money for the island school. In the early 1960s, they built their dream home, a sprawling house on a mountain overlooking the St. Thomas harbor. They named their new home Kyalami, a Zulu word meaning "Our Loving Home."

In 1963, Donald Stanford had a mild heart attack. This health crisis prompted the hardworking Stanfords to think about slowing down. They retired from their many businesses, though they continued to hold leases and collect rents on much of the St. Thomas property. They took a vacation to Portugal and loved the relaxed beauty of that country so much that they packed up the boys and moved to Lisbon for the next two years. While the Stanfords relaxed, their sons attended the French school in Lisbon. As the boys grew older, however, their parents decided that, in order to ensure the best possible education for them, they would move back to the United States. In 1966, the family moved to Washington, D.C., where young Donald and Bruce would attend an alternative school.

Remained Active Late in Life

While in Washington, Olivia Stanford found more work to do. In response to the civil rights movement of the 1960s, Congress had passed many new civil rights laws. In 1965, President Lyndon Johnson had set up a government commission to enforce these newly enacted laws. This organization, the Equal Employment Opportunity Commission (EEOC), was headed by Clifford Alexander, an African-American lawyer from New York who had held various government positions.

Olivia Stanford felt that the Commission's work was important enough to draw her out of retirement. She went to work for Alexander in the public relations and public awareness department of the EEOC. As part of her work, she produced a series of Public Service Announcement films informing the public about how the new civil rights laws would affect their lives. Her history in producing and performing in musical shows helped her feel comfortable working with such celebrities as Anthony Quinn and Billy Dee Williams, who starred in the government films.

In 1971, with her children on their own or in college, Stanford and her husband returned to their mountaintop home in St. Thomas. Once again, she became immersed in community events, and once again she took a leadership role. Donald Stanford had long been active in the Rotary Club, a social service club for businessmen. The first Rotary Club was formed in Chicago in 1905 as a network for businessmen who wanted to make a contribution to their communities. By the early 2000s, there were over 31,000 Rotary clubs in 166 countries.

Since women were not originally permitted in Rotary, wives and other women who wished to support the community service work of the Rotarians formed separate organizations, called the Inner Wheel. There was no Inner Wheel on St. Thomas, so Olivia Stanford started one. Among its other projects, the St. Thomas Inner Wheel opened and operated a gift shop in the island hospital to raise funds for community services. Next, Stanford helped to found an organization called Partners for Health, which raised money to buy sorely needed equipment for the island hospital. Once again, Olivia Stanford began organizing musical shows and film festivals to raise money for her cause, calling on the celebrities she had met while working for the EEOC to come to St. Thomas and help.

In 1990, Partners for Health held a formal ball to honor Olivia Stanford for all her work in the community. The organization she had founded honored her with the title, "My Fair Lady of St. Thomas."

In 1991, the Stanfords decided to move to Florida in order to have better access to health care. Though she had several different homes in Florida, Olivia Stanford took her Steinway baby grand piano with her everywhere she moved, always happy playing music for her friends, her family, and her church. Her lively spirit attracted people to her and she made friends wherever she went.

Donald Stanford died in 1996, and in 1998 Olivia moved in with her youngest son for a short time. However, her independent spirit soon prompted her to look for her own place, and she moved again. She spent the last two years of her life designing and decorating yet another dream home, a condominium in St. Augustine, Florida. She died of pneumonia in 2004, having been active up to the end of her life. At the celebration of her life in the fall of 2004, one of her granddaughters lovingly described the gracious and irrepressible Olivia Stanford as someone who "always had something on her to-do list, was always looking for someone else to meet, and was still looking for the perfect pair of shoes."

Sources

Periodicals

The African, January 1948.
Ebony, May 1946.
New York Age, May 28, 1949.
Jet, March 29, 2004.

On-line

"A Brief History," *Rotary International,* www.rotary. com (November 8, 2004).
"Early Rotary Issues Regarding Women and Rotary," *Rotary's Global History Fellowship,* www.ro taryhistoryfellowship.org/ women/issues-early/inne rwheel/begin.htm (November 8, 2004).

"Rose Morgan," *The History Makers,* www.thehisto rymakers.com/biography/biography.asp?bioindex =167&category=styleMakers (November 8, 2004).

"Obituary: Olivia Dilworth Stanford," *Virgin Islands Daily News*, www.virginislandsdailynews.com/in dex.pl/article_obituaries?id=4066814 (September 28, 2004).

Other

Information for this profile was obtained through an interview with Donald Stanford on November 5, 2004. Additional help was provided by Madalin Price and Inner Wheel of St. Thomas.

—Tina Gianoulis

Franklin A. Thomas

1934—

Philanthropist, administrator, lawyer

Thomas, Franklin A., photograph. © Bettmann/Corbis.

Franklin A. Thomas made a name for himself as an inspiring leader in America. For seventeen years Thomas was president of the Ford Foundation, a vast and self-perpetuating trust originally endowed by car manufacturer Henry Ford and his son Edsel. With a reported $7.7 billion in assets when Thomas resigned his post in 1996, Thomas and his Ford Foundation staff used strategic sums of money—more than $200 million annually—to help needy communities, finance educational and cultural institutions, support civil rights in the United States and around the world, and strengthen and empower policy influencing organizations. Since leaving the Foundation, Thomas has continued to serve in leadership positions in America's largest corporations and has continued to work in philanthropic ventures in South Africa.

Born in 1934 in the Bedford-Stuyvesant section of Brooklyn, Thomas is the youngest child of a proud but poverty-wracked West Indian family. When Thomas was just eleven years old, his father, James, a laborer, became disabled and later died. Left to support six children, Thomas's mother, Viola, worked as a housekeeper until World War II when she landed a job as a machinist at American Can. The stoic Viola returned to housekeeping at the end of the war when the availability of returning soldiers allowed manufacturers to again raise racial and gender barriers to hiring.

Despite living in a poor West Indian neighborhood that was riddled with the violence of gang wars, Thomas was raised in a family atmosphere that fostered pride and an upward-looking mindset. "We were taught," he told *Ebony,* "that there were no limits on what you could do in life except the limits that you set on yourself." Thomas was a good student, a superior basketball player, and a leader in the Concord Baptist Church Boy Scouts. "He was something of a hero in my neighborhood," Dr. Bernard Gifford, who also grew up in "Bed-Stuy," told *Black Enterprise.* "Teachers held him up as a model because he was a student as well as a basketball player and that was important."

At 6 feet 4 inches in height, Thomas, a star center at Franklin K. Lane High School, was offered basketball scholarships by several major universities. He refused the scholarships and instead—on the advice of his mother who felt that others would question his

At a Glance . . .

Born Franklin Augustine Thomas, May 27, 1934, in Brooklyn, NY; son of James (a laborer) and Viola (a housekeeper and machinist; maiden name, Atherley) Thomas; married Dawn Conrada (divorced, 1972); children: Keith, Hillary, Kerrie, Kyle. *Education:* Columbia University, BA, 1956, LLB, 1963. *Military/Wartime Service:* U.S. Air Force, Strategic Air Command navigator, 1956-60; became captain.

Career: Federal Housing and Home Finance Agency, New York office, attorney, 1963; Southern District of New York, assistant U.S. attorney, 1964-65; New York City Police Department, deputy police commissioner in charge of legal matters, 1965-67; Bedford-Stuyvesant Restoration Corporation, Brooklyn, president and chief executive officer, 1967-77; attorney in private practice, 1977-79; Ford Foundation, New York City, president, 1979-96; TFF Study Group, consultant, 1996–.

Memberships: Aluminum Company of America, Avaya, CBS Inc., Cummins Engine Co., Inc., Citicorp/Citibank, and Lucent Technologies, board of directors; Study Commission on United States Policy Toward Southern Africa, chairman; Secretary of State's Advisory Committee on South Africa, member, 1985-87; September 11th Fund, chairman.

Awards: Honorary degrees from Yale University, Fordham University, Pratt Institute, Pace University, and Columbia University; Lyndon B. Johnson Foundation, award for contribution to the betterment of urban life, 1974; Columbia University, medal of excellence, 1976; Columbia College, Alexander Hamilton Award, 1983.

intelligence if he accepted a sports scholarship—accepted an academic scholarship from Columbia University.

At Columbia, Thomas nevertheless continued his basketball career. He became the first African American to captain an Ivy League basketball team and was twice voted the league's most valuable player. In addition, he became involved with the NAACP's (National Association for the Advancement of Colored People) drive to increase black admissions at the university. But what was perhaps most important about his Columbia expe-

rience were the relationships he developed with others who would later become movers and shakers in the fields of business, law, and politics.

After graduating in 1956, Thomas took advantage of his ROTC training and did a four-year hitch with the Air Force, where he worked his way up to captain and flew missions as a navigator with the Strategic Air Command. In 1960 he returned to Columbia for his law degree. He opted for a career in law after seeing a con man swindle his mother out of a down payment on a house she wanted to buy.

Upon receiving his law degree in 1963, Thomas moved into a series of high-powered government jobs. He worked as an attorney for the Federal Housing and Home Finance Agency, was admitted to the New York State Bar the following year, served as an assistant U.S. attorney in New York from 1964 until 1965, and then worked for three years as New York's deputy police commissioner in charge of legal matters. Asked later how he made the remarkable transition from economic impoverishment to positions of leadership in the legal arena, he told the *New York Times Magazine*, "I grew up in a family that just assumed that one, you were smart and capable; two, that you were going to work hard, and three, the combination of these two meant that anything was possible."

In 1967 Thomas caught the attention of New York senator Robert Kennedy. Kennedy was looking for ways to improve living conditions in Bedford-Stuyvesant and wanted to create a nonprofit community development agency to raise and coordinate public and private redevelopment funds. To head up the agency, Kennedy sought a "Bed-Stuy" resident. On the advice of staff member and future *Black Enterprise* publisher Earl Graves, Kennedy met with Thomas. Impressed with the 33-year-old lawyer, in May of that year he appointed Thomas president of the newly created Bedford-Stuyvesant Restoration Corporation.

Thomas soon acquired the reputation of a man who gets the job done. During his ten years as president, the Restoration Corporation raised some $63 million in public and private funds—including a significant amount from the Ford Foundation. It built three apartment complexes and erected a 200,000 square foot shopping center. It rehabilitated 400 brownstone units, established the Billie Holiday Theater, helped to start or expand 120 businesses in the area, and developed a $21 million mortgage pool. Under Thomas's leadership, the Restoration Corporation lured an IBM facility into the neighborhood, placed 7,000 residents in jobs and helped engender a positive feeling among the neighborhood's residents. Perhaps most importantly, Thomas's Restoration Corporation became a model for the hundreds of community-based redevelopment corporations that would later come into being around the country.

During his tenure at Bedford-Stuyvesant Restoration Corporation, Thomas also became well known in public and private circles. CBS, Citicorp/Citibank, AT&T, and the Cummins Engine Company all paid him handsomely to serve on their boards of directors. He was a trustee of the Ford Foundation, and in 1976, then president-elect Jimmy Carter even asked him to serve as secretary of Housing and Urban Development. A flattered Thomas refused, telling Carter that the only federal job he wanted was the one Carter was about to occupy.

Thomas left the Restoration Corporation in 1977, worked in private practice for a time, and for nine months filled in as head of New York's John Hay Whitney Foundation. Early in 1979, Rockefeller Foundation head Dr. John Knowles convinced him to lead a year-long study of apartheid—a policy of political and economic discrimination against blacks practiced by the oppressive white minority government of South Africa. Several months later, officials at the Ford Foundation asked if he would take on the foundation's presidency following the retirement of longtime Ford head McGeorge Bundy. Thomas agreed, stipulating that he be allowed to honor his commitment to the Rockefeller Foundation. He served as chairman of the Study Commission on United States Policy Toward Southern Africa and wrote the forward to the commission's 1981 report *Time Running Out*.

Reaction to Thomas's appointment as president of the Ford Foundation was enthusiastic. Vernon Jordan, former National Urban League president, hailed it as "the most significant black appointment in my time…the first real example of a case where whites have turned meaningful power over to a black," according to *Black Enterprise*.

Ebony reported that Thomas viewed the Ford Foundation as "one of the few places that has social purpose as its objective and…controls the resources with which to do something about it." But while his appointment represented honor and opportunity, it was not without its downside. The foundation was hitting hard times. Declining stock prices and overextension during the previous administration had shrunken assets to $2.2 billion from a mid-1960s high of $4 billion. Annual spending was down to $108 million from $220 million. In addition, the Ford Foundation was committed to too many programs.

Among his first actions upon occupying the foundation's New York offices was the creation of the Local Initiative Support Corporation (LISC). Funded by Ford and six corporations, the LISC would help existing community development groups—like the one Thomas had run in Bedford-Stuyvesant—move from successfully managed small projects to major neighborhood revitalization efforts.

But while LISC was important, Thomas's main inaugural task was an exhaustive review of all of the foundation's administrative and grant-making activities. In order to turn things around financially, Thomas had to

be a tough manager; changing the institution would mean confronting the entrenched staff. Each officer had to undergo a performance review and justify the worth of his or her program. Longtime staffers resented the review. They reportedly saw Thomas as aloof and unwilling to talk to them on a personal basis. Siobhan Oppenheimer-Nicolau, a program officer with Ford for 14 years, told *New York* magazine, "There was a very drastic change in style after Frank arrived. This had always been a very collegial operation, with a great deal of feedback, of exchange. Much of that stopped because he isolated himself and people had no way of knowing whether or not he had any confidence in them."

Early in 1981 Thomas completed his review and began making changes at the foundation. He told *New York* his mandate was to address problems of overextension, to reduce the ratio of management costs to program dollars, and to reorganize the staff in order to break up the largely separate divisions and encourage staff interaction. As a result of the reorganization, 16 senior staff members left of their own accord and another 16 were laid off. By the end of his third year, Thomas had trimmed the entire Ford staff from over 442 to about 324.

Many staffers were angry at being forced to leave. Four older employees filed age discrimination complaints with the U.S. Equal Employment Opportunity Commission (EEOC). Thomas responded that he had the right to let these people go and that they should have known better than to expect lifetime employment at the Ford Foundation. "The foundation has hired people on term contracts in order to reinforce the fact that there is no tenure here," he told *New York*. "Besides, there is always the desirability of having a somewhat regular rotation of significant parts of your staff…. Age was just not a factor in the decision of retention or non-retention."

While most critics recognized that Thomas was acting in the interest of the organization, some questioned his tactics. As quoted in *New York*, Oppenheimer-Nicolau noted that Thomas "chose to make a drastic turnaround rather than an evolutionary one, and this necessarily created more of a sense of threat than would normally have been the case."

Along with the staff cuts, Thomas made many important changes in the foundation's organization and priorities. He phased out Ford's heavy involvement in population control, environmental protection, school-finance reform, public-interest law and some other areas, while allocating more than half the foundation's budget for urban poverty and rural poverty and resources. In terms of grant-making, he moved the foundation away from providing routine operating expenses for local groups and toward concentrating on broader programs with the potential to impact large groups of people. Finally, Thomas reorganized the institution's three nearly autonomous divisions into six thematic areas: human rights and social justice; urban poverty and the disadvantaged; rural poverty and resources; education; international, economic, and political issues; and governance and public policy.

In contrast to Thomas's detractors, some observers acknowledged the president's serious-minded approach to his work—especially at a time when the government was pulling back in its commitment to all sorts of programs. "Frank is very analytical, careful and deliberate," Ford staffer Susan Berresford told *Ebony*. "In a period of diminishing resources, the kind of care he brings is all the more important. And he brings freshness."

By 1990 Thomas had in many basic ways changed the operation of the world's largest charitable foundation: the previously sagging endowment reached the $5.8 billion mark. The grant-making focused more on issues of domestic poverty, with an emphasis on results-oriented programming rather than on studies.

In many ways Thomas had worked to bring the experience he gained at the Bedford-Stuyvesant Restoration Corporation to the hundreds of community redevelopment agencies the Ford Foundation was supporting through the LISC. "I would argue community development is emerging as a major revolution in the country," he told the *New York Times*, "one that engages people in ways that affect their lives and their localities. It may not be glamorous, but it should stimulate an excitement in all of us regardless of our politics or background."

Though not known for his public persona, Thomas was coaxed out of his quiet ways by the 1992 riots in Los Angeles. He blamed the riots at least partially on the U.S. government. "The weak partner in community revitalization in the last decade has been the federal government, which has retreated from participation," he told the *New York Times*. "The events in Los Angeles tell us we cannot continue to fail investing in our neighborhoods and our people. We are spending the capital invested years ago, and that capital needs to be renewed."

After seventeen years at the helm, Thomas ended his career at the Ford Foundation in 1996. Susan Berresford was his chosen successor. Thomas drew great satisfaction in leaving the Foundation as "tightly managed, tightly budgeted, ..." and with "a sense that the place functions on a basis that can be explained, that decisions are taken on a basis that seems rational and consistent with the program agenda," according to the *Ford Foundation Report*. Writing about Thomas' career for the *Ford Foundation Report*, Henry B. Schacht considered Thomas' tenure a "period of extraordinary leadership." Thomas offered his philosophy of leadership to Siobhan Oppenheimer-Nicolau in an interview by the National Film Archive of Philanthropy, saying, as quoted in the *Ford Foundation Report*: "[I]deally, you want to attract people who are smarter than you are. That's how you help an organi-

zation grow. But first you have to be willing to admit that there are people who are smarter than you are. And then you have to consciously and deliberately try and find them and induce them to come and work in an environment where they, too, are not necessarily going to be the smartest persons in the place. If you can build that into your own psyche, if you don't feel threatened by those differences but feel enriched by them, then you can have a great time in a foundation. If, on the other hand, you have to feel that you know everything and know more about each subject than anyone else in your institution, then you are letting your own individual limits hinder the institution's ability to function well. And that's not leadership."

Since 1996, Thomas has continued to lead. He has maintained his membership on the board of directors of several of the country's most powerful companies, including Citicorp, Lucent Technologies, and Pepsico, and worked as a consultant for the TFF Study Group, a nonprofit organization dedicated to development in South Africa. He was also hired to chair the September 11th Fund to offer relief to the victims of the September 11, 2001, terrorist attacks in New York and Washington, D.C. In 2003 *Fortune* magazine dubbed Thomas as one of four "kingmakers" in corporate America, noting that his position in some of the country's largest companies gave him the "power to make other people powerful." Given Thomas' dedication to wooing the best and the brightest to his organizations, corporate America seemed in good hands.

Sources

Periodicals

Black Enterprise, September 1980; February 1982; July 1990.
Ebony, October 1982.
Ford Foundation Report, Spring 1996.
Fortune, August 11, 2003.
Los Angeles Times, February 14, 1992.
Newsweek, September 7, 1981.
New York, September 28, 1981.
New Yorker, August 31, 1981.
New York Times, January 30, 1979; February 8, 1981; October 10, 1982; May 26, 1992.
U.S. News & World Report, March 31, 1981.
Wall Street Journal, February 15, 1979.

On-line

Ford Foundation, www.fordfound.org (January 31, 2005).
"Franklin A. Thomas," *Ford Foundation Report*, http://www.fordfound.org/publications/ff_report/ view_ff_report_detail.cfm?report_index=48 (January 31, 2005).

—Jordan Wankoff and Sara Pendergast

Stephen John Thurston

1952—

Pastor

Stephen John Thurston is the third generation to pastor the New Covenant Missionary Baptist Church. Like his grandfather and father before him, Thurston preaches every Sunday to his Southside Chicago congregation. A charismatic leader and dynamic preacher, his church has grown to over 2,000 members. He is also the president of the National Baptist Convention of America.

Thurston was born on July 20, 1945, in Chicago, Illinois, the second child of Rev. John and Ruth (Hall) Thurston. He grew up in Chicago and attended public school. The most significant influence in Thurston's young life was the church, namely, New Covenant Missionary Baptist Church. New Covenant was founded by Thurston's grandfather, Elijah Thurston, who entered the ministry in 1934 and immediately began pastoring Chicago's Salem Baptist Church at 37th and Langley Avenue. Three years later he moved the church to East 44th Street and reorganized it as the 44th Street Baptist Church. In 1956, after his son John Lee Thurston had joined him in the ministry, the church moved to its present location at 740 East 77th Street and was renamed New Covenant Missionary Baptist Church. John Lee Thurston served as co-pastor of the church until Thurston's grandfather died in 1968, at which time his father took over sole leadership of the church.

At an early age, Thurston was preparing and being prepared to step into his father's shoes to become the third generation to minister at New Covenant. In 1967 Thurston's father invited Martin Luther King, Jr., to preach at New Covenant. He asked King to address

three issues: achieving personal goals, improving the welfare those in need, and working to glorify God. Thurston, just 15 years old at the time, found inspiration in King's words.

Thurston graduated from John M. Harlan High School in Chicago in 1970 and attended the now-defunct Bishop College in Dallas, Texas, from where he received a Bachelor of Arts degree in religion in 1975. He also completed advanced studies at Wheaton Christian College in Wheaton, Illinois. He married his grade school sweetheart, Joyce D. Hand, on June 18, 1977. They have four children: Stephen John II, Nicole D'Vaugh, Teniece Rael, and Christian Avery Elijah.

Thurston first ascended to the pulpit of New Covenant Missionary Baptist Church on Easter Sunday of 1971, delivering the sermon "Where Did You Die?" On Easter Sunday three years later, in 1974, Thurston's father laid hands on his son and ordained him. Thurston thus entered the ministry as an assistant pastor under his father's tutelage. Again on an Easter Sunday, just one year later, Thurston made another step in his journey when his father appointed him as co-pastor to serve alongside him in equal capacity. When his father passed away on January 21, 1979, Thurston, like his father before him, became the sole spiritual leader of New Covenant.

Much of the tremendous growth of New Covenant, which has gone from a member of 50 in 1934 to over 2,000 in 2004, can be attributed to Thurston's dynamic and energetic ministry. He was named one of "America's Best and Brightest Young Business and

At a Glance . . .

Born on July 20, 1952, in Chicago, IL; son of John Lee and Ruth (Hall) Thurston; married Joyce DeVonne Hand, June 18, 1977; children: Stephen John II, Nicole D'Vaugh, Teniece Rael, Christian Avery Elijah. *Education:* Bishop College, BA, religion, 1975. *Religion:* Baptist.

Career: New Covenant Missionary Baptist Church, Chicago, IL, assistant pastor, 1974, co-pastor, 1975-79; pastor, 1979-.

Selected memberships: National Baptist Convention of America, president; Chicago Baptist Institute, chairman of finance; Broadcast Ministers Alliance of Chicago and Vicinity, member; Christian Education Congress, executive committee; Illinois National Baptist State Convention, president.

Awards: America's Best and Brightest Young Business and Professional Men, *Dollars and Sense Magazine,* 1987.

Addresses: *Office*—New Covenant Missionary Baptist Church, 740 E. 77th Street, Chicago, IL 60619-2553.

Professional Men" by *Dollars and Sense* magazine in 1987, and Manya A. Brachear of the *Chicago Tribune* reported in 2003, "Congregants who have known all three pastors said Stephen Thurston inherited his grandfather's booming voice and conservative values and his father's charisma and activist aspirations." Many of his sermons are available as a transcript or on tape or CD.

Thurston preaches at three services every Sunday morning, hosts two live Sunday radio broadcasts, and has two recorded television shows that broadcast in the greater Chicago area each week—and he is pushing his congregation to establish its own telecommunications systems to increase control of airtime. Conservative in his social values (he's against same-sex marriage and ordination of gays), he actively and unapologetically pushes a political platform.

Along with being a regular guest preacher around Chicago, during the 1990s, Thurston made several world trips. In 1990 he served as the coordinator for the Baptist World Alliance in Seoul, Korea, and traveled to Hong Kong and Honolulu. He visited Ghana and Zimbabwe in 1993, Argentina in 1995, and Australia in 2000. He has also toured Israel and the Holy Lands. Under Thurston's leadership, New Covenant has opened a hospital in Ghana and is building a polytechnical institute there.

Remembering the lessons of his youth, Thurston is a strong voice for the disenfranchised and the poor. He is also a leading advocate for the black community. His propensity to state his positions—both theological and political—from the pulpit have led some to suggest that Thurston is too opinionated and too political. Thurston rebuffs such critics, saying that it is his job to speak loudly and boldly. According to the *Online Baptist Standard*, Thurston, speaking at a Baptist conference, lamented, "Many of us bring this attitude of indifference into the pulpit. We're right down the middle—not for anything, not really against anything.... We compromise the word of God with the sins of men, so we will not declare the iniquities that are present and real."

Thurston's political involvement has included a push to get more blacks into elected office as a means to create a truly integrated society. "We live in a country where the United States Senate is made up of 100 individuals and not one of them is African American," he told the *Chicago Sun-Times* in 2003. "That's not integration at all, in any stretch of the imagination." Rev. Jesse Jackson, who has been close to both Thurston and his father, told the *Chicago Tribune*, "Many ministers are focused a lot on faith without works, faith without action, faith without challenge.... Stephen Thurston is a warrior."

In 2003 Thurston was elected as the president of the National Baptist Convention of America, the organizational body of denomination that includes some 3.5 million members of 1,500 churches in 31 states. It is the second-largest black Christian denomination in the country. He won by a very close margin of just 24 votes out of more than 2,000. Because of his political emphasis, his election was somewhat controversial, but many hope that Thurston's charismatic personality and leadership skills will pull together the denomination.

Thurston continued to serve as the pastor of New Covenant while fulfilling his duties as president of the National Baptist Convention. His son, Stephen, Jr., has already preached his first sermon at New Covenant and is preparing to carry on the tradition of the Thurston legacy at New Covenant. Thurston, however, has many more years of sermons to deliver before handing over the reins.

Sources

Periodicals

Chicago Sun-Times, September 6, 2003.
Chicago Tribune, October 13, 2003.

On-line

"Convention Presidents Address African-American Preachers," *The Online Baptist Standard,* www.

baptiststandard.com/postnuke/index.php?module=
htmlpages&func=display&pid=2397 (December 3,
2004).

"Meet the President," *National Baptist Convention of
America, Inc.,* www.nbcamerica.net/meet.htm (December 3, 2004).

"The Thurston Pastoral Legacy," *New Covenant
Missionary Baptist Church,* www.newcovenantmbc.
com/events/bios/ (December 3, 2004).

—Kari Bethel

William E. Trueheart

1942—

Educator, non-profit administrator

When William E. Trueheart became the first African American to lead a private New England college in 1989, his appointment made national headlines. However, he had long been a prominent figure in higher education. As a decorated Harvard scholar, doctoral graduate, and college administrator, Trueheart had made his mark in the world of educational theory and administration. However it would not be until he left the ivy-covered towers of academia that his dedication to education would reach those who needed it most—children, families, and community members. He has since been responsible for delivering free books to millions of children nationwide, promoting literacy programs in thousands of communities, and even going so far as to making sure inner-city children had a pool to cool off in during the long heat of summer. Though Harvard University put Trueheart on its board of overseers and city officials clamored for his advice, it is the children nationwide who, finishing their first book, taking their first breaststroke, stand as the true testament to Trueheart's career.

Read Way to Career in Education

William E. Trueheart was born to Louise Elnora Harris and Junious Elton Trueheart on July 10, 1942. He was raised in Stamford, Connecticut, where his early life was immersed in literature. "One of the most touching things I can remember in my life is when my fifth grade teacher, knowing my love of reading, bought me a book on the Wright brothers—something we didn't have in our library," Trueheart told the *Kennedy*

School of Government Bulletin. "It was her way of encouraging me to read." It worked. By the time Trueheart reached junior high he had read every autobiography and biography book in his elementary school library and had joined Stamford's public library in order to read more.

After finishing high school, Trueheart chose to stay close to home for college, enrolling in the University of Connecticut. After graduating with a bachelor's degree in political science in 1966, he began his career in education, also at the University of Connecticut. From 1966 to 1968 he was the assistant director of admissions. The following year he received a one-year fellowship from the American Council of Education, which he also carried out at Connecticut. In 1969 Trueheart served one year as assistant to the university president; then he became the director of the university's academic advisory center and assistant to the dean of the College of Liberal Arts and Sciences. He held these two positions concurrently until 1972.

Trueheart left Connecticut to become a graduate student at Harvard University's John F. Kennedy School of Government where he received a master's in public administration in 1973. While at Harvard, Trueheart proved his merit as a scholar by earning several prestigious fellowships. He was a Littauer Fellow in 1973 and from 1974 to 1979 he held consecutive fellowships from the Charles I. Travelli Foundation and the Ford Foundation. He used these fellowships to research the book *Production Function Analysis in High Education: General Methodology and Applications to Four Year Black Colleges*, which he co-

He then moved to Harvard's governing board as an associate secretary, a position he held for three years. In 1986 Trueheart went to Rhode Island to become the executive vice president of Bryant College, a small, private college in the suburbs of Providence. Three years later he was appointed president. Trueheart's promotion was historical. He was the first African American to hold the top spot at a four-year private college in New England.

During seven years as president of Bryant, Trueheart initiated several important programs. He was instrumental in helping Bryant qualify for Association to Advance Collegiate Schools of Business (AACSB) accreditation. Just over 25 percent of the nation's 1,000-plus business schools have met the rigorous standards of the AACSB. Because of Trueheart's efforts to achieve the accreditation, Bryant has received national recognition for its business program. Drawing on this reputation, Trueheart spearheaded the Center for Design & Business, a joint program between Bryant and the Rhode Island School of Design (RISD). The innovative program was designed to help entrepreneurs make the leap from idea to production with classes on marketing, production, patenting, and business basics. "They really did help shape our company," one graduate told the *Knight Ridder/Tribune Business News*. "What's so unique about it is it combines design with business—it's just not happening enough in the world."

While at Bryant, Trueheart also became heavily involved in civic and community work, particularly with groups focused on education. He joined the boards of the Public Education Fund Network, the Nellie Mae Education Foundation, the New England Education Loan Marketing Corporation, and the Rhode Island Independent Higher Education Association. On the business side he was appointed to the boards of Fleet National Bank, the Narragansett Electric Company, Blue Cross/Blue Shield, and various Chambers of Commerce. His expertise in higher education and public administration also made him a valuable consultant to organizations as varied as the Ford Foundation, Arthur D. Little, Inc., the United States National Parks Service, and the College of the Atlantic.

Led Country's Largest Literacy Program

Trueheart left Bryant in 1996 and—after a brief stint as a visiting scholar at Harvard University—moved from higher education to general education. He became the president and CEO of Reading Is Fundamental (RIF), the country's oldest and largest non-profit children's literacy program. It was a perfect fit for Trueheart who told the National Education Association, "As a child, I spent every day reading in the library, and that love of literacy spilled into my work."

When Trueheart took over at RIF, he was faced with a waiting list of over one million children needing books,

authored in 1977. Trueheart also used the fellowships to pursue doctoral studies at Harvard, earning a PhD in education in 1979.

Doctorate in hand, Trueheart returned to his career in higher education. From 1979 to 1983 he was the assistant dean at the Kennedy School of Government.

ongoing problems with funding, and a downward sliding national literacy rate. Trueheart tackled the problems head-on with the traits that have come to define his professional career—innovation, diplomacy, and scholarship. According to the *New Pittsburgh Courier*, upon joining RIF Trueheart "launched an ambitious strategy to expand RIF services to about 1.3 million more children by the end of 2001." To do this Trueheart undertook a round-the-clock schedule of lobbying, fundraising, and partnering with powerful allies.

One of the most high-profile programs created under Trueheart's watch at RIF was Read to Achieve, sponsored by the National Basketball Association (NBA). The program opened Reading and Learning Centers nationwide that provided young people with access to books and technology. "Children who face a future of low literacy also face limited job prospects, low salaries, poor health care, social isolation, and few educational opportunities," Trueheart said in a *PR Newswire* article. "To those children, NBA players are heroes and readers. RIF's long-term alliance with the NBA has already inspired millions of children to love reading and we look forward to an even stronger connection between our two organizations." In addition to the NBA, Trueheart nurtured partnerships with Coca-Cola, J. Crew, and Scholastic Publishers. He also turned to new ways to promote literacy including internet, cable, and satellite television programs.

Focused Skills on Community and Country

Trueheart's next move brought him to Pittsburgh. In July of 2001 he was appointed CEO and president of the Pittsburgh Foundation, the 17th largest community foundation in the country with assets in excess of $548 million. With his appointment, Trueheart moved further away from educational work and deeper into community work which encompasses not only education but economic, family, health, and cultural issues. "I'm eager to join The Pittsburgh Foundation leadership team to encourage and nurture more substantial, thorough community involvement and investment," Trueheart was quoted as saying in the *New Pittsburgh Courier*.

Trueheart wasted no time getting involved in the local community. In addition to his role with the foundation Trueheart co-chaired a city-sponsored evaluation of the Pittsburgh public school system. He was also instru-

mental in organizing SOS—Save Our Summer, a fundraising drive that helped reopen half of Pittsburgh's public swimming pools and several of its recreation centers. And in an unprecedented move for a major city, Pittsburgh found itself being bailed out of a financial crisis by a coalition of non-profit organizations. Trueheart and The Pittsburgh Foundation led the campaign, hosting emergency meetings and organizing details of the bail-out.

In just three years with The Pittsburgh Foundation, Trueheart had fulfilled the hopes he had expressed upon joining the organization. "I look forward to working with folks in the Pittsburgh and Allegheny County communities, in the schools, in the colleges and universities, and with Pittsburgh leaders at every level," the *New Pittsburgh Courier* quoted him as saying. "I particularly look forward to working collaboratively with other foundations to better serve the citizens of Pennsylvania, and in doing so, the nation." Considering the successful innovations he has implemented so far—at Bryant College, Reading Is Fundamental, the Pittsburgh Foundation, and in the city of Pittsburgh—there is no reason to doubt that other cities and organizations nationwide will turn to Trueheart's programs for guidance and inspiration.

Sources

Periodicals

Knight Ridder/Tribune Business News, March 17, 2002.
New Pittsburgh Courier, July 25, 2001.
PR Newswire, May 15, 2001; July 20, 2001.

On-line

"It's Not the RIF You Think You Know," *National Education Association*, www.nea.org/neatoday/01 05/innov.html (October 28, 2004).
"Reading Something Into It, Bill Trueheart MPA 1973," *Kennedy School of Government Bulletin*, www.ksg.harvard.edu/ksgpress/bulletin/spring20 01/profiletrueheart.html (October 28, 2004).
"William E. Trueheart, President and CEO," *The Pittsburgh Foundation*, www.pittsburghfoundation.org/ page11905.cfm (October 28, 2004).

—Candace LaBalle

Charleszetta "Mother" Waddles

1912-2001

Activist, spiritual leader

For nearly four decades, the Reverend Charleszetta Waddles, affectionately known as "Mother Waddles," devoted her life to providing food, hope, and human dignity to the downtrodden and disadvantaged people of Detroit. Founder, director, and spiritual leader of the Mother Waddles Perpetual Mission, Inc., a nonprofit, nondenominational organization run by volunteers and dependent on private donations, Waddles believed that the church must move beyond religious dogma to focus on the real needs of real people.

"We're trying to show what the church could mean to the world if it lived by what it preached," Mother Waddles told *Newsweek*. "I read the Bible. It didn't say just go to church. It said, 'Do something.'" In addition to operating a 35-cent dining room on Detroit's "skid row" that serves appetizing meals in cheerful, dignified surroundings, the mission offers health care, counseling, and job training to thousands of needy citizens. Still others benefit from an Emergency Services Program that provides food, clothing, shelter, and medicine. Well into her eighties, Waddles continued to work 12-hour days and to remain on call throughout the night. "We give a person the things he needs, when he needs them," she told Lee Edson of *Reader's Digest*. "We take care of him whether he's an alcoholic or a junkie, black or white, employed or unemployed. We don't turn anyone away."

Charleszetta Waddles was 36 years old and the mother of 10 children when she began what James K. Davis of *Life* described as her "one-woman war on poverty." Learning that a neighbor with two children was about to lose her home, Waddles took a pushcart and went up and down the street collecting food from local businesses. These donations were enough to feed the family for eight weeks, while whatever money the woman had went toward payments on her house. Having witnessed the power of Christian charity, Waddles began studying the Scriptures, and within a short time became ordained as a Pentecostal minister.

With the help of her husband, Payton Waddles, Charleszetta opened the Helping Hand Restaurant, and in 1956 established the Perpetual Mission. Over the years, Waddles's tireless work among the poor has earned her countless honors and awards, including the 1988 Humanitarian Award from the National Urban League, the Sojourner Truth Award, the Religious Heritage Award, and letters of commendation from U.S. vice-presidents Hubert H. Humphrey and Lyndon B. Johnson. In 1990 she and her mission were the subject of a highly acclaimed television documentary, *Ya' Done Good*.

Charleszetta Waddles, the eldest of seven children, was born in St. Louis, Missouri, in 1912. From her earliest years, helping others came naturally to her, whether it was looking after her younger brothers and sisters or doing chores for elderly neighbors. When she was 12 years old, her father died, and she was forced to drop

At a Glance . . .

Born Charleszetta Lena Campbell on October 7, 1912, in St. Louis, MO; died July 12, 2001, in Detroit, MI; daughter of Henry and Ella (Brown) Campbell; married Clifford Walker, c. 1926 (died); married second husband, c. 1933 (divorced); married Payton Waddles, Jr. (an automobile company employee); children: Beatrice, Lathet L., Latheda, Lorraine, Andrea, Dennis, Therese, Annette, Roosevelt, Charles.

Career: Established Mother Waddles Perpetual Mission, Inc., 1956, national director and pastor, 1956-2001.

Memberships: NAACP; Mayor's Task Force Committee; City of Detroit Bicentennial Committee.

Awards: Bell Ringer Award, Ford Motor Company; Lane Bryant Citizens Award; Sojourner Truth Award; Religious Heritage Award; Humanitarian Award, State of Michigan Legislative Body; Volunteer Leadership Award; A. Philip Randolph Institute Special Award; Humanitarian Award, National Urban League, 1988; Wolverine Frontiersman Award, State of Michigan; letters of commendation from President Richard M. Nixon and U.S. vice-presidents Lyndon B. Johnson and Hubert H. Humphrey.

Addresses: *Office*–Mother Waddles Perpetual Mission, 12330 Jos. Campau Rd., Detroit, MI 48212.

out of school to help support her family. The only job she could find was as a full-time housemaid. At the age of 14, she married 19-year-old Clifford Walker. He died five years later, leaving her with one child and dim prospects. Within two years, she had married again, and over the next 15 years had nine more children.

In 1936 Waddles and her family moved to Detroit, Michigan, where her husband hoped to find a better job. Instead, he ended up working in a restaurant for 11 dollars a week. His lack of ambition ultimately drove Waddles to leave him; she felt it was better to go on welfare to support her family than to remain with a man with such limited aspirations. What welfare and Aid to Dependent Children failed to provide, Waddles managed to scrape together on her own. "I've put tubs in front of my house on weekends and sold barbecue," she told Vern E. Smith of *Newsweek*. "I've picked up numbers in the neighborhood because that's what I had

to do if I wanted my kids to have the things they needed. It was an educational experience. You learn how to survive. I think that knowledge ought to be used to help somebody else get by."

Waddles was still struggling herself when she stepped forward to help save her neighbor's house. Shortly thereafter, she had a vision directing her to create a church with a social conscience—one that would feed, clothe, and shelter those in need. But it was her third husband, Ford Motor Company employee Payton Waddles, who made it all possible. She was selling barbecue to raise money for a church function when he first crossed her path. Waddles, she told Edson, was "the channel the Lord used to make me free to help others."

As a child, Charleszetta Waddles had witnessed firsthand the hypocrisy that can accompany the conventional church and many of its members. Her father, a successful St. Louis barber, was once the darling of his congregation. Then, unknowingly, he happened to give a haircut to a customer with impetigo, a contagious skin disease. His business was ruined overnight. From then on, he was unable to make a decent living. Dejected, he stood on street corners for hours at a time. When he died, few church members attended his funeral. Waddles identifies this heartless rejection of her father by so-called "religious" people as one of the most traumatic experiences of her childhood, and one that has strongly influenced the course of her life and work.

When, in the late 1940s, Waddles began holding prayer meetings at her house for small groups of local ladies, she emphasized practical, charitable actions rather than religious rhetoric. No one, she told her friends, is too poor to help those who are less fortunate. She advised each one to take a single can of food from their shelf and give it to someone in need. After a period of diligent bible study, Waddles became ordained as a minister in the First Pentecostal Church. She was later re-ordained in the International Association of Universal Truth. In 1950, her desire to give tangible shape to the teachings of Jesus Christ inspired her to open the Helping Hand Restaurant. "I started by begging free rent," she told Davis. "I went out to markets with a pushcart and collected scraps and cleaned and used them."

Situated on the edge of Detroit's skid row, surrounded by flophouses, all-night movies, and day-labor pools, the restaurant offered simple yet wholesome meals for just 35 cents—or free to those whose pockets were empty. Over the years, as Waddles's reputation grew and private donations trickled in, the entrees became heartier and the menu more varied, but the price of a meal remained the same. All patrons, no matter what their station in life, were warmly welcomed and made to feel at home.

"Unlike the soup kitchens of the Depression era, where the destitute lined up with a tin cup for a handout,

Mother Waddles's establishment boasts white table-cloths, a flower on every table, and uniformed wait-resses," wrote *Reader's Digest* contributor Edson. Those who could not pay could eat for free, while those who could afford to often paid as much as three dollars for a cup of coffee. At first, Waddles did all of the cooking, dishes, and laundry herself, but as time went by, dozens of dedicated volunteers joined her.

Waddles was not content to stop with her 35-cent "miracle meals," however. In order to feel truly useful, and to bring about lasting social change, she had to get at the root of urban poverty. To do this, she needed to expand her mission and enlarge its premises. One day in 1956, while thumbing through a Detroit newspaper, she came across an advertisement reading, "Store for Rent, two months rent free." She immediately con-tacted the landlord for further details and learned that the ad was misleading–that, in fact, the prospective occupant would have to pay two months' rent up front before receiving the discount–but she somehow man-aged to convince the owner to let her have the space for free.

This storefront property, located in a crime-ridden area of inner-city Detroit, was the original home of Wad-dles's church, the Perpetual Mission for Saving Souls of All Nations. Its name was later shortened to the Mother Waddles Perpetual Mission. Fires, financial setbacks, and other problems have forced the mission to move numerous times over the years, but its spirit and goals have remained the same. "We are," Waddles told Edson, "the most unorganized, successful operation in the world."

Since 1956, city agencies have referred thousands of needy people to Mother Waddles's mission. Thousands more have simply walked in off the street. "This is the last resort for a lot of people," mission worker Don Richardson told *Newsweek*. "If we don't solve the problem, it's not going to be solved, and this gives every case that much more urgency." Waddles was assisted in her work by a committed corps of volunteers that ranges in size from about 50 to more than 200. The type of help provided always varied greatly. Waddles "cajoled businessmen into providing tempo-rary aid for new arrivals to Detroit, outfitted a ragged teenager with clothes in which to graduate from high school and convinced drug addicts to seek out a new life," Edson wrote.

But perhaps more importantly, Waddles provided once hopeless and disenfranchised people with the spiritual strength and confidence to pull themselves out of poverty and desperation. "You can't give people pride," Waddles told Edson, "but you can provide the kind of understanding that makes people look to their inner strengths and find their own sense of pride."

In addition to helping countless people through miscel-laneous crises, over the years Waddles introduced a number of innovative social and educational programs.

These include a self-help center offering classes in typing, dressmaking, machine operating, and uphol-stery; a tutoring program designed to help keep teen-agers in school; and a job placement service for the unemployed. In 1972 she managed to persuade two young, white doctors to give up their lucrative suburban practices and open a clinic in the mission. Here, poor people could receive quality health care for free, or at minimal cost. Around the same time, she set up a halfway house for a handful of mental patients who had nowhere to go following their release from state insti-tutions. The state contributed $30 a week towards the care of each patient.

Other projects have included the Auto Safety Trouba-dours, a group of young people who came together to study African American history and sing safety songs at civic functions, and a special troop of Camp Fire Girls. "The ministry means administering to people whatever their interests, young or old," Waddles told *Life*'s Davis. "That's why I have such an octopus of a program." The mission also houses a simple chapel, where Waddles conducted Sunday services. The choir is composed of volunteers and members of Waddles's immediate family.

Because it receives no city, state, or federal funding, the mission is faced with constant financial crises. Churches and local businesses provide some money, and many of the people Waddles has assisted in the past—such as champion boxer Thomas Hearns—come back to help. Those who cannot give money donate food, clothes, or furniture. To generate addi-tional income, Waddles wrote books on philosophy, self-awareness, and self-esteem, as well as two soul food cookbooks.

The cookbooks have sold more than 85,000 copies since 1959, and all of the proceeds have been chan-neled back into the mission. Waddles also shared her inspirational message with radio and TV audiences in the Detroit area, and on numerous occasions, her public appeals for help have brought in generous donations. During one emergency, Michigan governor William Milliken was moved to donate a side of beef, and automaker Henry Ford sent in a check for $1,000. In 1984, a fire forced the 35-cent dining room to close its doors. Ten years later, just as Waddles was preparing to reopen it, another fire gutted the mission's ware-house, destroying a kitchen's worth of restaurant equipment and tons of donated clothes. When asked how she retained her optimism in the face of constant setbacks, Waddles's reply was simple: "I'm accustomed to change," she told the *Detroit Free Press*. Her son, Charles Sturkey, put it another way. "Mother has faith that God is working through her and will always provide her with what she needs," he told Edson. A second mission operates under Waddles's name in Kumast, Ghana, West Africa.

Throughout a lifetime of service to the poor, Mother Waddles accumulated dozens of awards. Among the most prestigious are Michigan's Volunteer Leadership and Wolverine Frontiersman awards, the Sojourner Truth Award, humanitarian awards from the State of Michigan Legislative Body and the National Urban League, and the Lane Bryant Citizens Award. For many years, the governor of Michigan and the mayor of Detroit sponsored an annual Mother Waddles Week, focusing local attention on the importance of community service.

In 1968 Waddles received an invitation to President Richard M. Nixon's inauguration, and three years later was honored with a special presidential commendation. She has also served as honorary chair of the Women's Conference of Concern and was featured in the Black Woman of Courage exhibits at the Smithsonian Institution and the Walter P. Reuther Library.

In August of 1967, trucks and cars carrying donations of food and clothing from Mother Waddles's mission were among the few vehicles to brave the riot-torn streets of inner-city Detroit. Inside a crumbling church, Waddles distributed food to needy citizens, many of whom had not eaten in days. In the early 1970s, a haggard woman wandered into Waddles's mission, downtrodden and despondent, not knowing where to go or what to do. In a few minutes, Waddles had given her a job in the mission kitchen, and within weeks, the once despairing woman was holding her head up high. When a leper in the Philippines heard of Waddles's work and asked for her help, Waddles borrowed money from a local businessman and sent off a donation. "I couldn't do otherwise," she told Edson. "God knows no distance."

One of the keys to Waddles's success was her ability to identify with those she helped. "There, but for the grace of God, goes me," she told Davis. "It can happen to anybody. Your husband or wife leaves you, you reach 50 and lose your job, the bottle, I don't know what, but it can happen to anybody. Hungry people can be dangerous people—it's the best excuse to do the lowest thing." But Waddles's motivation came from something much simpler and more profound. "I was born," she told Davis, "with the desire to love people."

Waddles died on July 12, 2001, at her Detroit, Michigan, home. She was 88. Detroit's mayor, Dennis Archer, told the *Detroit News,* "Mother Waddles loss is Detroit's loss. She was an icon to this city, having helped more people who have been in need and touched the lives of so many who have been down and out." Her mission continues to operate to this day.

Sources

Periodicals

Detroit Free Press, February 16, 1990; September 25, 1994, p. 1C.
Detroit News, July 13, 2001.
Ebony, May 1972.
Essence, October 1990, p. 48.
Jet, July 16, 1990, p. 24.
Life, March 21, 1969, pp. 87-88.
Michigan Chronicle, October 3, 1990.
Newsweek, May 1, 1972, p, 123.
People, August 20, 1990, p. 9.
Reader's Digest, October 1972, pp. 175-78.

On-line

Mother Waddles Perpetual Mission, www.mother-waddles.com (January 31, 2005).

Other

Additional information for this profile was obtained from the PBS television documentary *Ya' Done Good* (1990).

—Caroline B. D. Smith and Sara Pendergast

Joaquin Wallace

1965—

Founder, Project Transition Inc.

In 1998 former college baseball player Joaquin Wallace founded the non-profit Project Transition Inc., a welfare-to-work program that put long-term unemployed and "working poor" African-American clients into a corporate setting to build their confidence and self esteem. The project was based on the idea that giving people access to real-life, white-collar work situations would help them get white-collar jobs; something no welfare-to-work program had tried before. Starting as a "demonstration project," Project Transition eventually became a flagship scheme, receiving in over five years around $3 million in funding from California's Alameda County alone. The project also attracted national attention. Wallace was featured in magazine articles, received several awards, and even received a letter of encouragement from George W. Bush in the early days of his presidency. It is estimated that over 1,000 people benefited from Project Transition in its five-year existence.

Joaquin Wallace was born on September 11, 1965, in Oakland, California. His father is Emanuel Wallace, a laborer, and his mother is Dorothy Ann Wallace, a restaurant cook and hostess. An only child, he was raised in the Bay Area and attended Oakland Technical School, where he excelled at baseball and graduated in 1983. He attended San Francisco State University on an athletics scholarship—he was a college baseball player—and graduated in 1989 with a bachelor's degree in economics. In 1995 he graduated with an MBA in marketing from Golden Gate University, and in 2005 was working towards a PhD in public policy, also at Golden Gate. Wallace married Jamelle Simon in 1995, and they have three daughters: Jameela, Sasha, and Kendall.

Shaped by Experience

By 1987 Wallace was studying for his degree and had won a much sought-after internship with the San Francisco Giants; in August 1987 he was hired by the Giants to work in the front office. As the first black to do so Wallace appeared in newspaper and magazine articles, becoming an example of the franchise's willingness to promote blacks to public positions. Wallace's experience was not a happy one, however, and by 1988 he had been fired and was working as a gas station attendant. Wallace told *Contemporary Black Biography* (*CBB*) that this experience was one that inspired him to help others break out of the cycle of unemployment, low pay, and low self-esteem that seemed to him to bedevil the black community. He also explained that this was a moment when he realized that education was the key to breaking that cycle.

It was almost a decade before he had the idea behind Project Transition and was able to act on behalf of others. Wallace concentrated on his own education, studying marketing, while working as a computing instructor at Laney College in Alameda, and developing an interest in public policy that he would eventually pursue at the doctoral level. This academic mix of economics, marketing, and public policy is what Wallace credited for his insight into the problems faced by old-style welfare-to-work programs, as well as for some of his ideas about how to solve them.

An Idea from the Internet

Wallace told *CBB* that the idea behind Project Transition came to him one night in 1997 while he was browsing the Internet and came across articles about President Clinton's 1996 Personal Responsibility and Work Opportunity Reconciliation Act, which among other things aimed to help the unemployed and working poor support themselves through training. President Clinton declared the aim of the act was to "end welfare as we know it." Wallace said he realized that the existing model for welfare-to-work programs was not working. He noticed that training programs for the unemployed aimed to place people in blue-collar and service jobs paying low wages; such low expectations did nothing to improve their self esteem. The radical idea behind Project Transition was that it would help people leapfrog blue-collar work and find placements in well-paid white-collar industries.

The basic principles behind Project Transition were based on Abraham Maslow's "hierarchy of needs," a theory Wallace had come across while studying psychology. Maslow argued that after needs such as food, water, shelter, safety, and security are taken care of, human beings need self esteem, a place in society, and what he called "self-actualization." Wallace decided that Project Transition would address self-esteem and self-actualization, the two areas where he found poor black Americans to be most lacking. The project would raise its clients' self-esteem by offering them access to high-quality equipment and comfortable, corporate-style training facilities in business districts. The idea was to put clients in a corporate environment so they could see themselves working there and set their sights higher than before. Wallace likened this process of self-actualization to the techniques used in car sales: "If the salesman can get you into the driver's seat of that car, so you can see yourself driving it, well then he has a much easier job persuading you to buy it."

But before Wallace could begin working on selling the idea of white-collar work to his clients, he had to sell the idea of Project Transition to investors. In early 1998 he began researching for a business plan and persuading people to join the non-profit's board of directors, a task that took over a year to finalize. He raised money from local banks and Wells Fargo donated a free facility in the basement of one of its buildings in downtown Oakland. When the doors opened on September 7, 1998, Wallace had already spent half of his $40,000 startup budget on computers; he and his family had redecorated the neglected basement, buying high quality office equipment, leather armchairs, and good carpeting, and hanging framed pictures on the wall. Wallace told *CBB* that he wanted to break the assumption that non-profit meant "non-quality."

By the end of the year the project was out of money and facing a major setback. A grant application to Alameda County for $300,000 was put in the wrong category and rejected. Wallace appealed the decision and invited county officials to visit the Oakland facility. What they saw was impressive and soon Alameda became one of the project's key investors, inventing a whole new grant category, known as "Demonstration Project" to award an initial $100,000. Over five years Alameda County allocated $3 million to Project Transition.

Not Just Computers

Between 1999 and 2002 Project Transition delivered almost 300 free classes in basic literacy and computer skills. Working together with his wife Jamelle, Wallace offered after school clubs, a children's daycare service, and a girls' basketball program alongside its adult training programs. By 2002 Project Transition had three state of the art computer labs, networked together; the facilities were so good that corporate clients used them for their own training courses.

But Wallace's idea was not just about practical computing skills; he estimates that in fact computing was only about ten percent of what the project did. Aware that members of the poorest black communities often lack the communication and presentation skills that would make them valuable employees, the Wallaces provided well-rounded training to get people into good jobs. Wallace told *CBB* of his pride in the "rate of return" for his efforts: over 80 percent of Project Transition graduates found a job and 80 percent of them kept that job for 180 days or more, with average earnings over $30,000 a year after that time.

Wallace's tendency to use the language of business made it difficult for him to promote the project with public-sector organizations, and by 2002 the project seemed to have reached its natural limit. Over 1,000 people from the Oakland area had benefited, but Wallace said that by then he felt he had done all he could at a local level. Changes to the welfare system and reductions in the amount of money available for training of welfare recipients meant that the tide was turning against Project Transition at a national level too. For example, Wallace estimated that it cost $16,000 per year to train someone to the same level as through Project Transition, but that the return on that investment was that many of them found work paying well above the national average wage. Under the new system only $4,000 per year was available for training, far less than was necessary to provide the quality for which Project Transition had become known. In 2003 the scheme folded, leaving Wallace, his family, and those who had been helped to turn their lives around disappointed. Wallace told *CBB* that abandoning Project Transition was very hard, but he remained optimistic about the future. He hopes to persuade forward-looking investors and politicians to take up his idea on a national or even international level. In the meantime he had begun planning books about setting up a successful welfare-to-work program and a motivational book geared towards African-American men.

Sources

Periodicals

City Flight Magazine, March 5, 2002.
Essence Magazine, November, 2003.
Oakland Post, November 27, 1998.
Oakland Tribune, March 12, 2003.
San Francisco Chronicle, August 5, 2002.

Other

Additional material for this profile was obtained through an interview with Joaquin Wallace on November 29, 2004, and from material supplied by him.

—Chris Routledge

Forest Whitaker

1961—

Actor, director, producer

"A burly, good-natured Texan, soft-spoken and a little shy, Forest Whitaker doesn't exactly stand out in a crowd," wrote Associated Press correspondent Jay Sharbutt. "But in Hollywood, where unemployment is the rule, not the exception, he does OK." Whitaker, an award-winning actor, has graduated from important cameo roles to leading parts in major films. Not only has he won roles created specifically for a black actor—including jazz legend Charlie Parker in *Bird*—he has also received the opportunity to portray characters originally written for white actors. Whitaker commented to the Associated Press on his extraordinary range of roles: "I only care about doing characters I can grow from, someone I can learn from, people I can find some truth in. If I can do that, I can be happy."

As much as possible, Whitaker avoids the prying eyes of the Hollywood press. He grants interviews reluctantly and says little about his personal life or his work in the film industry. The actor explained in *Ebony* that the publicity surrounding his recent starring roles has proven difficult for him to accept. "I really appreciate that people enjoy my work, but most of my life has been in the background," he said. "I'm really just a

Whitaker, Forest, photograph. © Rufus R. Folkks/Corbis.

normal guy, hanging out trying to live my life…. I appreciate the attention and I am growing to understand it and deal with it better, but I would prefer to walk around in total obscurity."

It may be too late for Whitaker to return to the anonymity he longs for, but he zealously guards what privacy is left by offering few details about his childhood or formative years. He was born July 15, 1961, in Longview, Texas, but grew up in Carson and Los Angeles, California. The oldest of three children of an insurance salesman and a special education teacher, Whitaker attended Palisades High School in Los Angeles, where he was a good student and an All-League defensive back in football. He earned a sports scholarship to California State University at Pomona and became a drama and music major. Eventually, though, he felt that his singing talent would be better cultivated at the University of Southern California, and he transferred there to study voice.

Stage work proved tempting, however, and Whitaker began appearing in local equity productions in Southern California. "I was probably going to go to New York and work on stage and that was it," he recalled to

helped to launch the be-bop era—for his lead role in Clint Eastwood's *Bird*, a film treatment of Parker's life. In order to ensure he would be believable as a saxophone player, Whitaker took horn lessons and talked to numerous people who knew Parker during the years before the famous musician died an early, drug-related death. Whitaker even interviewed recovering heroin addicts in an effort to better understand the effects of drug abuse and dependency. "The research took on a very large scope," he remarked in *Ebony*. "I would wake up so depressed some mornings that I would really begin to understand why Charlie Parker tried to kill himself and why he took drugs. He led a very hard life, and it took quite a while to shake his thoughts from my head." Whitaker's portrayal of Parker in *Bird* won the young actor the top award at the 1988 Cannes Film Festival. *Jet* correspondent Lou Ransom declared that the role was "the crowning achievement in Whitaker's career, which has shown remarkable success." And Wheaton suggested that Whitaker's performance was "exceptional, the kind of acting that makes a star. He lets the late jazzman's self-destructive streak come through but also shows us Parker's charm and intelligence."

The success of *Bird* proved that Whitaker could handle a principal role. He has been busy ever since, acting in films such as *Diary of a Hitman* and *Article 99*. He also took on the task of producing several films. In *A Rage in Harlem*—a 1991 comedy-drama that he also co-produced—Whitaker played a mild-mannered accountant who falls hopelessly in love with a worldly songstress and subsequently becomes embroiled in danger when he seeks to save her from a sordid scheme involving stolen gold. The actor pointed out to the Associated Press that the film "takes on a kind of fable quality. It's really about being able to believe in something and not be changed and structured by the world, being true to yourself." *A Rage in Harlem*, which was shot in Cincinnati, Ohio, also featured Gregory Hines, Danny Glover, and Robin Givens.

Whitaker took on the challenge of assuming the role of Joe Louis—the heavyweight boxer who won a world championship against Germany's Max Schmeling in 1938. In order to prepare for this portrayal, Whitaker went into a gym and worked with boxing trainers. The actor expressed in the Los Angeles *Daily News* that he is particularly excited about the opportunity to play Louis. "I love boxing," he said. "Joe Louis was the beginning. He gave pride to the black community." More than that, the actor added, "Joe Louis united the country."

Whitaker also began directing films in the early 1990s. His directing debut was in 1993 with *Strapped*, an original film for HBO, for which he won the International Critics' Award for best new director at the Toronto Film Festival in 1993. He has also directed such feature films as *Waiting to Exhale* in 1995, *Hope Floats* in 1998, and *First Daughter* in 2004.

the Associated Press. "It just so happens I was working on a play and it turned into an opportunity to do a film." Since 1982 Whitaker has worked regularly in the movies, going from project to project and working his way from the ranks of the "extras" to the very best roles.

In 1982 Whitaker earned his first substantial role in a well-received teen film titled *Fast Times at Ridgemont High*. The actor's size and robust build helped him land the part of a tough guy whose cherished car gets trashed. That essentially comic role was followed by more important, serious ones; in *The Color of Money*, for example, Whitaker appeared as a pool shark who tries to beat the best players in the game. Although he was on screen only briefly, Whitaker studied the nuances of pool for months in order to perfect his moves and timing. As a result, observed Robert Wheaton in *Ebony*, "his one-scene cameo...almost stole the show from high-powered stars Paul Newman and Tom Cruise." Whitaker's performance in *The Color of Money* brought him to the attention of director Barry Levinson, who gave the actor a substantial part in the big-budget *Good Morning, Vietnam*. Whitaker was particularly pleased with that opportunity, because the part was not originally written for a black actor; he later portrayed another character intended for a white actor in *Johnny Handsome*. For all of these roles, Whitaker has done homework—in the form of reading and interviews—in order to assure that his performance would be realistic.

Whitaker put his greatest energy into researching the life of Charlie "Yardbird" Parker—the jazz giant who

To support his efforts, Whitaker established his own multimedia company called Spirit Dance Entertainment. Based in both the United States and the United Kingdom, Spirit Dance Entertainment, includes film, television, and music production. In London, the company mentors black and Asian filmmakers. His work continued to earn acclaim throughout the industry. In 2001 Whitaker produced his first feature film through Spirit Dance, *Green Dragon*. Soon, his television efforts were winning awards; *Door to Door*, a made for television movie about a man's efforts to become a successful salesman despite his cerebral palsy, won an Emmy award in 2003. In 2004, Whitaker was one of the first two directors selected for the First Amendment Project, a collaboration between the Sundance Channel and Court TV. For the project, Whitaker will direct a film that will portray an aspect of the First Amendment in a creative, fresh, innovative way.

Whitaker lives quietly in Los Angeles near his retired parents. He remains devoted to music, especially singing and playing the saxophone, and has been writing screenplays to support his own productions. Married in 1996, Whitaker is rarely seen on the Hollywood party scene—he shuns the limelight whenever possible. *Ebony* contributor Rhoda E. McKinney noted that despite his hard work and success, "Whitaker is truly a reluctant star. He is a humble man who shies from excess and pretense." Pressed about his views in *Ebony*, the star would only reply: "I hope through my work to help people understand themselves and others better."

Selected works

Films

Fast Times at Ridgemont High, 1982.
Platoon, 1986.
Stakeout, 1987.
Good Morning, Vietnam, 1987.
Bird, 1988.
Bloodsport, 1988.
Johnny Handsome, 1989.
Downtown, 1990.
Diary of a Hitman, 1991.
A Rage in Harlem, 1991.

Article 99, 1992.
The Crying Game, 1992.
Consenting Adults, 1992.
Body Snatchers, 1993.
Bank Robber, 1993.
Blown Away, 1994.
Jason's Lyric, 1994.
Ready to Wear, 1994.
Smoke, 1995.
Species, 1995.
Phenomenon, 1996.
Body Count, 1998.
Ghost Dog: The Way of the Samurai, 1999.
Light It Up, 1999.
Battlefield Earth: A Saga of the Year 3000, 2000.
Four Dogs Playing Poker, 2000.
Green Dragon, 2001.
The Hire: The Follow, 2001.
The Fourth Angel, 2001.
Panic Room, 2002.
Phone Booth, 2002.
Jiminy Glick in La La Wood, 2004.
First Daughter, 2004.

Sources

Periodicals

Associated Press wire reports, October 16, 1988; September 6, 1990; May 5, 1991.
Business Wire, January 15, 2004.
Chicago Tribune, May 25, 1988; May 3, 1991.
Daily News (Los Angeles), May 7, 1991.
Ebony, October 1988; November 1988.
Jet, November 7, 1988.
Journal and Constitution (Atlanta), November 5, 1988.
Los Angeles Times, May 3, 1991.
New York Times, May 24, 1988; September 11, 1988; May 3, 1991.
Phoenix Gazette, June 8, 1991.
Post and Courier (Charleston, SC), March 6, 2003.
Washington *Post,* August 2, 1990; May 3, 1991.

—Mark Kram and Sara Pendergast

Gerald Wilson

1918—

Jazz bandleader, composer, trumpeter

Jazz is often thought to be a young person's art, with soloists and bandleaders becoming best known for innovations they have developed early in their careers. In the hands of bandleader, composer, and trumpeter Gerald Wilson, however, jazz has inspired a process of lifelong musical growth over a seven-decade career. As a jazz musician, Wilson explained to the *New York Times,* "Your first ten years are thrown away. If you did pretty good for ten years, you're just starting." Sometimes, in other interviews, he lengthened the interval to 20 years.

Gerald Stanley Wilson was born in Shelby, Mississippi, on September 4, 1918. His mother started giving him piano lessons when he was six. The pair moved to Memphis, Tennessee, where Wilson heard the then-new music of the big bands on the radio. By the time he was ten, Wilson had decided that he wanted to become a bandleader. "To tell you the truth, I don't know if I had the talent for it or not," he told the *Washington Post.* "Maybe I just had the will and that got me in."

That willpower led Wilson to purchase a trumpet from the Sears mail-order catalog, paying $9.95 including postage. In 1934, Wilson and his mother went north to see the World's Fair in Chicago. Wilson wanted to stay on and study music in Chicago, but his mother couldn't afford the city's top-dollar music lessons. They moved on to Detroit, where Wilson studied theory and orchestration at Cass Technical High School.

Band Members Encouraged Arranging Efforts

Wilson kept up his trumpet studies, and after finishing high school he soon signed on with a group called the Plantation Music Orchestra at one of Detroit's leading nightclubs. That propelled him to a slot with a nationally famous band, the Jimmie Lunceford Orchestra, which he joined in 1939. One day Wilson gave Lunceford an arrangement he had written of a tune called "Sometimes I'm Happy." The bandleader turned it down, but other band members encouraged Wilson to keep trying. He proved a quick study of what Lunceford wanted as his very next arrangement, "Hi Spook," became part of the band's regular repertoire. Wilson also contributed several original compositions to the Lunceford orchestra, one of which, the influential and modern-sounding "Yarddog Mazurka," became a jazz standard.

The atmosphere in the Lunceford band was intoxicating and did much to shape Wilson's musical imagination. "We threw the trumpets high in the air, we twirled them high up there," he told the *Boston Globe.* "We had all kinds of moves and put on a big show–but we played great music. Listen to it. We were the avant-garde then, and we would have two or three hits going on the jukebox at the same time."

But Wilson left Lunceford in 1942, hoping to squeeze in some touring with bandleaders Les Hite and Benny Carter before being inducted into the U.S. Navy. He then played in a band with a group of other Navy members that was led by former Lunceford sideman Willie Smith and also included future trumpet star Clark Terry. Wilson was stationed at the Great Lakes Naval Training Center near his home in Detroit, but after his discharge he headed for Los Angeles and its growing jazz scene. In 1944 he formed his own big band.

Disbanded Group

This first incarnation of the Gerald Wilson Orchestra found immediate success, launching an eastward tour that stopped off for a 13-week run in Salt Lake City, Utah, and an additional two weeks in St. Louis. On another trip the group appeared at the Harlem neighborhood's famed Apollo Theater in New York. Wilson also waxed some 45 recordings with the band, as well as a number of others with smaller groups and other ensembles. Then, with his career seemingly on the rise, Wilson disbanded his orchestra. "We had over $100,000 worth of contracts," he told the *Boston Globe*. "But I realized I had just started and that this was not what I was looking for musically. I had to study some more."

Some of those studies occurred as Wilson joined one of the greatest of the big bands, the Count Basie Orchestra, in 1948. "They needed a trumpeter, and I wanted to sit in that band and play and learn," Wilson told the *Globe*. "This was the All-American rhythm section–Walter Page, Jo Jones, Freddie Green, and Count. What school could have been better than to sit right there and watch them and listen?" Wilson also played in and wrote music for the band of trumpeter Dizzy

Gillespie, where he took the bandstand next to a radical young saxophonist named John Coltrane.

Still gathering his creative ideas as he entered middle age, Wilson took a break from music in the early 1950s. For a time he ran a small grocery store. But he kept in touch with music, soaking up new sounds as he encountered them. He immersed himself in classical music, studying the works of such modern composers as Aram Khachaturian and Manuel de Falla. On the other hand, even as many jazz musicians were rejecting popular music, Wilson contributed arrangements to recordings by Nancy Wilson, Ray Charles, and even middle-of-the-road pop-rocker Bobby Darin. "I wanted to equip myself so that whatever kind of music my client wanted to hear, I was capable of making it," he explained to the *Washington Post*. Some of the arrangements heard on Charles's pioneering country albums of the early 1960s were done by Wilson. Employed for a time by the Mercury and Capitol labels, he wrote movie and television scores and also became the bandleader for African-American comedian Redd Foxx at one point.

Reviving an on-and-off arranging relationship with the Duke Ellington Orchestra, Wilson made his way back to jazz. Building up his sound with several smaller groups, he re-formed the Gerald Wilson Orchestra in 1961. The group recorded a series of albums on the Pacific Jazz label in the 1960s. These recordings benefited from a Latin tinge inspired in Wilson's music partly by his Mexican-born wife, Josephina. The strong vogue for Latin rhythms in the 1960s even brought Wilson a pop hit when his "Viva Tirado," from the *Moment of Truth* album (1962) was covered by the Latin rock group El Chicano in 1970. The album *The Golden Sword* (1966) contained a number dedicated to a famous Mexican bullfighter and another, the "Teotihuacan Suite," that evoked that pyramid-shaped landmark near Mexico City.

Work Showed Orchestral Influences

Once again, Wilson sought out new challenges instead of resting on his musical laurels. Commissioned by conductor Zubin Mehta to write a piece for the Los Angeles Philharmonic Orchestra in 1972, Wilson began to stretch his wings as a composer. His original jazz pieces became substantial, complex creations that might incorporate influences ranging from classical music to rock and rhythm and blues, and his band gained a reputation as the top large ensemble on the West Coast. Talented young soloists, such as guitarist Joe Pass, vied for places in Wilson's group. "Gerald's pieces are all extended, with long solos and long backgrounds," American Jazz Orchestra saxophonist Loren Schoenberg told the *New York Times* in 1988. "They're almost hypnotic. Most are seven to ten minutes long. Only a master can keep the interest going that long, and he does." In 1982, Wilson was awarded a $20,000 fellowship by the National Endowment for the Arts.

The profits from his commercially successful enterprises of the 1950s and 1960s helped finance the creative experiments of Wilson's remarkable old age. "I made a good living," he told the *Boston Globe*. "I made a living so now I don't have to go hustling any jobs. I have written for the symphony. I have written for the movies, and I have written for television. I arrange anything. I wanted to do all these things. I've done that. Now I'm doing exactly what I want, musically, and I do it when I please."

Wilson's dense harmonies taxed musicians' abilities, but a new generation of well-schooled players learned to keep up with him. The aging Wilson had little patience for jazz nostalgia, always looking toward new sounds. "Kids play now things those guys [early jazz players] couldn't even imagine," he told the *Globe*. Wilson passed on a great deal of his own knowledge as a jazz educator in later years, teaching at San Fernando Valley State College (later California State University at Northridge) beginning in 1970 and later moving on to California State University at Los Angeles and finally joining the faculty of the University of California at Los Angeles (UCLA) in 1991. His jazz history classes there drew upwards of 500 students. He looked back on his life and career in a 1996 spoken-word release with music, *Suite Memories: Reflections on a Jazz Journey.*

Wilson and his orchestra recorded consistently in the 1980s and barely slowed down after that, releasing the successful *State Street Sweet* in 1994, following up a successful Monterey Jazz Festival appearance in 1997 with *Theme for Monterey* (1998), and scoring a Grammy nomination in the Best Large Jazz Ensemble category with *New York, New Sound* in 2003, by which time Wilson was 85 years old. "I'm constantly learning, stretching out where I've never been before," he had told the *New York Times* some years earlier. "I'm always figuring out new directions where to go."

Selected discography

Moment of Truth, Pacific Jazz, 1962.
Portraits, Pacific Jazz, 1963.
Gerald Wilson: On Stage, Pacific Jazz, 1965.
The Best of the Gerald Wilson Orchestra, Pacific Jazz, ca. 1968.
Eternal Equinox, Pacific Jazz, 1969.
Love You Madly, Discovery, 1981.
Orchestra of the '80s, Trend, 1983.
Jenna, Discovery, 1989.
State Street Sweet, MAMA Jazz, 1994.
Suite Memories, MAMA Jazz, 1996.
Theme for Monterey, MAMA Jazz, 1998.
New York, New Sound, Mack Avenue, 2003.

Sources

Books

Contemporary Musicians, volume 19, Gale, 1997.

Periodicals

Boston Globe, November 10, 1988, p. 89.
Chicago Sun-Times, September 2, 1994, p. 55.
New York Times, October 20, 1988, p. C23; January 2, 1990, p. C17.
Plain Dealer (Cleveland, OH), February 4, 2000, p. Friday-16.
San Francisco Chronicle, September 14, 1997, p. Datebook-51.
Seattle Times, July 21, 2000, p. H15.
Washington Post, June 5, 1996, p. C7.

On-line

"Gerald Wilson," *All Music Guide,* www.allmusic.com (November 24, 2004).

Other

Suite Memories: Reflections on a Jazz Journey (spoken word recording), MAMA Jazz Foundation, 1996.

—James M. Manheim

James Worthy

1961—

Basketball player

Worthy, James, photograph. Mark Mainz/Getty Images.

In 12 years with the Los Angeles Lakers basketball team, "Big Game" James Worthy was known for his ability to maneuver around opposing players at a dizzying pace. "I just decide I'm going to go around [a defensive opponent] when I'm setting up and when I get the ball, I go," he told *Sports Illustrated*. He also thrilled fans with trademark one-handed swooping dunks. With the Lakers, Worthy helped his team capture three NBA championships. "I don't think there has been or will be a better small forward than James," former Lakers coach Pat Riley told the *Knight Ridder/Tribune News Service*. "He was always such a quiet guy. But when he was in his prime, I can guarantee you, there wasn't anybody who could touch him."

Played Basketball to Help Parents

James Ager Worthy was born on February 27, 1961, the youngest son of Ervin and Gladys Worthy. He was raised in Gastonia, North Carolina, where his father was a Baptist minister. Worthy started playing basketball around the age of four, though he acknowledged during his Basketball Hall of Fame acceptance speech, "I just hated the sport," according to *Newsday*. His parents inadvertently changed his mind. The Worthy family believed in hard work and hard study and it was expected that their children would go to college. However, on a minister's salary that was not so easy to accomplish. Worthy saw his parents struggling to pay college tuition for his brothers and decided to get a scholarship to help out. "[That] was the only reason I wanted to play ball," Worthy continued.

By ninth grade Worthy was making local headlines. By tenth grade colleges were after him. Already nearing his full height of six feet, nine inches, Worthy was very big, very fast, and very good. As he led Ashbrook High to victory after victory, even his opponents cheered for him. By his senior year he had played on five All-American teams, earned Conference Player of the Year, and amassed an incredible average of 21.5 points per game (ppg) and 12.5 rebounds per game (rpg). Scholarship offers poured in. Worthy stayed close to home, choosing the University of North Carolina (UNC). His decision again was influenced by his family. "[UNC Coach Dean Smith] talked to my parents and promised two things; I would go to class and I had to go

At a Glance . . .

Born on February 27, 1961, in Gastonia, NC; married Angela Wilder, 1984 (divorced); two children. *Education:* Attended University of North Carolina, 1979-82.

Career: Los Angeles Lakers, professional basketball player, 1982-94; professional speaker, 1994–; broadcaster.

Selected memberships: Big Brothers of Los Angeles; Special Olympics; Boys and Girls Club of America.

Selected awards: NCAA, Most Outstanding Player of the Final Four, 1982; NBA, Most Valuable Player of the Finals, 1988; LA Lakers, jersey retired, 1995; NBA, 50 Greatest Players in NBA History, 1996; enshrined in Naismith Memorial Basketball Hall of Fame, 2003.

Addresses: *Home*—Los Angeles, CA.

to church unless I had a letter from my parents," Worthy told *Hoophall*, the Web site of the Basketball Hall of Fame. "From that point I knew I wanted to play for Coach Smith."

Worthy donned the UNC Tar Heel uniform in 1980 but midway through his freshman year he slipped and shattered his ankle. Doctors had to implant two screws and a six-inch metal rod to repair the damage. He missed 14 games and began to doubt his future in basketball. "I wasn't sure I would be able to come back with the same type of intensity I'd always had," the *NBA* Web site quoted him. His fears were unfounded. His sophomore year, with the screws still intact, Worthy stormed back onto the court. He averaged 14.2 ppg and 8.4 rpg, helping to lead the Tar Heels to the NCAA championships. Though they lost to Indiana, Worthy's reputation as a top college player was cemented.

Went from College Champion to Superstar Shadows

Worthy entered his junior year at UNC at the top of his game. "He was the quickest guy on our North Carolina team," a former UNC coach told *Knight Ridder/ Tribune News Service*. "And we had Michael Jordan as a freshman. But James was a man among boys underneath. And when the big games came, his eyes got big." With an average of 15.6 ppg in the regular season, Worthy led his team to the 1982 NCAA

championships. In a pattern that came to characterize him, Worthy shifted into high gear during the playoffs and scored 28 points in the final game to seal the championship.

In three years at UNC Worthy was named to 11 All-American teams, voted Most Outstanding Player of the 1982 NCAA Final Four, chosen Helms Foundation National Player of the Year, and of course, earned an NCAA championship. He was ready to go pro. He left UNC just before his senior year and threw his name into the 1982 NBA draft. The Los Angeles Lakers did not hesitate to make him the number one draft choice.

In 1982 the Lakers were the reigning NBA champions and their roster boasted superstars Kareem Abdul Jabbar and Magic Johnson. The team also had Jamaal Wilkes as small forward—the position Worthy was drafted to play. On just about any other team, Worthy would have become an immediate star. On the Lakers, he was relegated to the background. "We could all see he was a big-time player, but I think what everybody appreciated most under the circumstances was that he kept his mouth shut," Johnson told *Sports Illustrated*. In fact Worthy gained a league-wide reputation for his stoicism. He did not scream for joy over a win, nor complain loudly about a loss. He shunned media attention and did not engage in locker room banter. "We know him, but we don't know him," Johnson told *Sports Illustrated*. This quiet demeanor came to be an essential part of his success in pro ball. "James was a great player within a system," Jerry West, former general manager of the Lakers, told the *Knight Ridder/ Tribune News Service*.

Earned First NBA Championship

While he was still a rookie, *Sports Illustrated* called Worthy "one of the best players to come into the NBA in the last decade." He earned that praise, playing in 77 games and scoring the highest field goal percentage of any rookie in the league. He also became the fourth rookie in Lakers history to score 1,000 points. Worthy's feats landed him on the NBA All-Rookie team. Coaches and fellow teammates were also impressed. "He has unbelievable footwork," Lakers forward Maurice Lucas told *Sports Illustrated*. West agreed, telling the *Knight Ridder/Tribune News Service*, "James was an impossible matchup. Put a smaller guy on him and he'd go over him. Put a taller guy on him and he'd go around him. Put a smaller, quicker guy on him and he'd still go around him. That was his special skill." Unfortunately, near the end of the season Worthy broke his leg and was sidelined during the playoffs.

Back on court by the middle of the 1984 season, Worthy racked up a 14.5 ppg average. Again, he turned up the heat during the playoffs, increasing his average to 17.7 ppg. Worthy and team went on to face long-time rivals the Boston Celtics in the championships series. According to *Sports Illustrated*, "[Worthy dominated] the first three games." By the fourth game, the Celtics—and their fans, known for taunting opposing teams in order to unnerve them—had had enough. As Worthy took the floor for a potentially game-tying free-throw, the heckling began, not only from the fans, but also from Celtic players. Worthy missed and the Lakers went on to lose the series. "I really didn't appreciate that," Worthy told *Sports Illustrated*. "I just thought it was kind of low. It was my first experience with the Boston mystique. It was kind of cheap—but that's the Celtics."

In 1985 the Lakers returned to face Boston in the NBA championships. After losing the first game by 40 points, the usually quiet Worthy spoke up. "Before Game 2, I remember James saying, 'Let's go out and play like the Lakers,'" teammate Michael Cooper recalled to the *Knight Ridder/Tribune News Service*. "Now, that doesn't sound like anything special. But it reminded us that we hadn't been ourselves." Taking his own advice, Worthy, whose season average had been 17.6 ppg, increased his average to 21.5 in the playoffs. In the finals against Boston he nudged even higher, to 23.7. "The bigger the game, the more important the situation, the better James plays," Riley told *Sports Illustrated*. Playing like a Laker, Worthy helped the team win the championship. "That was the one I cherish the most," the *NBA* Web site quoted Worthy. From 1959 to 1969, the Lakers had faced the Celtics seven times in the championships, losing each time. In breaking that losing streak, Worthy and crew became Los Angeles heroes.

Became "Big Game" James

For the first time in his professional career Worthy's scoring average topped 20 ppg in the 1986 regular season. He also made the first of seven consecutive appearances in the NBA All-Star Game. The All-Star series—held mid-season each year—features players voted on by fans. Worthy's inclusion proved that he had finally come out of the shadow of Jabbar and Johnson. Worthy and the Lakers faced the Celtics again in the 1986 championship. Boston won but the Lakers bounced back the following year. In 1987 the Lakers tore through the playoffs and then trounced the Celtics in six games to retake the NBA crown.

By 1988 Worthy was a superstar. During home games the stadium shook as the crowds chanted his name. Sports journalists across the country wrote that Worthy was indeed "worthy"—of praise, fame, even basketball history. Characteristically, Worthy stayed focused on basketball. His scoring average again topped 20 ppg, helping the Lakers coast to another championship appearance. This time their opponents were the Detroit Pistons. The series came down to the wire in the seventh game. Worthy, again proving his grace under pressure, pulled off the best game of his career. He scored an astounding 36 points, 16 rebounds, and 10 assists. In basketball, when a player attains double-digits in three different game statistics, it is called a triple-double;—an amazing feat that attests to a player's versatility. By scoring the first triple-double of his career, Worthy helped the Lakers beat the Pistons, 108 to 105. Worthy donned his third championship ring and was named Most Valuable Player of the Finals. He also earned the nickname that has come to define him: "Big Game" James.

The Lakers lost the NBA championship to the Pistons in 1989 and did not make it past the semi-finals in 1990. They returned to the finals in 1991, but lost to the Chicago Bulls. As the Lakers fell, Worthy's play also declined. In 1991 he posted the best scoring average of his career with 21.4 ppg, yet his field goal percentage dropped for the first time in eight seasons. The following year Worthy had surgery on his knee and sat out most of the season. When he came back in 1993 he had record low averages in every category. He was suffering tendonitis and knee pain. "Physically, he's beat up," teammate Sam Bowie told the *Knight Ridder/Tribune News Service*. Worthy decided to retire a week into his thirteenth season with the Lakers. He was 33. In addition to his physical ailments, Worthy admitted to *Hoophall*, "I lost the love of [playing] the game."

Following retirement, the previously media-shy Worthy took on several high-profile jobs. He covered the NCAA Final Four for CBS and appeared on *Fox Sports News*. He guest-starred on *Everyone Loves Raymond* and *Star Trek: The Next Generation*. On the professional speaking route, he began commanding up to $20,000 an appearance. He also wrote a basketball column for *Sports Ya!*, a Spanish-language Web site. Meanwhile, he received several prestigious honors for his years with the Lakers. On December 10, 1995, Worthy became only the sixth player in Lakers history to have his jersey—number 42—retired. In 1996, the NBA named Worthy one of the 50 greatest basketball players in history. And in September of 2003 Worthy was inducted into the Naismith Memorial Basketball Hall of Fame. "This is the ultimate," *Sports Network* quoted Worthy as saying during his acceptance speech. "It is more than an honor to be amongst the Hall of Famers tonight." However, in typical modesty, he clarified to *Hoophall*, "of all my goals, this was not one of them.... I played basketball to try to get my parents from working so hard." He not only succeeded, he became a basketball legend in the process.

Sources

Periodicals

Knight Ridder/Tribune News Service, November 9, 1994; November 10, 1994.
Newsday, September 7, 2003.

Sports Illustrated, February 21, 1983; May 19, 1986.

Sports Network, September 6, 2003.

On-line

"James Worthy," *NBA,* www.nba.com/history/players/worthy_bio.html (October 24, 2004).

"James Worthy," *Biography Resource Center,* www.galenet.com/servlet/BioRC (December 8, 2004).

"The Worthy File," *Hoophall,* www.hoophall.com/halloffamers/worthy_james_feature.htm (October 24, 2004).

—Candace LaBalle

Cumulative Nationality Index

*Volume numbers appear in **bold***

American

Aaliyah **30**
Aaron, Hank **5**
Abbott, Robert Sengstacke **27**
Abdul-Jabbar, Kareem **8**
Abdur-Rahim, Shareef **28**
Abernathy, Ralph David **1**
Abu-Jamal, Mumia **15**
Ace, Johnny **36**
Adams Earley, Charity **13, 34**
Adams, Eula L. **39**
Adams, Floyd, Jr. **12**
Adams, Johnny **39**
Adams, Leslie **39**
Adams, Oleta **18**
Adams, Osceola Macarthy **31**
Adams, Sheila J. **25**
Adams, Yolanda **17**
Adams-Ender, Clara **40**
Adderley, Julian "Cannonball" **30**
Adderley, Nat **29**
Adkins, Rod **41**
Adkins, Rutherford H. **21**
Agyeman, Jaramogi Abebe **10**
Ailey, Alvin **8**
Al-Amin, Jamil Abdullah **6**
Albright, Gerald **23**
Alert, Kool DJ Red **33**
Alexander, Archie Alphonso **14**
Alexander, Clifford **26**
Alexander, Joyce London **18**
Alexander, Khandi **43**
Alexander, Margaret Walker **22**
Alexander, Sadie Tanner Mossell **22**
Ali, Laila **27**
Ali, Muhammad **2, 16**
Allain, Stephanie **49**
Allen, Byron **3, 24**
Allen, Debbie **13, 42**
Allen, Ethel D. **13**
Allen, Marcus **20**
Allen, Robert L. **38**
Allen, Samuel W. **38**
Allen, Tina **22**
Alston, Charles **33**
Ames, Wilmer **27**
Amos, John **8**
Amos, Wally **9**
Anderson, Carl **48**
Anderson, Charles Edward **37**
Anderson, Eddie "Rochester" **30**
Anderson, Elmer **25**
Anderson, Jamal **22**

Anderson, Marian **2, 33**
Anderson, Michael P. **40**
Anderson, Norman B. **45**
Andrews, Benny **22**
Andrews, Bert **13**
Andrews, Raymond **4**
Angelou, Maya **1, 15**
Ansa, Tina McElroy **14**
Anthony, Carmelo **46**
Anthony, Wendell **25**
Archer, Dennis **7, 36**
Archie-Hudson, Marguerite **44**
Arkadie, Kevin **17**
Armstrong, Louis **2**
Armstrong, Robb **15**
Armstrong, Vanessa Bell **24**
Arnwine, Barbara **28**
Arrington, Richard **24**
Arroyo, Martina **30**
Asante, Molefi Kete **3**
Ashanti **37**
Ashe, Arthur **1, 18**
Ashford, Emmett **22**
Ashford, Nickolas **21**
Ashley-Ward, Amelia **23**
Atkins, Cholly **40**
Atkins, Erica **34**
Atkins, Russell **45**
Atkins, Tina **34**
Aubert, Alvin **41**
Auguste, Donna **29**
Austin, Junius C. **44**
Austin, Lovie **40**
Austin, Patti **24**
Avant, Clarence **19**
Ayers, Roy **16**
Babatunde, Obba **35**
Bacon-Bercey, June **38**
Badu, Erykah **22**
Bailey, Buster **38**
Bailey, Clyde **45**
Bailey, DeFord **33**
Bailey, Radcliffe **19**
Bailey, Xenobia **11**
Baines, Harold **32**
Baiocchi, Regina Harris **41**
Baisden, Michael **25**
Baker, Anita **21, 48**
Baker, Augusta **38**
Baker, Dusty **8, 43**
Baker, Ella **5**
Baker, Gwendolyn Calvert **9**
Baker, Houston A., Jr. **6**
Baker, Josephine **3**

Baker, LaVern **26**
Baker, Maxine B. **28**
Baker, Thurbert **22**
Baldwin, James **1**
Ballance, Frank W. **41**
Ballard, Allen Butler, Jr. **40**
Ballard, Hank **41**
Bambaataa, Afrika **34**
Bambara, Toni Cade **10**
Bandele, Asha **36**
Banks, Ernie **33**
Banks, Jeffrey **17**
Banks, Tyra **11**
Banks, William **11**
Baraka, Amiri **1, 38**
Barber, Ronde **41**
Barboza, Anthony **10**
Barclay, Paris **37**
Barden, Don H. **9, 20**
Barker, Danny **32**
Barkley, Charles **5**
Barlow, Roosevelt **49**
Barnes, Roosevelt "Booba" **33**
Barnett, Amy Du Bois **46**
Barnett, Marguerite **46**
Barney, Lem **26**
Barnhill, David **30**
Barrax, Gerald William **45**
Barrett, Andrew C. **12**
Barrett, Jacquelyn **28**
Barry, Marion S(hepilov, Jr.) **7, 44**
Barthe, Richmond **15**
Basie, Count **23**
Basquiat, Jean-Michel **5**
Bass, Charlotta Spears **40**
Bassett, Angela **6, 23**
Bates, Daisy **13**
Bates, Karen Grigsby **40**
Bates, Peg Leg **14**
Bath, Patricia E. **37**
Baugh, David **23**
Baylor, Don **6**
Baylor, Helen **36**
Beach, Michael **26**
Beal, Bernard B. **46**
Beals, Jennifer **12**
Beals, Melba Patillo **15**
Bearden, Romare **2**
Beasley, Jamar **29**
Beasley, Phoebe **34**
Beatty, Talley **35**
Bechet, Sidney **18**
Beckford, Tyson **11**
Beckham, Barry **41**

Belafonte, Harry **4**
Bell, Derrick **6**
Bell, James "Cool Papa" **36**
Bell, James Madison **40**
Bell, Michael **40**
Bell, Robert Mack **22**
Bellamy, Bill **12**
Belle, Albert **10**
Belle, Regina **1**
Belton, Sharon Sayles **9, 16**
Benét, Eric **28**
Ben-Israel, Ben Ami **11**
Benjamin, Andre **45**
Benjamin, Regina **20**
Bennett, George Harold "Hal" **45**
Bennett, Lerone, Jr. **5**
Benson, Angela **34**
Berry, Bertice **8**
Berry, Chuck **29**
Berry, Fred "Rerun" **48**
Berry, Halle **4, 19**
Berry, Mary Frances **7**
Berry, Theodore **31**
Berrysmith, Don Reginald **49**
Bethune, Mary McLeod **4**
Betsch, MaVynee **28**
Beverly, Frankie **25**
Bibb, Eric **49**
Bickerstaff, Bernie **21**
Biggers, John **20, 33**
Bing, Dave **3**
Bishop, Sanford D. Jr. **24**
Black, Barry C. **47**
Black, Keith Lanier **18**
Blackburn, Robert **28**
Blackwell, Unita **17**
Blair, Paul **36**
Blake, Asha **26**
Blake, Eubie **29**
Blake, James **43**
Blakey, Art **37**
Blanchard, Terence **43**
Bland, Bobby "Blue" **36**
Bland, Eleanor Taylor **39**
Blanks, Billy **22**
Blanton, Dain **29**
Blassingame, John Wesley **40**
Blige, Mary J. **20, 34**
Blockson, Charles L. **42**
Blow, Kurtis **31**
Bluford, Guy **2, 35**
Bluitt, Juliann S. **14**
Bogle, Donald **34**
Bolden, Buddy **39**

Cumulative Occupation Index

*Volume numbers appear in **bold***

Art and design
Adjaye, David **38**
Allen, Tina **22**
Alston, Charles **33**
Andrews, Benny **22**
Andrews, Bert **13**
Armstrong, Robb **15**
Bailey, Radcliffe **19**
Bailey, Xenobia **11**
Barboza, Anthony **10**
Barnes, Ernie **16**
Barthe, Richmond **15**
Basquiat, Jean-Michel **5**
Bearden, Romare **2**
Beasley, Phoebe **34**
Biggers, John **20, 33**
Blacknurn, Robert **28**
Brandon, Barbara **3**
Brown, Donald **19**
Burke, Selma **16**
Burroughs, Margaret Taylor **9**
Camp, Kimberly **19**
Campbell, E. Simms **13**
Campbell, Mary Schmidt **43**
Catlett, Elizabeth **2**
Chase-Riboud, Barbara **20, 46**
Cortor, Eldzier **42**
Cowans, Adger W. **20**
Crite, Alan Rohan **29**
De Veaux, Alexis **44**
DeCarava, Roy **42**
Delaney, Beauford **19**
Delaney, Joseph **30**
Delsarte, Louis **34**
Donaldson, Jeff **46**
Douglas, Aaron **7**
Driskell, David C. **7**
Edwards, Melvin **22**
El Wilson, Barbara **35**
Ewing, Patrick A. **17**
Fax, Elton **48**
Feelings, Tom **11, 47**
Freeman, Leonard **27**
Fuller, Meta Vaux Warrick **27**
Gantt, Harvey **1**
Gilliam, Sam **16**
Golden, Thelma **10**
Goodnight, Paul **32**
Guyton, Tyree **9**
Harkless, Necia Desiree **19**
Harrington, Oliver W. **9**
Hathaway, Isaac Scott **33**
Hayden, Palmer **13**

Hayes, Cecil N. **46**
Hope, John **8**
Hudson, Cheryl **15**
Hudson, Wade **15**
Hunt, Richard **6**
Hunter, Clementine **45**
Hutson, Jean Blackwell **16**
Jackson, Earl **31**
Jackson, Vera **40**
John, Daymond **23**
Johnson, Jeh Vincent **44**
Johnson, William Henry **3**
Jones, Lois Mailou **13**
Kitt, Sandra **23**
Knox, Simmie **49**
Lawrence, Jacob **4, 28**
Lee, Annie Francis **22**
Lee-Smith, Hughie **5, 22**
Lewis, Edmonia **10**
Lewis, Norman **39**
Lewis, Samella **25**
Loving, Alvin **35**
Manley, Edna **26**
Mayhew, Richard **39**
McGee, Charles **10**
McGruder, Aaron **28**
Mitchell, Corinne **8**
Moody, Ronald **30**
Morrison, Keith **13**
Motley, Archibald Jr. **30**
Moutoussamy-Ashe, Jeanne **7**
Mutu, Wangechi **44**
N'Namdi, George R. **17**
Nugent, Richard Bruce **39**
Olden, Georg(e) **44**
Ouattara **43**
Perkins, Marion **38**
Pierre, Andre **17**
Pinderhughes, John **47**
Pinkney, Jerry **15**
Pippin, Horace **9**
Porter, James A. **11**
Prophet, Nancy Elizabeth **42**
Puryear, Martin **42**
Ringgold, Faith **4**
Ruley, Ellis **38**
Saar, Alison **16**
Saint James, Synthia **12**
Sallee, Charles **38**
Sanders, Joseph R., Jr. **11**
Savage, Augusta **12**
Sebree, Charles **40**
Serrano, Andres **3**
Shabazz, Attallah **6**

Simpson, Lorna **4, 36**
Sims, Lowery Stokes **27**
Sklarek, Norma Merrick **25**
Sleet, Moneta, Jr. **5**
Smith, Marvin **46**
Smith, Morgan **46**
Smith, Vincent D. **48**
Tanksley, Ann **37**
Tanner, Henry Ossawa **1**
Thomas, Alma **14**
Thrash, Dox **35**
Tolliver, William **9**
VanDerZee, James **6**
Wainwright, Joscelyn **46**
Walker, A'lelia **14**
Walker, Kara **16**
Washington, Alonzo **29**
Washington, James, Jr. **38**
Wells, James Lesesne **10**
White, Charles **39**
White, Dondi **34**
White, John H. **27**
Williams, Billy Dee **8**
Williams, O. S. **13**
Williams, Paul R. **9**
Williams, William T. **11**
Wilson, Ellis **39**
Woodruff, Hale **9**

Business
Abbot, Robert Sengstacke **27**
Abdul-Jabbar, Kareem **8**
Adams, Eula L. **39**
Adkins, Rod **41**
Ailey, Alvin **8**
Al-Amin, Jamil Abdullah **6**
Alexander, Archie Alphonso **14**
Allen, Byron **24**
Ames, Wilmer **27**
Amos, Wally **9**
Auguste, Donna **29**
Avant, Clarence **19**
Beal, Bernard B. **46**
Beamon, Bob **30**
Baker, Dusty **8, 43**
Baker, Ella **5**
Baker, Gwendolyn Calvert **9**
Baker, Maxine **28**
Banks, Jeffrey **17**
Banks, William **11**
Barden, Don H. **9, 20**
Barrett, Andrew C. **12**
Beasley, Phoebe **34**
Bennett, Lerone, Jr. **5**

Bing, Dave **3**
Bolden, Frank E. **44**
Borders, James **9**
Boston, Kelvin E. **25**
Boston, Lloyd **24**
Boyd, Gwendolyn **49**
Boyd, John W., Jr. **20**
Boyd, T. B., III **6**
Bradley, Jennette B. **40**
Bridges, Shelia **36**
Bridgforth, Glinda **36**
Brimmer, Andrew F. **2, 48**
Bronner, Nathaniel H., Sr. **32**
Brown, Eddie C. **35**
Brown, Les **5**
Brown, Marie Dutton **12**
Brunson, Dorothy **1**
Bryant, John **26**
Burrell, Thomas J. **21**
Burroughs, Margaret Taylor **9**
Burrus, William Henry "Bill" **45**
Busby, Jheryl **3**
Cain, Herman **15**
CasSelle, Malcolm **11**
Chamberlain, Wilt **18, 47**
Chapman, Nathan A. Jr. **21**
Chappell, Emma **18**
Chase, Debra Martin **49**
Chenault, Kenneth I. **4, 36**
Cherry, Deron **40**
Chisholm, Samuel J. **32**
Clark, Celeste **15**
Clark, Patrick **14**
Clay, William Lacy **8**
Clayton, Xernona **3, 45**
Cobbs, Price M. **9**
Colbert, Virgis William **17**
Coleman, Donald A. **24**
Combs, Sean "Puffy" **17, 43**
Connerly, Ward **14**
Conyers, Nathan G. **24**
Cooper, Barry **33**
Cooper, Evern **40**
Corbi, Lana **42**
Cornelius, Don **4**
Cosby, Bill **7, 26**
Cottrell, Comer **11**
Creagh, Milton **27**
Cullers, Vincent T. **49**
Daniels-Carter, Valerie **23**
Darden, Calvin **38**
Dash, Darien **29**
Davis, Ed **24**
Dawson, Matel "Mat," Jr. **39**

189

Cumulative Subject Index

Volume numbers appear in **bold**

Cumulative Name Index

Volume numbers appear in **bold**